Mastering Apache Maven 3

Enhance developer productivity and address exact
enterprise build requirements by extending Maven

Prabath Siriwardena

[PACKT] open source*
PUBLISHING   community experience distilled

BIRMINGHAM - MUMBAI

Mastering Apache Maven 3

Copyright © 2014 Packt Publishing

First published: December 2014

Production reference: 1221214

Published by Packt Publishing Ltd.
Livery Place
35 Livery Street
Birmingham B3 2PB, UK.

ISBN 978-1-78398-386-5

www.packtpub.com

Credits

Author
Prabath Siriwardena

Reviewers
Petri Kainulainen
Michał Kozik
Pavithra Gunasekara
Sagara Gunathunga
Bhavani P Polimetla

Commissioning Editor
Akram Hussain

Acquisition Editor
Subho Gupta

Content Development Editor
Ruchita Bhansali

Technical Editors
Shubhangi Dhamgaye
Shweta Pant
Mohita Vyas

Project Coordinator
Kranti Berde

Copy Editors
Roshni Banerjee
Deepa Nambiar
Rashmi Sawant

Proofreaders
Simran Bhogal
Mario Cecere
Lucy Rowland

Indexer
Tejal Soni

Graphics
Valentina D'silva
Abhinash Sahu

Production Coordinator
Manu Joseph

Cover Work
Manu Joseph

About the Author

Prabath Siriwardena is the Director of Security Architecture at WSO2 Inc.,
a company that produces a wide variety of open source software from data to screen.
He is a member of OASIS Identity Metasystem Interoperability (IMI) TC, OASIS
eXtensible Access Control Markup Language (XACML) TC, OASIS Security Services
(SAML) TC, OASIS Identity in the Cloud TC, and OASIS Cloud Authorization
(CloudAuthZ) TC. Prabath is also a member of PMC Apache Axis and has spoken at
numerous international conferences, including OSCON, ApacheCon, WSO2Con, EIC,
IDentity Next, and OSDC. He has more than 10 years of industry experience and has
worked with many Fortune 100 companies.

Acknowledgments

I would first like to thank Subho Gupta, a senior acquisition editor at Packt Publishing, who came up with the idea of writing a book on mastering Apache Maven; then I would like to thank, Ruchita Bhansali, a content development editor at Packt Publishing, who I worked with closely throughout the project—thank you very much, Ruchita, for your patience and flexibility. Also, I would like to thank all the others at Packt who helped me throughout to make this book a reality from the initial idea. Thank you very much for all your continuous support.

Dr. Sanjiva Weerawarana, the CEO of WSO2, and Paul Fremantle, the CTO of WSO2, have always been my mentors. I am truly grateful to both of them for everything they have done for me.

I'd like to thank my beloved wife, Pavithra, and my loving little daughter, Dinadi. Pavithra wanted me to write this book even more than I wanted. If I say she is the driving force behind this book, I am not exaggerating. She simply went beyond by not only feeding me with all the encouragement, but also by helping immensely in reviewing the book and developing samples. She was always the first reader. Thank you very much, Pavithra. Also, thanks to little Dinadi for your patience—it was your time I spent on writing the book.

I would also like to thank all the technical reviewers of the book. All your suggestions and thoughts were extremely valuable and are much appreciated.

My parents and my sister have been the driving force behind me since my birth. If not for them, I wouldn't be who I am today. I am grateful to them for everything they have done for me. Last but not least, I'd like to thank my wife's parents; they were amazingly helpful in making sure that the only thing I had to do was to write this book, taking care of almost all the other things that I was supposed to do.

Although this would sounds like a one-man effort, it's actually a team effort. Thanks to everyone who supported me in different ways.

About the Reviewers

Petri Kainulainen is a software developer who lives in Tampere, Finland. He specializes in application development with the Java programming language and the Spring framework.

Petri has 15 years of experience in software development, and during his career, he has participated in the development projects of Finland's leading online market places as a software architect. He is currently working at Vincit Oy as a passionate architect.

Petri is the author of *Spring Data*, *Packt Publishing*, which was published in 2012, and writes regularly on his blog at `http://www.petrikainulainen.net/blog/`.

Michał Kozik is an enthusiastic freelance developer. He has gained broad experience in Java while working for companies in the e-commerce, telecommunication, and government sectors. Michał is always looking for new technologies to help him meet the challenges of customers. He enjoys sports and spending time with his family.

Pavithra Gunasekara is a programmer, blogger, and keen enthusiast of big data and data science. She received her Bachelor's degree in Computer Science from the University of Colombo. She has worked as a software engineer at a leading IT company in Sri Lanka and has hands-on experience in Java, R, Python, and Hadoop. Being a huge fan of Massive Open Online Courses(MOOC), she currently follows the data science specialization course provided by Coursera to extend her knowledge of data science. She regularly writes technical content on her blog at `http://blog.eviac.net`.

Sagara Gunathunga is a long-term contributor to Apache Software Foundation and a PMC member of Apache Axis and Apache Web Services projects. He actively contributes to Apache Axis2, Apache Web Services, and Apache Synapse projects. He currently serves as the Vice President of the Apache Web Services project.

In his day job, he works for WSO2, where he previously led the WSO2 Application Server project and now leads the WSO2 Governance Registry project. Sagara has more than 8 years of industry experience in Java EE, Spring, Web Service, API management, and enterprise-integration-related technologies. Sagara holds a degree in Computer Science from the University of Peradeniya, Sri Lanka and also holds a Bachelor's degree in Information Technology from University of Colombo School of Computing.

Sagara usually writes his technical expertise on his blog at `http://ssagara.blogspot.com/`.

Bhavani P Polimetla has been learning and working in IT Industry since 1990. He graduated with Bachelor of Computer Science and Master of Computer Applications degrees from Andhra University, India. He worked on standalone Swing applications on Grid computing and Multitier Architecture. He has worked with clients that include three fortune 50 companies. At present, he is working as a software architect at Mountain View, California, USA.

To demonstrate his skills he has completed, more than 25 Certifications in the spectrum of Java, database, project management, and architecture subjects. He has also received awards for many of his projects. He likes to spend his free time doing social service activities. More information is available on his website at `www.polimetla.com`.

www.PacktPub.com

Support files, eBooks, discount offers, and more

For support files and downloads related to your book, please visit www.PacktPub.com.

Did you know that Packt offers eBook versions of every book published, with PDF and ePub files available? You can upgrade to the eBook version at www.PacktPub.com and as a print book customer, you are entitled to a discount on the eBook copy. Get in touch with us at service@packtpub.com for more details.

At www.PacktPub.com, you can also read a collection of free technical articles, sign up for a range of free newsletters and receive exclusive discounts and offers on Packt books and eBooks.

https://www2.packtpub.com/books/subscription/packtlib

Do you need instant solutions to your IT questions? PacktLib is Packt's online digital book library. Here, you can search, access, and read Packt's entire library of books.

Why subscribe?

- Fully searchable across every book published by Packt
- Copy and paste, print, and bookmark content
- On demand and accessible via a web browser

Free access for Packt account holders

If you have an account with Packt at www.PacktPub.com, you can use this to access PacktLib today and view 9 entirely free books. Simply use your login credentials for immediate access.

This book is dedicated with great honor, to my father – the greatest human being that I have ever met.

Table of Contents

Preface

Maven is the number one build tool used by developers, and it has been available for more than a decade. Maven stands out among other build tools due to its extensible architecture, which is built on the concept of *convention over configuration*. This has made Maven the de-facto tool to manage and build Java projects. It's being widely used by many open source Java projects under Apache Software Foundation, SourceForge, Google Code, and many more.

Mastering Apache Maven 3 provides a step-by-step guide that will show you how to use Apache Maven in an optimal way to address enterprise build requirements. After reading this book, you will be able to:

- Apply Maven's best practices in designing a build system to improve developers' productivity
- Customize the build process to suit your enterprise needs by developing custom Maven plugins, lifecycles, and archetypes
- Troubleshoot build issues with greater confidence
- Implement and deploy a Maven repository manager to manage the build process in a better way
- Design the build with proper dependency management, avoiding any maintenance nightmares
- Optimize the Maven configuration settings
- Build your own distribution archive using Maven assemblies
- Build custom Maven lifecycles and lifecycle extensions

What this book covers

Chapter 1, Apache Maven Quick Start, focuses on giving an introduction to Apache Maven. If you are an advanced Maven user, you can simply jump to the next chapter. It will show how to install and configure Maven on different operating systems such as Linux, Mac, and Microsoft Windows and tips and tricks to use Maven.

Chapter 2, Demystifying Project Object Model, focuses on core concepts and best practices related to Project Object Model (POM) in building a large-scale multimodule Maven project.

Chapter 3, Maven Configuration, discusses how to customize the Maven configuration at three different levels: the global level, the user level, and the project level for optimal use.

Chapter 4, Build Lifecycles, discusses the Maven build lifecycles in detail. A Maven build lifecycle consists of a set of well-defined phases. Each phase groups a set of goals defined by Maven plugins and the lifecycle defines the order of execution of the phases.

Chapter 5, Maven Plugins, explains the usage of key Maven plugins and demonstrates how to build custom plugins. All the useful functionalities in the build process are developed as Maven plugins. One could also easily call Maven, a plugin execution framework.

Chapter 6, Maven Assemblies, explains how to build custom assemblies with the Maven assembly plugin. The Maven assembly plugin produces a custom archive, which adheres to a user-defined layout. This custom archive is also known as the Maven assembly. In other words, it's a distribution unit that is built according to a custom layout.

Chapter 7, Maven Archetypes, explains how to use existing archetypes and how to build custom Maven archetypes. Maven archetypes provide a way of reducing repetitive work in building Maven projects. There are thousands of archetypes out there that are available freely to assist you in building different types of projects.

Chapter 8, Maven Repository Management, discusses the pros and cons of using a Maven repository manager. This chapter further explains how to use Nexus as a repository manager and configure it as a hosted, proxied, and group repository.

Chapter 9, Best Practices, looks at and highlights some of the best practices to be followed in a large-scale development project with Maven. It is always recommended to follow best practices, as they will drastically improve developers' productivity and reduce maintenance nightmares.

What you need for this book

To proceed with the examples that are presented in this book, you will need the following software:

- Apache Maven 3.2.x, which can be downloaded from `http://maven.apache.org/download.cgi`

- Java 1.6+ SDK, which can be downloaded from `http://www.oracle.com/technetwork/java/javase/downloads/index.html`

- Microsoft Windows, Linux, or Mac OS X operating systems

Who this book is for

If you are working with Java or Java EE projects and you want to take the fullest advantage of Maven in designing, executing, and maintaining your build system for optimal developer productivity, then this book is ideal for you. It is also particularly useful if you are a developer or an architect. You should be well versed with Maven and its basic functionalities if you wish to get the most out of this book.

Conventions

In this book, you will find a number of text styles that distinguish between different kinds of information. Here are some examples of these styles and an explanation of their meaning.

Code words in text, database table names, folder names, filenames, file extensions, pathnames, dummy URLs, user input, and Twitter handles are shown as follows: "When you type `mvn clean install`, Maven will execute all the phases in the default lifecycle up to and including the `install` phase."

A block of code is set as follows:

```
<project>
  [...]
  <build>
    [...]
    <plugins>
      <plugin>
        <groupId>org.apache.maven.plugins</groupId>
        <artifactId>maven-compiler-plugin</artifactId>
        <version>3.1</version>
        <configuration>
          <source>1.7</source>
          <target>1.7</target>
```

```
        </configuration>
      </plugin>
    </plugins>
    [...]
  </build>
  [...]
</project>
```

When we wish to draw your attention to a particular part of a code block, the relevant lines or items are set in bold:

```
<project>
  [...]
  <build>
    [...]
    <plugins>
      <plugin>
        <groupId>org.apache.maven.plugins</groupId>
        <artifactId>maven-compiler-plugin</artifactId>
        <version>3.1</version>
        <configuration>
          <source>1.7</source>
          <target>1.7</target>
        </configuration>
      </plugin>
    </plugins>
    [...]
  </build>
  [...]
</project>
```

Any command-line input or output is written as follows:

```
$ mvn install:install
```

New terms and **important** words are shown in bold. Words that you see on the screen, for example, in menus or dialog boxes, appear in the text like this: "Click on the **Add** button in the **Role Management** section and select **Repo: All Maven Repositories (Full Control)**, as shown in the upcoming screenshot."

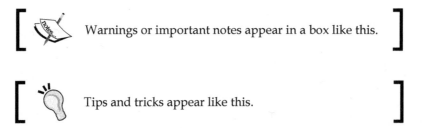

Warnings or important notes appear in a box like this.

Tips and tricks appear like this.

Reader feedback

Feedback from our readers is always welcome. Let us know what you think about this book — what you liked or disliked. Reader feedback is important for us as it helps us develop titles that you will really get the most out of.

To send us general feedback, simply e-mail feedback@packtpub.com, and mention the book's title in the subject of your message.

If there is a topic that you have expertise in and you are interested in either writing or contributing to a book, see our author guide at www.packtpub.com/authors.

Customer support

Now that you are the proud owner of a Packt book, we have a number of things to help you to get the most from your purchase.

Downloading the example code

You can download the example code files from your account at http://www.packtpub.com for all the Packt Publishing books you have purchased. If you purchased this book elsewhere, you can visit http://www.packtpub.com/support and register to have the files e-mailed directly to you.

Errata

Although we have taken every care to ensure the accuracy of our content, mistakes do happen. If you find a mistake in one of our books — maybe a mistake in the text or the code — we would be grateful if you could report this to us. By doing so, you can save other readers from frustration and help us improve subsequent versions of this book. If you find any errata, please report them by visiting http://www.packtpub.com/submit-errata, selecting your book, clicking on the **Errata Submission Form** link, and entering the details of your errata. Once your errata are verified, your submission will be accepted and the errata will be uploaded to our website or added to any list of existing errata under the Errata section of that title.

To view the previously submitted errata, go to https://www.packtpub.com/books/content/support and enter the name of the book in the search field. The required information will appear under the **Errata** section.

Piracy

Piracy of copyrighted material on the Internet is an ongoing problem across all media. At Packt, we take the protection of our copyright and licenses very seriously. If you come across any illegal copies of our works in any form on the Internet, please provide us with the location address or website name immediately so that we can pursue a remedy.

Please contact us at `copyright@packtpub.com` with a link to the suspected pirated material.

We appreciate your help in protecting our authors and our ability to bring you valuable content.

Questions

If you have a problem with any aspect of this book, you can contact us at `questions@packtpub.com`, and we will do our best to address the problem.

1
Apache Maven Quick Start

This chapter will introduce Apache Maven. If you are an advanced Maven user, you can simply jump into the next chapter. Even for an advanced user, it is highly recommended that you at least brush through this chapter, as it will be helpful to make sure that we are on the same page as we proceed.

In this chapter, we will be discussing about the following topics:

- Installing and configuring Maven on Ubuntu, Mac OS X, and Microsoft Windows
- IDE integration
- Tips and tricks to use Maven effectively

A quick introduction

Apache Maven is popular as a build tool. However, in reality, it goes beyond being just a build tool. It provides a comprehensive build management platform. Prior to Maven, developers had to spend a lot of time in building a build system. There was no common interface. It differed from project to project—each time a developer moved from one project to another, there was a learning curve. Maven filled this gap by introducing a common interface. It ended the era of "the build engineer."

Installing Apache Maven

Installing Maven on any platform is a straightforward task. At the time of writing this book, the latest version is 3.2.3, which is available to download from `http://maven.apache.org/download.cgi`. This version requires JDK 1.6.0 or above. You should keep a note of the Java requirement for version 3.2.3 if you are planning to upgrade from version 3.0.0 family or 3.1.0 family. Prior to Maven 3.2.1, the only requirement was JDK 1.5.0.

Apache Maven is an extremely lightweight distribution. It does not have any hard requirements in terms of memory, disk space, or CPU. Maven is built on top of Java and will work on any operating system that runs a **Java Virtual Machine (JVM)**.

Installing Apache Maven on Ubuntu

Installing Maven on Ubuntu just needs a single-line command. Proceed with the following steps:

1. Run the following `apt-get` command in the command prompt; you need to have the `sudo` privileges to execute this:

   ```
   $ sudo apt-get install maven
   ```

2. The installation takes a few minutes to complete. Upon the completion of the installation, you can run the following command to verify the installation:

   ```
   $ mvn -version
   ```

3. You should get an output similar to the following one if Apache Maven has been installed successfully:

   ```
   $ mvn -version
   Apache Maven 3.2.3
   Maven home: /usr/share/maven
   Java version: 1.7.0_60, vendor: Oracle Corporation
   Java home: /usr/lib/jvm/java-7-oracle/jre
   Default locale: en_US, platform encoding: UTF-8
   OS name: "linux", version: "3.13.0-24-generic", arch: "amd64",
     family: "unix"
   ```

4. Maven is installed under the `/usr/share/maven` directory. To check the directory structure behind the Maven installation directory, use the following command:

   ```
   $ ls /usr/share/maven
   bin   boot   conf   lib   man
   ```

5. Maven configuration files can be found under the `/etc/maven` directory using the following command:

   ```
   $ ls /etc/maven
   m2.conf   settings.xml
   ```

If you don't want to work with the apt-get command, there is another way of installing Maven under any Unix-based operating system. We will discuss this in the next section. Since Mac OS X has a kernel built on top of the Unix kernel, installing Maven on Mac OS X would be the same as installing it on any Unix-based operating system.

Installing Apache Maven on Mac OS X

Most of the OS X distributions prior to OS X Mavericks had Apache Maven preinstalled. To verify that you've got Maven installed in your system, try out the following command:

```
$ mvn -version
```

If it does not result in a version, this means you do not have Apache Maven installed.

The following steps will guide you through the Maven installation process:

1. First, we need to download the latest version of Maven. Throughout this book, we will use Maven 3.2.3, which is the latest version at the time of writing this book. The Maven 3.2.3 ZIP distribution can be downloaded from http://maven.apache.org/download.cgi.

2. Unzip the downloaded ZIP file and extract it to /usr/share/java directory. You need to have the sudo privileges to execute the following command:

   ```
   $ sudo unzip  apache-maven-3.2.3-bin.zip -d /usr/share/java/
   ```

3. If you already have Maven installed in your system, use the following command to unlink:

   ```
   $ sudo unlink /usr/share/maven
   ```

4. Use the following command to create a symlink to the latest Maven distribution, which you just unzipped. You need to have the sudo privileges to execute the following command:

   ```
   $ sudo ln -s /usr/share/java/apache-maven-3.2.3  /usr/share/maven
   ```

5. Verify the Maven installation with the following command:

   ```
   $ mvn -version
   Apache Maven 3.2.3 (33f8c3e1027c3ddde99d3cdebad2656a31e8fdf4;
   2014-08-12T02:28:10+05:30)
   Maven home: /usr/share/maven
   Java version: 1.6.0_65, vendor: Apple Inc.
   ```

```
Java home: /System/Library/Java/JavaVirtualMachines/1.6.0.jdk/
Contents/Home
Default locale: en_US, platform encoding: MacRoman
OS name: "mac os x", version: "10.8.5", arch: "x86_64",
   family: "mac"
```

 Maven can also be installed on Mac OS X with Homebrew. Check out the video at this link, `https://www.youtube.com/watch?v=xTzLGcqUf8k`, which explains the installation process in detail.

Installing Apache Maven on Microsoft Windows

First, we need to download the latest version of Maven. The Apache Maven 3.2.3 ZIP distribution can be downloaded from `http://maven.apache.org/download.cgi`. Next, perform the following steps:

1. Unzip the downloaded ZIP file and extract it to `C:\Program Files\ASF` folder.

2. Set the `M2_HOME` environment variable and point it to `C:\Program Files\ASF\apache-maven-3.2.3`.

3. Verify the Maven installation with the following command on the command prompt:

   ```
   mvn -version
   ```

 To learn how to set the environment variables on Microsoft Windows, you can refer `http://www.computerhope.com/issues/ch000549.htm`.

Configuring the heap size

Once you have installed Maven in your system, the next step is to fine-tune it for optimal performance. By default, the maximum heap allocation is 256 - 512 MB (`-Xms256m` to `-Xmx512m`). This default limit does not work while building a large, complex Java project, and it is recommended that you have at least 1024 MB of maximum heap. If you encounter the `java.lang.OutOfMemoryError` error at any point during a Maven build, it is mostly due to the lack of memory. You can use the `MAVEN_OPTS` environment variable to set the maximum allowed heap size for Maven at a global level.

The following command will set the heap size in Linux. Make sure that the value set as the maximum heap size does not exceed your system memory of the machine that runs Maven.

```
$ export MAVEN_OPTS="-Xmx1024m -XX:MaxPermSize=128m"
```

If you are on Microsoft Windows, use the following command:

```
$ set MAVEN_OPTS=-Xmx1024m -XX:MaxPermSize=128m
```

Here `-Xmx` takes the maximum heap size and `-XX:MaxPermSize` takes the maximum PermGen size.

Maven runs as a Java process on JVM. As Java proceeds with a build, it keeps on creating Java objects. These objects are stored in the memory allocated to Maven. This area of memory where Java objects are stored is known as heap. Heap is created at the JVM start, and it increases as more and more objects are created up to the defined maximum limit. The `-Xms` JVM flag is used to instruct JVM the minimum value it should set at the time it creates the heap. The `-Xmx` JVM flag sets the maximum heap size.

Permanent Generation (PermGen) is an area of memory managed by JVM, which stores the internal representations of Java classes. The maximum size of PermGen can be set by the `-XX:MaxPermSize` JVM flag.

To learn about the Maven `OutOfMemoryError` error, check out the information at this link: `https://cwiki.apache.org/confluence/display/MAVEN/OutOfMemoryError`.

Monitoring the build

The most popular way of starting a Maven build is by using the `mvn clean install` command. This will build all the Maven modules under your project and install the artifacts to your local repository. For a simple project, the entire build process will take less than a minute. However, for a large project, to create an online build with a clean repository could even take more than 3 hours: this is not an exaggeration. If you look at the WSO2 Carbon complete code base, the complete build process takes more than four hours to run with all the test cases. During a long-running build process, it is extremely important that we monitor the build properly.

WSO2 Carbon is a framework that is written on top of OSGi to build servers. All WSO2 products, which are 100 percent open source and released under Apache 2.0 license, are built on top of WSO2 Carbon. WSO2 Carbon code base is available at `https://svn.wso2.org/repos/wso2/carbon/`.

The following screenshot shows an overview of the JVisualVM tool running a Maven build:

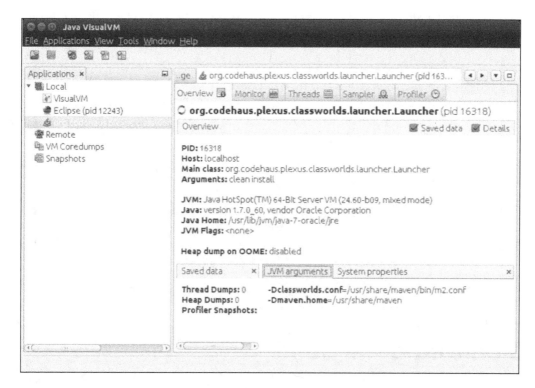

 JVisualVM is a Java virtual machine monitoring, troubleshooting, and profiling tool. To learn more about it, refer `http://docs.oracle.com/javase/6/docs/technotes/tools/share/jvisualvm.html`.

The JVisualVM tool that comes with the JDK distribution can be used to monitor a running Maven build. First, we need to start the Maven build and then start JVisualVM using the following command:

```
$ jvisualvm
```

This command will start the JVisualVM tool. Once the tool gets started, select `org.codehaus.plexus.classworlds.launcher.Launcher` from the **Applications** tab to monitor the running Maven build. You can gather many important statistics using JVisualVM, and based on that you can optimize your system resources for an optimal Maven build.

The following screenshot shows JVisualVM statistics of a running Maven build:

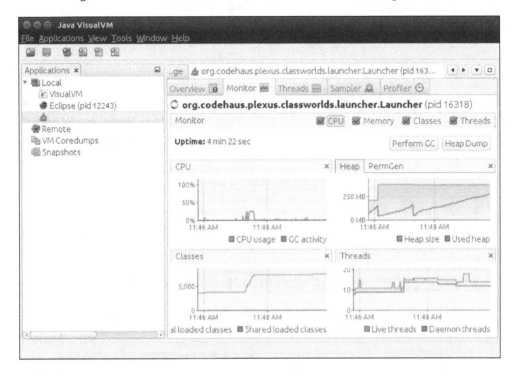

Remote debugging

For a developer, remote debugging is a must-have feature for any build system. Why do we need remote debugging for a build system? This is extremely useful when you run your tests through the build itself. If any of the tests fail during the build, you should be able to debug and pinpoint the problem. The following command will run Maven in the debugging mode:

```
$ mvn clean install -Dmaven.surefire.debug
```

When the build starts to execute tests, it will be paused to connect with an IDE. You can connect Eclipse, NetBeans, or your favorite IDE to port 5005 in order to start remote debugging. By default, Maven opens up port 5005 for remote debugging.

```
-----------------------------------------------------
 T E S T S
-----------------------------------------------------
Listening for transport dt_socket at address: 5005
```

The default listening port number can be changed by setting the value of `address` appropriately. When you set the value of the `suspend` variable to `y`, the Maven build will stop until an IDE gets connected to it. If you want the build to continue and connect the IDE later, then set the value to `n`. To get full control over the debugging options, you can use the following command:

```
$ mvn clean install -Dmaven.surefire.debug="-Xdebug -
  Xrunjdwp:transport=dt_socket,server=y,suspend=y,address=8000 -
  Xnoagent -Djava.compiler=NONE"
```

> Refer to the corresponding IDE documentation to see how it can be remotely connected to an externally running process for remote debugging.

Convention over configuration

Convention over configuration is one of the main design philosophies behind Apache Maven. Let's go through a few examples.

A complete Maven project can be created using the following code snippet in `pom.xml` file:

```xml
<project>
  <modelVersion>4.0.0</modelVersion>
  <groupId>com.packt</groupId>
  <artifactId>sample-one</artifactId>
  <version>1.0.0</version>
</project>
```

Downloading the example code

The Maven POM file starts with the `<project>` element. Always define the `<project/>` element with the corresponding schema. Some tools can't validate the file without it.

```
<project xmlns=http://maven.apache.org/POM/4.0.0
    xmlns:xsi=.........
    xsi:schemaLocation="…">
```

Copy the previous configuration element and create a `pom.xml` file out of it. Then, place it in a directory called `chapter-01` and create the following child directories under it:

- `chapter-01/src/main/java`
- `chapter-01/src/test/java`

Now, you can place your Java code under `chapter-01/src/main/java` and test cases under `chapter-01/src/test/java`. Use the following command to run the Maven build:

$ mvn clean install

This little configuration is tied up with many conventions:

- The Java source code is available at `{base-dir}/src/main/java`
- Test cases are available at `{base-dir}/src/test/java`
- A JAR file type of artifact is produced
- Compiled class files are copied into `{base-dir}/target/classes`
- The final artifact is copied into `{base-dir}/target`
- The link `http://repo.maven.apache.org/maven2` is used as the repository

If someone needs to override the default, conventional behavior of Maven, that is possible too. The following sample `pom.xml` file shows how to override some of the preceding default values:

```
<project>
  <modelVersion>4.0.0</modelVersion>
  <groupId>com.packt</groupId>
  <artifactId>sample-one</artifactId>
  <version>1.0.0</version>
  <packaging>jar</packaging>
```

```
<build>
  <sourceDirectory>${basedir}/src/main/java</sourceDirectory>
  <testSourceDirectory>${basedir}/src/test/java
  </testSourceDirectory>
  <outputDirectory>${basedir}/target/classes
  </outputDirectory>
</build>
</project>
```

IDE integration

Most of the hardcore developers never want to leave their IDE. Not just coding, building, deploying, and testing, they would be happy to do everything (if possible) from the IDE itself. Most popular IDEs have support for Maven integration and they have developed their own plugins to support Maven.

NetBeans integration

NetBeans 6.7 or newer ships with inbuilt Maven integration, while NetBeans 7.0 and newer versions bundle a complete copy of Maven 3 and run it for builds just like you would from the command line. For Version 6.9 or older, you have to download a Maven build and configure the IDE to run that. More information corresponding to Maven and NetBeans integration is available at `http://wiki.netbeans.org/MavenBestPractices`.

IntelliJ IDEA integration

IntelliJ IDEA has inbuilt support for Maven; hence, you don't need to perform any additional steps to install it. More information corresponding to Maven and IntelliJ IDEA integration is available at `http://wiki.jetbrains.net/intellij/Creating_and_importing_Maven_projects`.

Eclipse integration

The M2Eclipse project provides first class Maven support through the Eclipse IDE. More information corresponding to Maven and Eclipse integration is available at `https://www.eclipse.org/m2e/`.

 The book *Maven for Eclipse, Packt Publishing*, discusses Maven and Eclipse integration in detail (`https://www.packtpub.com/application-development/maven-eclipse`).

Troubleshooting

If everything works fine, we don't have to worry about troubleshooting. However, most of the time this is not the case. A Maven build could fail for many reasons—some are under your control, while others are beyond your control. Knowing proper troubleshooting tips helps you pinpoint the exact problem. The following sections list out some of the commonly used troubleshooting tips. We will expand the list as we proceed in this book.

Enabling Maven debug-level logs

Once Maven debug level logging is enabled, it will print all the actions it takes during the build process. To enable debug level logging, use the following command:

```
$ mvn clean install -X
```

Building dependency tree

If you find any issues with any dependencies in your Maven project, the first step is to build a dependency tree. This shows where each dependency comes from. To build the dependency tree, run the following command against your project POM file:

```
$ mvn dependency:tree
```

The following result shows the truncated output of the previous command executed against the Apache Rampart project:

```
[INFO] ------------------------------------------------------------
[INFO] Building Rampart - Trust 1.6.1-wso2v12
[INFO] ------------------------------------------------------------
[INFO]
[INFO] --- maven-dependency-plugin:2.1:tree (default-cli) @ rampart-
trust ---
[INFO] org.apache.rampart:rampart-trust:jar:1.6.1-wso2v12
[INFO] +- org.apache.rampart:rampart-policy:jar:1.6.1-wso2v12:compile
[INFO] +- org.apache.axis2:axis2-kernel:jar:1.6.1-wso2v10:compile
[INFO] |  +- org.apache.ws.commons.axiom:axiom-api:jar:1.2.11-
wso2v4:compile (version managed from 1.2.11)
[INFO] |  |  \- jaxen:jaxen:jar:1.1.1:compile
```

```
[INFO] |   +- org.apache.ws.commons.axiom:axiom-impl:jar:1.2.11-
wso2v4:compile (version managed from 1.2.11)
[INFO] |   +- org.apache.geronimo.specs:geronimo-ws-
metadata_2.0_spec:jar:1.1.2:compile
[INFO] |   +- org.apache.geronimo.specs:geronimo-
jta_1.1_spec:jar:1.1:compile
[INFO] |   +- javax.servlet:servlet-api:jar:2.3:compile
[INFO] |   +- commons-httpclient:commons-httpclient:jar:3.1:compile
[INFO] |   |  \- commons-codec:commons-codec:jar:1.2:compile
[INFO] |   +- commons-fileupload:commons-fileupload:jar:1.2:compile
```

Viewing all environment variables and system properties

If you have multiple JDKs installed in your system, you may wonder what is being used by Maven. The following command will display all the environment variables and system properties set for a given Maven project:

```
$ mvn help:system
```

The following result is the truncated output of the previous command:

```
========================Platform Properties Details===================


======================================================================
System Properties

======================================================================

java.runtime.name=Java(TM) SE Runtime Environment
sun.boot.library.path=/System/Library/Java/JavaVirtualMachines/1.6.0.
  jdk/Contents/Libraries
java.vm.version=20.65-b04-462
awt.nativeDoubleBuffering=true
gopherProxySet=false
mrj.build=11M4609
java.vm.vendor=Apple Inc.
java.vendor.url=http://www.apple.com/
```

```
guice.disable.misplaced.annotation.check=true
path.separator=:
java.vm.name=Java HotSpot(TM) 64-Bit Server VM
file.encoding.pkg=sun.io
sun.java.launcher=SUN_STANDARD
user.country=US
sun.os.patch.level=unknown


============================================================
Environment Variables
============================================================


JAVA_HOME=/System/Library/Frameworks/JavaVM.framework/Versions/Curren
   tJDK/Home
HOME=/Users/prabath
TERM_SESSION_ID=9E4F0D49-180D-45F6-B6FB-DFA2DCBF4B77
M2_HOME=/usr/share/maven/maven-3.2.3/
COMMAND_MODE=unix2003
Apple_PubSub_Socket_Render=/tmp/launch-w7NZbG/Render
LOGNAME=prabath
USER=prabath
```

Viewing the effective POM file

Maven uses default values for the configuration parameters when those are not overridden at the project level configuration. This is exactly what we discussed under the *convention over configuration* section. If we take the same sample POM file we used before in this chapter, we can see how the effective POM file would look using the following command.

```
$ mvn help:effective-pom
```

This is also the best way to see what default values are being used by Maven. More details about the `effective-pom` command are discussed in *Chapter 2, Demystifying Project Object Model*.

Viewing the dependency classpath

The following command lists all the JAR files and directories in the `build` classpath:

```
$ mvn dependency:build-classpath
```

The following result shows the truncated output of the previous command, executed against the Apache Rampart project:

```
[INFO] ------------------------------------------------------------
[INFO] Building Rampart - Trust 1.6.1-wso2v12
[INFO] ------------------------------------------------------------
[INFO]
[INFO] --- maven-dependency-plugin:2.1:build-classpath (default-cli)
@ rampart-trust ---
[INFO] Dependencies classpath:
/Users/prabath/.m2/repository/bouncycastle/bcprov-jdk14/140/bcprov-
jdk14-140.jar:/Users/prabath/.m2/repository/commons-cli/commons-
cli/1.0/commons-cli-1.0.jar:/Users/prabath/.m2/repository/commons-
codec/commons-codec/1.2/commons-codec-
1.2.jar:/Users/prabath/.m2/repository/commons-collections/commons-
collections/3.1/commons-collections-3.1.jar
```

Summary

This chapter focused on building a basic foundation of Maven to bring all the readers to a common ground. We discussed the basic steps to install and configure Maven in Ubuntu, Mac OS X, and Microsoft Windows operating systems. Then, we covered some of the common, useful Maven tips and tricks. As we proceed with the book, some of the concepts that we touched on in this chapter will be discussed in detail later.

In the next chapter, we will discuss **Maven Project Object Model (POM)** in detail.

2
Demystifying Project Object Model

Project Object Model (POM) is at the heart of any Maven project. This chapter focuses on core concepts and best practices related to POM in building a large-scale, multimodule Maven project.

As we proceed with this chapter, we will be discussing the following topics:

- The POM hierarchy, super POM, and parent POM
- Extending and overriding POM files
- Maven coordinates
- Managing dependencies
- Transitive dependencies
- Dependency scopes and optional dependencies

 In Maven 1, the equivalent to today's pom.xml file was identified as project.xml. Maven 2 renamed it to pom.xml. More details about the POM are available at http://maven.apache.org/pom.html.

Project Object Model

Any Maven project must have a `pom.xml` file. POM is the Maven project descriptor, just like the `web.xml` file in your Java EE web application or the `build.xml` file in your Ant project. The following code lists out all the key elements in a Maven `pom.xml` file. As we proceed with the book, we will discuss how to use each element in the most effective manner:

```
<project>
  <parent>...</parent>
  <modelVersion>4.0.0</modelVersion>
  <groupId>...</groupId>
  <artifactId>...</artifactId>
  <version>...</version>
  <packaging>...</packaging>

  <name>...</name>
  <description>...</description>
  <url>...</url>
  <inceptionYear>...</inceptionYear>
  <licenses>...</licenses>
  <organization>...</organization>
  <developers>...</developers>
  <contributors>...</contributors>


  <dependencies>...</dependencies>
  <dependencyManagement>...</dependencyManagement>
  <modules>...</modules>
  <properties>...</properties>

  <build>...</build>
  <reporting>...</reporting>

  <issueManagement>...</issueManagement>
  <ciManagement>...</ciManagement>
  <mailingLists>...</mailingLists>
  <scm>...</scm>
  <prerequisites>...</prerequisites>

  <repositories>...</repositories>
  <pluginRepositories>...</pluginRepositories>

  <distributionManagement>...</distributionManagement>

  <profiles>...</profiles>
</project>
```

The POM hierarchy

POM files maintain a parent-child relationship between them. A child POM file inherits all the configuration elements from its parent POM file. This is how Maven sticks to its design philosophy, which is *convention over configuration*. The minimal POM configuration for any Maven project is extremely simple, which is as follows:

```
<project>
  <modelVersion>4.0.0</modelVersion>
  <groupId>com.packt</groupId>
  <artifactId>sample-one</artifactId>
  <version>1.0.0</version>
</project>
```

Super POM

Any POM file can point to its parent POM. If the parent POM element is missing, then there is a system-wide POM file that is automatically treated as the parent POM file. This POM file is well known as the super POM. Ultimately, all the application POM files get extended from the super POM. The super POM file is at the top of the POM hierarchy, and it is bundled inside MAVEN_HOME/lib/maven-model-builder-3.2.3.jar - org/apache/maven/model/pom-4.0.0.xml. In Maven 2, this was bundled inside maven-2.X.X-uber.jar. All the default configurations are defined in the super POM file. Even the simplest form of a POM file will inherit all the configurations defined in the super POM file. Whatever configuration you need to override, you can do it by redefining the same section in your application POM file. The following lines of code show the super POM file configuration, which comes with Maven 3.2.3:

```
<project>
  <modelVersion>4.0.0</modelVersion>
```

The Maven central is the only repository defined under the repositories section. It will be inherited by all the Maven application modules. Maven uses the repositories defined under the repositories section to download all the dependent artifacts during a Maven build. The following code snippet shows the configuration block in pom.xml, which is used to define repositories:

```
<repositories>
  <repository>
    <id>central</id>
    <name>Central Repository</name>
    <url>http://repo.maven.apache.org/maven2</url>
    <layout>default</layout>
```

```
        <snapshots>
          <enabled>false</enabled>
        </snapshots>
      </repository>
    </repositories>
```

Plugin repositories define where to find Maven plugins. We'll be discussing about Maven plugins in *Chapter 5, Maven Plugins*. The following code snippet shows the configuration related to plugin repositories:

```
<pluginRepositories>
  <pluginRepository>
    <id>central</id>
    <name>Central Repository</name>
    <url>http://repo.maven.apache.org/maven2</url>
    <layout>default</layout>
    <snapshots>
      <enabled>false</enabled>
    </snapshots>
    <releases>
      <updatePolicy>never</updatePolicy>
    </releases>
  </pluginRepository>
</pluginRepositories>
```

The `build` configuration section includes all the information required to build a project:

```
<build>
  <directory>${project.basedir}/target</directory>
  <outputDirectory>${project.build.directory}/classes
  </outputDirectory>
  <finalName>${project.artifactId}-${project.version}
  </finalName>
  <testOutputDirectory>${project.build.directory}/test-classes
  </testOutputDirectory>
  <sourceDirectory>${project.basedir}/src/main/java
  </sourceDirectory>
  <scriptSourceDirectory>${project.basedir}/src/main/scripts
  </scriptSourceDirectory>
  <testSourceDirectory>${project.basedir}/src/test/java
  </testSourceDirectory>

  <resources>
    <resource>
```

```
        <directory>${project.basedir}/src/main/resources
        </directory>
      </resource>
    </resources>
    <testResources>
      <testResource>
        <directory>${project.basedir}/src/test/resources
        </directory>
      </testResource>
    </testResources>

    <pluginManagement>
      <plugins>
        <plugin>
          <artifactId>maven-antrun-plugin</artifactId>
          <version>1.3</version>
        </plugin>
        <plugin>
          <artifactId>maven-assembly-plugin</artifactId>
          <version>2.2-beta-5</version>
        </plugin>
        <plugin>
          <artifactId>maven-dependency-plugin</artifactId>
          <version>2.8</version>
        </plugin>
        <plugin>
          <artifactId>maven-release-plugin</artifactId>
          <version>2.3.2</version>
        </plugin>
      </plugins>
    </pluginManagement>

  </build>
```

The reporting section includes the details of report plugins, which are used to generate reports that will be later displayed on the site generated by Maven. The super POM only provides a default value for the output directory. The code is as follows:

```
<reporting>
  <outputDirectory>${project.build.directory}/site
  </outputDirectory>
</reporting>
```

The following code snippet defines the default build profile. When no profiles are defined at the application level, this will get executed. We will be talking about profiles in *Chapter 9, Best Practices*:

```xml
<profiles>
  <profile>
    <id>release-profile</id>

    <activation>
      <property>
        <name>performRelease</name>
        <value>true</value>
      </property>
    </activation>

    <build>
      <plugins>
        <plugin>
          <inherited>true</inherited>
          <artifactId>maven-source-plugin</artifactId>
          <executions>
            <execution>
              <id>attach-sources</id>
              <goals>
                <goal>jar</goal>
              </goals>
            </execution>
          </executions>
        </plugin>
        <plugin>
          <inherited>true</inherited>
          <artifactId>maven-javadoc-plugin</artifactId>
          <executions>
            <execution>
              <id>attach-javadocs</id>
              <goals>
                <goal>jar</goal>
              </goals>
            </execution>
          </executions>
        </plugin>
        <plugin>
          <inherited>true</inherited>
          <artifactId>maven-deploy-plugin</artifactId>
```

```
      <configuration>
        <updateReleaseInfo>true</updateReleaseInfo>
      </configuration>
    </plugin>
   </plugins>
  </build>
 </profile>
</profiles>

</project>
```

The following figure shows an abstract view of the super POM file, with the key configuration elements:

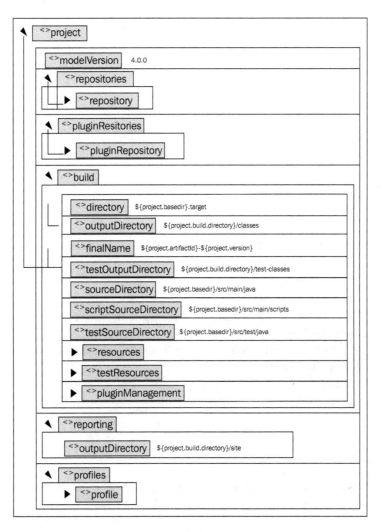

POM extending and overriding

Let's see how POM overriding works. In the following example, we extend the `repositories` section to add one more repository to what is defined in the Maven super POM file:

```
<project>
  <modelVersion>4.0.0</modelVersion>
  <groupId>com.packt</groupId>
  <artifactId>sample-one</artifactId>
  <version>1.0.0</version>

  <repositories>
    <repository>
      <id>wso2-nexus</id>
      <name>WSO2 internal Repository</name>
      <url>http://maven.wso2.org/nexus/content/groups/wso2-
        public/
      </url>
      <releases>
        <enabled>true</enabled>
        <updatePolicy>daily</updatePolicy>
        <checksumPolicy>ignore</checksumPolicy>
      </releases>
    </repository>
  </repositories>

</project>
```

Type the following command from the directory, where you have the previous POM file:

```
$ mvn help:effective-pom
```

This will display the effective POM file for the application, which combines all the default settings from the super POM file and the configuration defined in your application POM. In the following code snippet, you can see that the `<repositories>` section in the super POM file is being extended by your application specific configuration. Now the `<repositories>` section has the central repository defined in the super POM file as well as your application specific repository:

```
<repositories>
  <repository>
      <releases>
        <enabled>true</enabled>
        <updatePolicy>daily</updatePolicy>
        <checksumPolicy>ignore</checksumPolicy>
```

```
      </releases>
      <id>wso2-nexus</id>
      <name>WSO2 internal Repository</name>
      <url>
        http://maven.wso2.org/nexus/content/groups/wso2-public/
      </url>
    </repository>
    <repository>
      <snapshots>
        <enabled>false</enabled>
      </snapshots>
      <id>central</id>
      <name>Central Repository</name>
      <url>https://repo.maven.apache.org/maven2</url>
    </repository>
  </repositories>
```

If you want to override any of the configuration elements corresponding to the Maven central repository, inherited from the super POM file, then you have to define a repository in your application POM with the same repository id (as of the Maven central repository) and override the configuration element you need.

One main advantage of the POM hierarchy in Maven is that you can extend as well as override the configuration inherited from the top. Say for example, you might need to keep all the plugins defined in the super POM file, but just want to override the version of maven-release-plugin. The following configuration shows how to do it. By default, in the super POM, the maven-release-plugin version is 2.3.2, and here we update it to 2.5 in our application POM. If you run mvn help:effective-pom again against the updated POM file, you will notice that the plugin version is updated while the rest of the plugin configuration from the super POM file remain unchanged:

```
<project>

  <modelVersion>4.0.0</modelVersion>
  <groupId>com.packt</groupId>
  <artifactId>sample-one</artifactId>
  <version>1.0.0</version>

  <build>
    <pluginManagement>
      <plugins>
        <plugin>
          <artifactId>maven-release-plugin</artifactId>
          <version>2.5</version>
```

```
        </plugin>
      </plugins>
    </pluginManagement>
  </build>

</project>
```

To override the configuration of a given element or an artifact in the POM hierarchy, Maven should be able to uniquely identify the corresponding artifact. In the preceding scenario, the plugin was identified by its `artifactId`. In *Chapter 5, Maven Plugins*, we will further discuss how Maven locates plugins.

Maven coordinates

Maven coordinates identify uniquely a project, a dependency, or a plugin defined in POM. Each entity is uniquely identified by the combination of a group identifier, an artifact identifier, and the version (and, of course, with the packaging and the classifier). The group identifier is a way of grouping different Maven artifacts. For example, a set of artifacts produced by a company can be grouped under the same group identifier. The artifact identifier is the way you identify an artifact, which could be JAR, WAR, or any other type of an artifact uniquely within a given group. The `version` element lets you keep the same artifact in different versions in the same repository.

 A valid Maven POM file must have `groupId`, `artifactId`, and `version`. The groupId and the version elements can also be inherited from the parent POM file.

All these three coordinates of a given Maven artifact are used to define its path in the Maven repository. If we take the following example, the corresponding JAR file is installed in the local repository with the `USER_HOME/.m2/repository/com/packt/sample-one/1.0.0/` path:

```
<groupId>com.packt</groupId>
<artifactId>sample-one</artifactId>
<version>1.0.0</version>
```

If you have gone through the elements of the super POM file carefully, you might have noticed that it does not have any of the previously mentioned elements. No `groupId`, `artifactId`, or `version`. Does this mean that the super POM file is not a valid POM? The super POM file is like an abstract class in Java. It does not work by itself; it must be inherited by a child POM file. Another way to look at the super POM file is that it's the Maven's way of sharing default configurations.

Once again, if you look at the `<pluginManagement>` section of the super POM file, as shown in the following code snippet, you will notice that a given plugin artifact is identified only by its `artifactId` and `version` elements. This contradicts what we mentioned before; a given artifact is uniquely identified by the combination of `groupId`, `artifactId`, and `version`. How is this possible?

```
<plugin>
  <artifactId>maven-antrun-plugin</artifactId>
  <version>1.3</version>
</plugin>
```

There is an exception for plugins. You need not specify `groupId` for a plugin in the POM file; it's optional. By default, Maven uses `org.apache.maven.plugins` or `org.codehaus.mojo` as `groupId`. Have a look at the following section in `MAVEN_HOME/conf/settings.xml`. If you want to add additional group IDs for plugin lookup, you have to uncomment the section below and add them there:

```
<!-- pluginGroups
 | This is a list of additional group identifiers that
 | will be searched when resolving plugins by their prefix, i.e.
 | when invoking a command line like "mvn prefix:goal".
 | Maven will automatically add the group identifiers
 | "org.apache.maven.plugins" and "org.codehaus.mojo"
 | if these are not already contained in the list.
 |-->
<pluginGroups>
  <!-- pluginGroup
    | Specifies a further group identifier to use for plugin
    | lookup.
  <pluginGroup>com.your.plugins</pluginGroup>
  -->
</pluginGroups>
```

 We will be discussing Maven plugins in detail in *Chapter 5, Maven Plugins*.

Parent POM file

When we deal with hundreds of Maven modules, we need to structure the project to avoid any redundancies or any duplicate configurations. If not, it will lead to a huge maintenance nightmare. Let's have a look at some popular open source projects.

The WSO2 Carbon Turing branch, which is available at `https://svn.wso2.org/repos/wso2/carbon/platform/branches/turing/`, has more than 1000 Maven modules. Anyone who downloads the source code from the root should be able to build the complete source, with all components. The `pom.xml` file at the root acts as a module-aggregating POM. It defines all Maven modules that need to be built under the `<modules>` element. Each module element defines the relative path (from the root POM file) to the corresponding Maven module. There needs to be another POM file under the defined relative path. The root POM in the WSO2 Carbon Turing project only acts as an aggregator module. It does not build any parent-child relationships with other Maven modules. The following code snippet shows the module configuration in the root `pom.xml` file

```
<modules>
  <module>parent</module>
  <module>dependencies</module>
  <module>service-stubs</module>
  <module>components</module>
  <module>platform-integration/clarity-framework</module>
  <module>features</module>
  <module>samples/shopping-cart</module>
  <module>samples/shopping-cart-global</module>
</modules>
```

Now, let's have a look at the POM file inside the `parent` module. This POM file defines plugin repositories, a distribution repository, plugins, and a set of properties. This does not have any dependencies, and this is the POM file that acts as the parent for other Maven submodules. The parent POM file has the following coordinates:

```
<groupId>org.wso2.carbon</groupId>
<artifactId>platform-parent</artifactId>
<version>4.2.0</version>
<packaging>pom</packaging>
```

If you look at the POM file inside the `components` module, it refers `parent/pom.xml` as the parent Maven module. The value of the `relativePath` element, by default, refers to the `pom.xml` file one level above, that is, `../pom.xml`. However, in this case, it is not the parent POM file; hence, the value of the element must be overridden and set to `../parent/pom.xml`, as shown here:

```
<groupId>org.wso2.carbon</groupId>
<artifactId>carbon-components</artifactId>
<version>4.2.0</version>
<parent>
  <groupId>org.wso2.carbon</groupId>
  <artifactId>platform-parent</artifactId>
```

```
    <version>4.2.0</version>
    <relativePath>../parent/pom.xml</relativePath>
</parent>
```

If you go inside the `components` module and run `mvn help:effective-pom`, you will notice that the effective POM aggregates both the configurations defined in `parent/pom.xml` and `components/pom.xml`. Parent POM files help to propagate common configuration elements to the downstream Maven modules, and it can go up to many levels. The `components/pom.xml` file acts as a parent POM file for Maven modules below that. For example, let's have a look at the following `components/identity/pom.xml` file. It has a reference to the `components/pom.xml` file as its parent. Note that here we do not need to use the `relativePath` element, as the corresponding parent POM is at the default location:

```
<groupId>org.wso2.carbon</groupId>
<artifactId>identity</artifactId>
<version>4.2.0</version>
<parent>
    <groupId>org.wso2.carbon</groupId>
    <artifactId>carbon-components</artifactId>
    <version>4.2.0</version>
</parent>
```

 The complete list of elements in a POM file is explained in detail at `http://maven.apache.org/ref/3.2.3/maven-model/maven.html`.

Managing POM dependencies

In a large-scale development project with hundreds of Maven modules, managing dependencies could be a hazardous task. There are two effective ways to manage dependencies: POM inheritance and dependency grouping. With POM inheritance, the parent POM file has to define all the common dependencies used by its child modules under the `dependencyManagement` section. This way we can avoid any duplicate dependencies. Also, if we have to update the version of a given dependency, then we only have to make a change in one place. Let's take the same example we discussed before using the WSO2 Carbon Turing project. Let's have a look at the `dependencyManagement` section of `parent/pom.xml` (only a part of the POM file is shown here):

```
<dependencyManagement>
  <dependencies>
    <dependency>
```

```
          <groupId>org.apache.axis2</groupId>
          <artifactId>axis2-transport-mail</artifactId>
          <version>${axis2-transports.version}</version>
        </dependency>
        <dependency>
          <groupId>org.apache.ws.commons.axiom.wso2</groupId>
          <artifactId>axiom</artifactId>
          <version>${axiom.wso2.version}</version>
        </dependency>
      </dependencies>
    </dependencyManagement>
```

 To know more about dependency management, refer to *Introduction to the Dependency Mechanism* at `http://maven.apache.org/guides/ introduction/introduction-to-dependency-mechanism.html`.

Let's have a look at the `dependency` section of `identity/org.wso2.carbon. identity.core/4.2.3/pom.xml`, which extends from `components/pom.xml`. Here, you will see only `groupId` and `artifactId` of a given dependency but not `version`. The version of each dependency is managed through the `dependencyManagement` section of the parent POM file. If any child Maven module wants to override the version of an inherited dependency, it can simply add the `version` element:

```
<dependencies>
  <dependency>
    <groupId>org.apache.axis2.wso2</groupId>
    <artifactId>axis2</artifactId>
  </dependency>
  <dependency>
    <groupId>org.apache.ws.commons.axiom.wso2</groupId>
   <artifactId>axiom</artifactId>
  </dependency>
</dependencies>
```

Another best practice to highlight here is the way dependency versions are specified in the parent POM file, which is as follows:

```
<version>${axiom.wso2.version}</version>
```

Instead of specifying the version number inside the `dependency` element itself, here we have taken it out and represented the version as a property. The value of the property is defined under the `properties` section of the parent POM file, as shown in the following line of code. This makes POM maintenance extremely easy:

```
<properties>
  <axis2.wso2.version>1.6.1.wso2v10</axis2.wso2.version>
</properties>
```

The second approach to manage dependencies is through dependency grouping. All the common dependencies can be grouped into a single POM file. This approach is much better than POM inheritance. Here, you do not need to add references to individual dependencies. Let's go through a simple example. First, we need to logically group all dependencies into a single POM file.

Apache Axis2 is an open source SOAP engine. To build an Axis2 client, you need to have all the following dependencies added into your project. If you have multiple Axis2 client modules, in each module, you need to duplicate all these dependencies:

```
<dependency>
  <groupId>org.apache.axis2</groupId>
  <artifactId>axis2-kernel</artifactId>
  <version>1.6.2</version>
</dependency>
<dependency>
  <groupId>org.apache.axis2</groupId>
  <artifactId>axis2-adb</artifactId>
  <version>1.6.2</version>
</dependency>
<dependency>
  <groupId>org.apache.axis2</groupId>
  <artifactId>axis2-transport-http</artifactId>
  <version>1.6.2</version>
</dependency>
<dependency>
  <groupId>org.apache.axis2</groupId>
  <artifactId>axis2-transport-local</artifactId>
  <version>1.6.2</version>
</dependency>
<dependency>
  <groupId>org.apache.axis2</groupId>
  <artifactId>axis2-xmlbeans</artifactId>
  <version>1.6.2</version>
</dependency>
```

To avoid the dependency duplication, we can create a Maven module with all the previously mentioned five dependencies as shown in the following code. Make sure to set the value of the packaging element to pom:

```
<project>

  <modelVersion>4.0.0</modelVersion>
  <groupId>com.packt</groupId>
  <artifactId>axis2-client</artifactId>
  <version>1.0.0</version>
  <packaging>pom</packaging>

  <dependencies>
    <dependency>
      <groupId>org.apache.axis2</groupId>
      <artifactId>axis2-kernel</artifactId>
      <version>1.6.2</version>
    </dependency>
    <dependency>
      <groupId>org.apache.axis2</groupId>
      <artifactId>axis2-adb</artifactId>
      <version>1.6.2</version>
    </dependency>
    <dependency>
      <groupId>org.apache.axis2</groupId>
      <artifactId>axis2-transport-http</artifactId>
      <version>1.6.2</version>
    </dependency>
    <dependency>
      <groupId>org.apache.axis2</groupId>
      <artifactId>axis2-transport-local</artifactId>
      <version>1.6.2</version>
    </dependency>
    <dependency>
      <groupId>org.apache.axis2</groupId>
      <artifactId>axis2-xmlbeans</artifactId>
      <version>1.6.2</version>
    </dependency>
  </dependencies>

</project>
```

Now, in all of your Axis2 client projects, you only need to add a dependency to the `com.packt.axis2-client` module, as follows:

```
<project>

  <modelVersion>4.0.0</modelVersion>
  <groupId>com.packt</groupId>
  <artifactId>my-axis2-client</artifactId>
  <version>1.0.0</version>

  <dependencies>
    <dependency>
      <groupId>com.packt</groupId>
      <artifactId>axis2-client</artifactId>
      <version>1.0.0</version>
    </dependency>
  </dependencies>

</project>
```

Transitive dependencies

The transitive dependency feature was introduced in Maven 2.0, which automatically identifies the dependencies of your project dependencies and get them all into the build path of your project. Let's take the following POM as an example; it has only a single dependency:

```
<project>

  <modelVersion>4.0.0</modelVersion>
  <groupId>com.packt</groupId>
  <artifactId>jose</artifactId>
  <version>1.0.0</version>

  <dependencies>
    <dependency>
      <groupId>com.nimbusds</groupId>
      <artifactId>nimbus-jose-jwt</artifactId>
      <version>2.26</version>
    </dependency>
  </dependencies>

</project>
```

If you try to create an Eclipse project from the previous POM file using the `mvn eclipse:eclipse` command, it will result in the following `.classpath` file. Here you can see, in addition to the `nimbus-jose-jwt-2.26.jar` file, three more JAR files have been added. These are the transitive dependencies of the `nimbus-jose-jwt` dependency:

```
<classpath>
  <classpathentry kind="src" path="src/main/java"
    including="**/*.java"/>
  <classpathentry kind="output" path="target/classes"/>
  <classpathentry kind="con"
    path="org.eclipse.jdt.launching.JRE_CONTAINER"/>
  <classpathentry kind="var" path="M2_REPO/com/nimbusds/nimbus-
    jose-jwt/2.26/nimbus-jose-jwt-2.26.jar"/>
  <classpathentry kind="var" path="M2_REPO/net/jcip/jcip-
    annotations/1.0/jcip-annotations-1.0.jar"/>
  <classpathentry kind="var" path="M2_REPO/net/minidev/json-
    smart/1.1.1/json-smart-1.1.1.jar"/>
  <classpathentry kind="var"
    path="M2_REPO/org/bouncycastle/bcprov-jdk15on/1.50/bcprov-
    jdk15on-1.50.jar"/>
</classpath>
```

If you look at the POM file of the `nimbus-jose-jwt` project, you will see that the previously mentioned transitive dependencies are defined here as dependencies. Maven does not define a limit for transitive dependencies. One transitive dependency can have a reference to another transitive dependency, and it can go on like this endlessly, given that there are no cyclic dependencies found.

Transitive dependencies can cause some pain too if not used with care. If we take the same Maven module we discussed before as an example and have the following Java code inside `src/main/java directory`, it will compile without any errors/complaints. This has only a single dependency, which is `nimbus-jose-jwt-2.26.jar`. However, the `net.minidev.json.JSONArray` class comes from a transitive dependency, which is `json-smart-1.1.1.jar`. The build works fine, because Maven gets all the transitive dependencies into the project build path. Everything will work fine till one fine day, you update the version of `nimbus-jose-jwt`, and the new version could have a reference to a new version of `json-smart` jar, which is not compatible with your code. This could easily break your build or might cause test cases to fail. This would create hazards and it would be a nightmare to find out the root cause. The following Java code uses the `JSONArray` class from `json-smart-1.1.1.jar`:

```
import net.minidev.json.JSONArray;
import com.nimbusds.jwt.JWTClaimsSet;

public class JOSEUtil {
```

```
public static void main(String[] args) {

    JWTClaimsSet jwtClaims = new JWTClaimsSet();

    JSONArray jsonArray = new JSONArray();

    jsonArray.add("maven-book");

    jwtClaims.setIssuer("https://packt.com");

    jwtClaims.setSubject("john");

    jwtClaims.setCustomClaim("book", jsonArray);

    }

}
```

To avoid such a nightmare, you need to follow a simple rule of thumb. If you have any import statements in a Java class, you need to make sure that the dependency JAR file corresponding to this is being added to the project POM file.

The Maven dependency plugin helps you to find out such inconsistencies in your Maven module. Run the following command and observe its output;

```
$ mvn dependency:analyze

[INFO] --- maven-dependency-plugin:2.8:analyze (default-cli) @
  jose ---

[WARNING] Used undeclared dependencies found:

[WARNING] net.minidev:json-smart:jar:1.1.1:compile
```

Note the two warnings in the previous output. It clearly says we have an undeclared dependency for json-smart jar.

 The Maven dependency plugin has several goals to find out inconsistencies and possible loopholes in your dependency management. For more details on this, refer to http://maven. apache.org/plugins/maven-dependency-plugin/.

Dependency scopes

Maven defines the following six scope types; if there is no scope element defined for a given dependency, the default scope, compile, will get applied:

- compile: This is the default scope. Any dependency defined under the compile scope will be available in all the class paths and also packaged into the final artifact produced by the Maven project. If you are building a WAR type artifact, then the referred JAR file with the compile scope will be embedded into the WAR file itself.

- `provided`: This scope expects that the corresponding dependency will be provided either by JDK or a container, which runs the application. The best example is the servlet API. Any dependency with the `provided` scope will be available in the build time class path, but it won't be packaged into the final artifact. If it's a WAR file, the servlet API will be available in the class path during the build time, but won't get packaged into the WAR file.

```
<dependency>
  <groupId>javax.servlet</groupId>
  <artifactId>javax.servlet-api</artifactId>
  <version>3.0.1</version>
  <scope>provided</scope>
</dependency>
```

- `runtime`: Dependencies defined under the `runtime` scope will be available only during the runtime, not in the build time class path. These dependencies will be packaged into the final artifact. You can have a web app that in runtime talks to a MySQL database. Your code does not have any hard dependency to the MySQL database driver. Code is written against the Java JDBC API, and it does not need the MySQL database driver at the build time. However, during the runtime, it needs the driver to talk to the MySQL database. For this, the driver should be packaged into the final artifact.

- `test`: Dependencies are only needed for test compilation (for example, JUnit and TestNG), and execution must be defined under the `test` scope. These dependencies won't get packaged into the final artifact.

- `system`: This is very similar to the scope `provided`. The only difference is with the `system` scope, you need to tell Maven how to find it. System dependencies are useful when you do not have the referred dependency in a Maven repository. With this, you need to make sure that all system dependencies are available to download with the source code itself. It is always recommended to avoid using system dependencies. The following code snippets shows how to define a system dependency:

```
<dependency>
  <groupId>com.packt</groupId>
  <artifactId>jose</artifactId>
  <version>1.0.0</version>
  <scope>system</scope>
  <systemPath>${basedir}/lib/jose.jar</systemPath>
</dependency>
```

 $basedir is a built-in property defined in Maven to represent the directory, which has the corresponding POM file.

- `import`: This is only applicable for dependencies defined under the `dependencyManagement` section with the `pom` packaging type. Let's take the following POM file; it has the packaging type defined as `pom`:

```
<project>
  <modelVersion>4.0.0</modelVersion>
  <groupId>com.packt</groupId>
  <artifactId>axis2-client</artifactId>
  <version>1.0.0</version>
  <packaging>pom</packaging>

  <dependencyManagement>
    <dependencies>
      <dependency>
        <groupId>org.apache.axis2</groupId>
        <artifactId>axis2-kernel</artifactId>
        <version>1.6.2</version>
      </dependency>
      <dependency>
        <groupId>org.apache.axis2</groupId>
        <artifactId>axis2-adb</artifactId>
        <version>1.6.2</version>
      </dependency>
    </dependencies>
  </dependencyManagement>
</project>
```

Now, from a different Maven module, we add a dependency under the `dependencyManagement` section to the previous module, with the scope value set to `import` and the value of type set to `pom`:

```
<project>

  <modelVersion>4.0.0</modelVersion>
  <groupId>com.packt</groupId>
  <artifactId>my-axis2-client</artifactId>
  <version>1.0.0</version>

  <dependencyManagement>
    <dependencies>
      <dependency>
        <groupId>com.packt</groupId>
        <artifactId>axis2-client</artifactId>
        <version>1.0.0</version>
```

```
            <type>pom</type>
            <scope>import</scope>
         </dependency>
      </dependencies>
   </dependencyManagement>
<project>
```

Now, if we run `mvn help:effective-pom` against the last POM file, we will see the dependencies from before are being imported, as shown here:

```
<dependencyManagement>
  <dependencies>
    <dependency>
      <groupId>org.apache.axis2</groupId>
      <artifactId>axis2-kernel</artifactId>
      <version>1.6.2</version>
    </dependency>
    <dependency>
      <groupId>org.apache.axis2</groupId>
      <artifactId>axis2-adb</artifactId>
      <version>1.6.2</version>
    </dependency>
  </dependencies>
</dependencyManagement>
```

Optional dependencies

Let's say that we have a Java project that has to work with two different OSGi runtimes. We have written almost all the code to the OSGi API, but there are certain parts in the code that consume OSGi runtime-specific APIs. In runtime, only the code path related to the underneath OSGi runtime will get executed, not both. This raises the need to have both OSGI runtime JAR files at the build time. However, at runtime, we do not need both the code execution paths, only the one related to the OSGi runtime is needed. We can meet these requirements by optional dependencies, which is as follows:

```
<project>

  <modelVersion>4.0.0</modelVersion>
  <groupId>com.packt</groupId>
  <artifactId>osgi.client</artifactId>
  <version>1.0.0</version>

  <dependencies>
    <dependency>
```

```
            <groupId>org.eclipse.equinox</groupId>
            <artifactId>osgi</artifactId>
            <version>3.1.1</version>
            <scope>compile</scope>
            <optional>true</optional>
        </dependency>
        <dependency>
            <groupId>org.apache.phoenix</groupId>
            <artifactId>phoenix-core</artifactId>
            <version>3.0.0-incubating</version>
            <scope>compile</scope>
            <optional>true</optional>
        </dependency>
    </dependencies>

</project>
```

For any client project that needs `com.packt.osgi.client` to work in an Equinox OSGi runtime, it must explicitly add a dependency to the Equinox JAR file.

```
<project>

    <modelVersion>4.0.0</modelVersion>
    <groupId>com.packt</groupId>
    <artifactId>my.osgi.client</artifactId>
    <version>1.0.0</version>

    <dependencies>
        <dependency>
            <groupId>org.eclipse.equinox</groupId>
            <artifactId>osgi</artifactId>
            <version>3.1.1</version>
            <scope>compile</scope>
        </dependency>
        <dependency>
            <groupId>com.packt</groupId>
            <artifactId>osgi.client</artifactId>
            <version>1.0.0</version>
            <scope>compile</scope>
        </dependency>
    </dependencies>

</project>
```

Dependency exclusion

Dependency exclusion helps avoid getting a selected set of transitive dependencies. Say for example, we have the following POM file with two dependencies, one for the nimbus-jose-jwt and the other for the json-smart artifact:

```
<project>

    <modelVersion>4.0.0</modelVersion>
    <groupId>com.packt</groupId>
    <artifactId>jose</artifactId>
    <version>1.0.0</version>

    <dependencies>
      <dependency>
        <groupId>com.nimbusds</groupId>
        <artifactId>nimbus-jose-jwt</artifactId>
        <version>2.26</version>
      </dependency>
      <dependency>
        <groupId>net.minidev</groupId>
        <artifactId>json-smart</artifactId>
        <version>1.0.9</version>
      </dependency>
    </dependencies>

</project>
```

If we try to run mvn eclipse:eclipse against the previous POM file, you will see the following .classpath file that has a dependency to json-smart version 1.0.9 as rightly expected:

```
<classpathentry kind="var" path="M2_REPO/net/minidev/json-
    smart/1.0.9/json-smart-1.0.9.jar"/>
```

Let's say we have another project that refers to the same nimbus-jose-jwt artifact and a newer version of the json-smart JAR file:

```
<project>

    <modelVersion>4.0.0</modelVersion>
    <groupId>com.packt</groupId>
    <artifactId>jose.ext</artifactId>
    <version>1.0.0</version>

    <dependencies>
      <dependency>
        <groupId>com.nimbusds</groupId>
```

```
      <artifactId>nimbus-jose-jwt</artifactId>
      <version>2.26</version>
    </dependency>
    <dependency>
      <groupId>net.minidev</groupId>
      <artifactId>json-smart</artifactId>
      <version>1.1.1</version>
    </dependency>
  </dependencies>

</project>
```

If we try to run `mvn eclipse:eclipse` against the previous POM file, you will see the following `.classpath` file that has a dependency to the `json-smart` artifact version 1.1.1:

```
<classpathentry kind="var" path="M2_REPO/net/minidev/json-
  smart/1.1.1/json-smart-1.1.1.jar"/>
```

We still did not see a problem. Now, say we build a WAR file that has dependencies to both the previous Maven modules:

```
<project>

  <modelVersion>4.0.0</modelVersion>
  <groupId>com.packt</groupId>
  <artifactId>jose.war</artifactId>
  <version>1.0.0</version>
  <version>war</version>

  <dependencies>
    <dependency>
      <groupId>com.packt</groupId>
      <artifactId>jose</artifactId>
      <version>1.0.0</version>
    </dependency>
    <dependency>
      <groupId>com.packt</groupId>
      <artifactId>jose.ext</artifactId>
      <version>1.0.0</version>
    </dependency>
  </dependencies>

</project>
```

Once the WAR file is created, inside WEB-INF/lib, we can see only the 1.1.1 version of json-smart JAR file. This comes as a transitive dependency of the com.packt. jose.ext project. There can be a case where the WAR file does not need the 1.1.1 version in its runtime, but needs the 1.0.9 version. To achieve this, we need to exclude the 1.1.1 version of the json-smart JAR file from the com.packt.jose.ext project, as shown in the following code:

```
<project>

  <modelVersion>4.0.0</modelVersion>
  <groupId>com.packt</groupId>
  <artifactId>jose.war</artifactId>
  <version>1.0.0</version>
  <version>war</version>

  <dependencies>
    <dependency>
      <groupId>com.packt</groupId>
      <artifactId>jose</artifactId>
      <version>1.0.0</version>
    </dependency>
    <dependency>
      <groupId>com.packt</groupId>
      <artifactId>jose.ext</artifactId>
      <version>1.0.0</version>
      <exclusions>
        <exclusion>
          <groupId>net.minidev</groupId>
          <artifactId>json-smart</artifactId>
        </exclusion>
      </exclusions>
    </dependency>
  </dependencies>

</project>
```

Now, if you look inside WEB-INF/lib, you can see only the 1.0.9 version of the json-smart JAR file.

Summary

In this chapter, we focused our discussion around Maven Project Object Model (POM) and how to adhere to industry-wide accepted best practices to avoid maintenance nightmares. The key elements of a POM file, POM hierarchy and inheritance, managing dependencies, and related topics were covered here. In the next chapter, we will have a look at different options available to configure Maven.

3

Maven Configuration

Maven maintains its configuration at three different levels: global, user, and project. This chapter discusses how to customize Maven configuration at all three levels for optimal use:

- The global-level configuration is maintained at MAVEN_HOME/conf/ settings.xml

- The user-level configuration is maintained at USER_HOME/.m2/settings.xml

- The project-level configuration is maintained at PROJECT_HOME/pom.xml

> The settings.xml file is the God of all Maven configurations. The XML schema of the configuration elements defined in settings.xml is available at http://maven.apache.org/ xsd/settings-1.0.0.xsd. The following snippet shows a high-level outline of the settings.xml file:
>
> ```
> <settings>
> </settings>
> ```

As we proceed with this chapter, the following topics will be covered:

- Maven Wagon
- Proxy authentication
- Secured repositories
- Integration with Source Control Management systems
- Mirrored repositories
- Deploying artifacts
- Enabling logging

Maven Wagon

Maven Wagon provides a layer of abstraction over the underlying transport protocols to transfer resources or artifacts to and from Maven repositories. At the time of writing this book, the unified API provided by Maven Wagon has implementations for seven transports. The following figure shows the layered architecture of Maven Wagon:

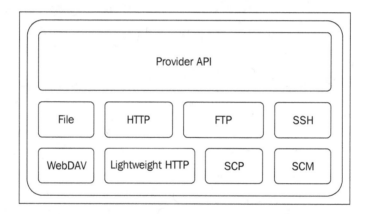

Due to the decoupled architecture, Maven does not have a hard dependency on the communication protocols supported by the repository. It can be over HTTP, FTP, SSH, WebDAV, or any other custom protocol.

 More details about Maven Wagon can be found at http://maven.apache.org/wagon/.

Wagon HTTP(S) transport

From Maven 3.0.4 onwards, Wagon HTTP(S) transport is based on Apache HTTP client 4.1.2. This also added the HTTP connection pooling support. By default, the connection pool size is 20 per destination. Wagon HTTP transport can be further tuned via `settings.xml`.

Maven artifact repositories can be defined in the application POM and will also inherit from the super POM file. The super POM file has defined the following repository with the id `central` tag:

```
<repositories>
  <repository>
    <snapshots>
      <enabled>false</enabled>
    </snapshots>
    <id>central</id>
    <name>Central Repository</name>
    <url>http://repo.maven.apache.org/maven2</url>
  </repository>
</repositories>
```

As the connectivity to the repository defined in the previous configuration is over HTTP, Wagon will use its HTTP implementation. You can see that the value of the `url` element is set to an HTTP endpoint.

The Wagon HTTP connection can be configured per repository by its id via `MAVEN_HOME/conf/settings.xml`. If we want to change the read timeout period of the HTTP connection to the previous Maven repository with the id `central` tag, add the following child element under the `<servers/>` element. The value of the `readTimeout` element defines the timeout period in milliseconds. If needed, the timeout can be defined per HTTP verb. Here, it's defined only for HTTP GET. The value of the `id` element must match with what is defined under `<repository>` element in the `pom.xml` file.

```
<server>
  <id>central</id>
  <configuration>
    <httpConfiguration>
      <get>
        <readTimeout>100000</readTimeout>
      </get>
    </httpConfiguration>
  </configuration>
</server>
```

The default read timeout in Maven HTTP connection is 30 minutes.

How about the connection timeout? The connection timeout is different from the connection read timeout, as discussed before. The connection timeout is the waiting time to make the initial connection, while the connection read timeout is the waiting time to read data from the connection after it is established. The following configuration shows how to change the default connection timeout. The value of the connectionTimeout element is defined in milliseconds:

```
<server>
  <id>central</id>
  <configuration>
    <httpConfiguration>
      <get>
        <connectionTimeout>100000</connectionTimeout>
      </get>
    </httpConfiguration>
  </configuration>
</server>
```

 The default connection timeout in the Maven HTTP connection is 100 seconds.

There can be a case where a remote repository server expects certain HTTP headers in the request. To add custom headers, you can have the following configuration:

```
<server>
  <id>central</id>
  <configuration>
    <httpHeaders>
      <httpHeader>
        <name>CUSTOM_HEADER_NAME</name>
        <value>CUSTOM_HEADER_VALUE</value>
      </httpHeader>
    </httpHeaders>
  </configuration>
</server>
```

As we discussed before, Wagon HTTP(S) transport is based on Apache HTTP client 4.1.2. Apache HTTP client has many configuration parameters to alter its default behavior. Any of these parameters can be configured in Wagon HTTP transport for Maven, as shown in the following configuration:

```
<server>
  <id>central</id>
  <configuration>
    <httpConfiguration>
      <get>
        <params>
          <param>
            <name>PARAM_NAME</name>
            <value>PARAM_VALUE</value>
          </param>
        </params>
      </get>
    </httpConfiguration>
  </configuration>
</server>
```

To ask an HTTP client to ignore cookies for all HTTP GET requests, you need to set the value of `http.protocol.cookie-policy` to `ignore`:

```
<server>
  <id>central</id>
  <configuration>
    <httpConfiguration>
      <get>
        <params>
          <param>
            <name>http.protocol.cookie-policy</name>
            <value>ignore</value>
          </param>
        </params>
      </get>
    </httpConfiguration>
  </configuration>
</server>
```

Wagon system properties

Maven Wagon's default behavior can be altered with the following system properties:

- `maven.wagon.http.pool`: This enables or disables the HTTP connection pooling. The default value is `true`. The following command shows how to set it:

  ```
  $ mvn clean install -Dmaven.wagon.http.pool=true
  ```

- `maven.wagon.httpconnectionManager.maxPerRoute`: This specifies the maximum number of HTTP connections that can be created against a given destination/repository. The default value is `20`.

  ```
  $ mvn clean install
  -Dmaven.wagon.httpconnectionManager.maxPerRoute=20
  ```

- `maven.wagon.httpconnectionManager.maxTotal`: This specifies the maximum number of total HTTP connections that can be created against all the destinations/repositories. The default value is `40`. The following command shows how to set it:

  ```
  $ mvn clean install
  -Dmaven.wagon.httpconnectionManager.maxTotal=40
  ```

- `maven.wagon.http.ssl.insecure`: When Maven talks to a server over TLS, it validates whether the server's TLS certificate is signed by a trusted **Certificate Authority (CA)**; if not, it will display an error. By setting this system property to `true`, you can avoid such errors and work with repositories that have self-signed certificates or untrusted certificates. The default value is `false`. The following command shows how to set it:

  ```
  $ mvn clean install -Dmaven.wagon.http.ssl.insecure=false
  ```

- `maven.wagon.http.ssl.allowall`: By default, when it talks to a TLS endpoint, Maven will check whether the hostname of the endpoint matches the **CN (Common Name)** value of its certificate. If not, it will display an error. By setting this system property to `true`. you can avoid such errors. The default value is `false`. The following command shows how to set it:

  ```
  $ mvn clean install -Dmaven.wagon.http.ssl.allowall=false
  ```

- `maven.wagon.http.ssl.ignore.validity.dates`: By default, when it talks to a TLS endpoint, Maven will check whether the expiration date of the certificate is valid. If not, it will display an error. By setting this system property to `true`, you can avoid such errors. The default value is `false`. The following command shows how to set it:

  ```
  $ mvn clean install -
  Dmaven.wagon.http.ssl.ignore.validity.dates=false
  ```

- `maven.wagon.rto`: This shows the connection read timeout in milliseconds. The default value is `30` minutes. The following command shows how to set it:

  `$ mvn clean install -Dmaven.wagon.rto=1800000`

Proxy authentication

During a Maven build, you need to connect to external repositories outside your firewall. In a tight and secured environment, any outbound connection has to go through an internal proxy server. The following configuration in `MAVEN_HOME/conf/settings.xml` shows how to connect to an external repository via a secured proxy server:

```
<proxy>
  <id>internal_proxy</id>
  <active>true</active>
  <protocol>http</protocol>
  <username>proxyuser</username>
  <password>proxypass</password>
  <host>proxy.host.net</host>
  <port>80</port>
  <nonProxyHosts>local.net|some.host.com</nonProxyHosts>
</proxy>
```

The `proxy` child element must be defined under the `proxies` element, with the appropriate configuration. There can be multiple `proxy` elements, but only the first `proxy` element where the value is `active` will be picked by Maven. If you also have a corporate Maven repository deployed behind a firewall, then the corresponding hostname should be defined under the `nonProxyHosts` element. When Maven talks to this repository, it won't go through the proxy.

Secured repositories

Maven repositories can be protected for legitimate access. If a given repository is protected with HTTP Basic authentication, the corresponding credentials should be defined, as shown in the following configuration, under the `server` element of `MAVEN_HOME/conf/settings.xml`. The value of the `id` element should match the value of the repository id element:

```
<server>
  <id>central</id>
  <username>my_username</username>
  <password>my_password</password>
</server>
```

If a given repository uses HTTP Basic authentication-based security, make sure that you talk to the server over **Transport Layer Security (TLS)**. Plain HTTP will carry your credentials in cleartext. Read more about TLS from `http://en.wikipedia.org/wiki/Transport_Layer_Security`.

Encrypting credentials in settings.xml

Maven keeps confidential data such as passwords in `settings.xml`. For example, in the previous two sections, the passwords for the proxy server and the repository are kept in cleartext. The following configuration repeats the server configuration of a repository secured with HTTP Basic authentication:

```
<server>
  <id>central</id>
  <username>my_username</username>
  <password>my_password</password>
</server>
```

More details about encrypting Maven passwords can be found at `http://maven.apache.org/guides/mini/guide-encryption.html`.

Keeping confidential data in configuration files in cleartext is a security threat that must be avoided. Maven provides a way to encrypt configuration data in `settings.xml`, which is as follows:

1. First, we need to create a master encryption key by using the following command:

   ```
   $ mvn -emp mymasterpassword
   {1J1MrCQRnngHIpSadxoyEKyt2zIGbm3Y1OClKdTtRR6TleNaEfGOEoJaxNc
     dMr+G}
   ```

2. With the output from the previous command, we need to create a file called `settings-security.xml` under `USER_HOME/.m2/` and add the encrypted master password there as shown here:

   ```
   <settingsSecurity>
     <master>
     {1J1MrCQRnngHIpSadxoyEKyt2zIGbm3Y1OClKdTtRR6TleNaEfGOEoJaxN
       cdMr+G}
     </master>
   </settingsSecurity>
   ```

3. Once the master password is configured properly, we can start encrypting rest of the confidential data in `settings.xml`. Let's see how to encrypt the server password. First, we need to generate the encrypted password for the cleartext one using the following command. Note that, earlier we used `emp` (encrypt master password) and now we are using `ep` (encrypt password):

```
$ mvn -ep my_password
{PbYw8YaLb3cHA34/5EdHzoUsmmw/u/nWOwb9e+x6Hbs=}
```

4. Copy the value of the encrypted password and replace the corresponding value in the `settings.xml` file, as shown here:

```
<server>
  <id>central</id>
  <username>my_username</username>
  <password>
    {PbYw8YaLb3cHA34/5EdHzoUsmmw/u/nWOwb9e+x6Hbs=}
  </password>
</server>
```

5. If you are still concerned about keeping the encrypted master key in the computer itself, use the following approach to remove it from the computer and take it with you in a USB stick. However, the disadvantage in this approach is that to trigger a build, Maven always looks for your USB stick, and this will prevent any scheduled online builds. To read the master key from the USB stick, use the following configuration in `settings-security.xml` under `USER_HOME/.m2/`:

```
<settingsSecurity>
  <relocation>
    /Volumes/MyUSBPEN/settings-security.xml
  </relocation>
</settingsSecurity>
```

For any inquisitive mind, there remains a question. How does Maven encrypt the password? What is the key used to encrypt the master password and where does Maven keep it?

Maven uses AES 128 with the PBE SHA-256 algorithm for encryption. **Password-Based Encryption (PBE)** is a way of performing symmetric key encryption using a password or a passphrase. Once Maven gets the master password in cleartext, it will calculate the salted hash against it using the SHA256 algorithm. This will be performed for a few iterations to end up with the encrypted master key. Even though we call it encrypted, it is not really encrypted using another key.

If you run the following command multiple times against the same cleartext password, you will end up with different encrypted passwords each time. The reason is that each time you run the command, Maven generates a random salt value and uses this to derive the encrypted master key:

```
$ mvn -emp mymasterpassword
```

To encrypt confidential data in `settings.xml`, Maven uses this master key along with the AES 128-bits symmetric-key encryption algorithm. Anyone with access to the master key will be able to decrypt all the encrypted passwords kept in `settings.xml`.

 How does Maven find what to decrypt from the `settings.xml` file? If you keep the data in the `settings.xml` file in the {xxxxx} format, Maven will try to decrypt it using the master key.

Source Control Management systems

At the time of this writing, Maven has complete support for integrating with Subversion (SVN), Git, Concurrent Versions System (CVS), Bazzar, Jazz, Mercurial, Perforce, StarTeam, and CM Synergy. Support for Visual SourceSafe, Team Foundation Server, Rational ClearCase, and AccuRev is partially completed.

Maven with Subversion

Let's try out a simple sample here, which integrates Maven with Subversion. You can download the complete sample from https://svn.wso2.org/repos/wso2/people/prabath/maven/chapter03/jose:

```
<project>
  <modelVersion>4.0.0</modelVersion>
  <groupId>com.packt</groupId>
  <artifactId>jose</artifactId>
  <version>1.0.0</version>

  <scm>
    <connection>
      scm:svn:https://svn.wso2.org/repos/wso2
        /people/prabath/maven/jose/src
    </connection>
    <developerConnection>
      scm:svn:https://svn.wso2.org/repos/wso2/
        people/prabath/maven/jose/src
```

```
      </developerConnection>
      <url>
        https://svn.wso2.org/repos/wso2/people/prabath/maven/jose
      </url>
    </scm>

    <build>
      <plugins>
        <plugin>
          <groupId>org.apache.maven.plugins</groupId>
          <artifactId>maven-scm-plugin</artifactId>
          <version>1.9</version>
          <configuration>
            <connectionType>
              connection
            </connectionType>
          </configuration>
        </plugin>
      </plugins>
    </build>

    <dependencies>
      <dependency>
        <groupId>com.nimbusds</groupId>
        <artifactId>nimbus-jose-jwt</artifactId>
        <version>2.26</version>
      </dependency>
    </dependencies>

  </project>
```

Here, we used a Maven SCM plugin to connect to Subversion. The plugin reads Subversion connection details from the <scm> section at the top. The <scm> configuration allows defining two types of connections: connection and developerConnection. The value of the connection element should have read-only access to the source-controlling system while the value of the developerConnection element should have read-write access. Most of the source-controlling systems let anyone check out the source code over plain HTTP while for commits or check-ins, it mandates the use of HTTPS. From the maven-scm-plugin configuration, you can pick which type of connection you need by setting the value of the connectionType element either to connection or developerConnection. If you are going to use the plugin only for read-only operations, then you should set the value of connectionType to connection. The value of the url element under the SCM configuration should point to the browsable URL of the SCM.

According to the Subversion SCM plugin documentation available at `http://maven.apache.org/scm/maven-scm-plugin/`, it supports the following SCM goals:

- `scm:add`: This is the command to add files
- `scm:bootstrap`: This is the command to check out and build a project
- `scm:branch`: This is used to branch the project
- `scm:changelog`: This is the command to show the source code revisions
- `scm:check-local-modification`: This fails the build if there are any local modifications
- `scm:checkin`: This is the command to commit changes
- `scm:checkout`: This is the command to get the source code
- `scm:diff`: This is the command to show the differences between the working copy and the remote one
- `scm:edit`: This is the command to start editing on the working copy
- `scm:export`: This is the command to get a fresh exported copy
- `scm:list`: This is the command to get the list of project files
- `scm:remove`: This is the command to mark a set of files for deletion
- `scm:status`: This is the command to show the SCM status of the working copy
- `scm:tag`: This is the command to tag a certain revision
- `scm:unedit`: This is the command to stop editing the working copy
- `scm:update`: This is the command to update the working copy with the latest changes
- `scm:update-subprojects`: This is the command to update all projects in a multi project build
- `scm:validate`: This validates the SCM information in the POM file

Let's a go through a few examples. The following command will check out the latest code before starting the build:

```
$ mvn scm:update clean install
```

The following command will find any local code modifications and will show the differences:

```
$ mvn scm:diff
```

Most of the source control systems (in fact all) protect the write operations with the username and password. In order to perform a write operation, we need to set up SVN credentials. There are two ways to do this. The first one is through the SCM plugin itself. Inside the SCM plugin configuration, we can define the SVN username and password as follows. In addition to this, the value of the `connectionType` element must be set to `developerConnection`:

```
<plugin>
  <groupId>org.apache.maven.plugins</groupId>
  <artifactId>maven-scm-plugin</artifactId>
  <version>1.9</version>
  <configuration>
    <connectionType>developerConnection</connectionType>
    <username>username</username>
    <password>password</password>
  </configuration>
</plugin>
```

> The previous approach can lead to certain security issues. When you maintain your credentials in a POM file, these credentials cannot be encrypted. Also, you maintain your POM files in Subversion itself. In this case, the POM file with the credentials will be checked-in and any Subversion user can see your credentials.

The second approach is to set up the Subversion credentials via `USER_HOME/.m2/settings.xml`. If you cannot find a `settings.xml` file inside `USER_HOME/.m2/`, you can copy the `settings.xml` file from `MAVEN_HOME/conf`. The id tag of the server configuration must point to the hostname of the Subversion connection URL. The configuration is as follows:

```
<server>
  <id>svn.wso2.org</id>
  <username>my_username</username>
  <password>my_password</password>
</server>
```

The password in the previous configuration can be encrypted by following the approach defined in the *Encrypting credentials in settings.xml* section of this chapter.

The following command will check in the updated code after a successful build:

```
$ mvn clean install scm:checkin -Dmessage="updated source"
```

Local repository location

By default, the Maven local repository is created at USER_HOME/.m2/repository. This can be changed to a preferred location by editing MAVEN_HOME/conf/settings. xml to update the value of the localRepository element, as follows:

```
<localRepository>/path/to/local/repo</localRepository>
```

Mirrored repositories

Most of the Maven repositories maintain a set of mirrored repositories to cater to high demand. Maven repositories are defined in the application pom.xml file in a project specific manner. Mirrored repositories are defined outside the application POM, either in MAVEN_HOME/conf/settings.xml or USER_HOME/.m2/settings.xml. A given repository can have multiple mirrored repositories in multiple geographical locations, for example, one in the US, one in Europe, and another in Asia. Based on the user's proximity, they can pick the mirrored repository. Due to the same reason, we cannot define it in the application POM file. In a large-scale project, developers can come from every corner of the world, and we cannot define a mirrored repository in the application POM. Each developer can define the most appropriate mirrored repository for him/her in USER_HOME/.m2/settings.xml under the <mirrors> configuration element, as follows:

```
<mirror>
  <id>mirrorId</id>
  <mirrorOf>repositoryId</mirrorOf>
  <name>Human Readable Name for this Mirror.</name>
  <url>http://my.repository.com/repo/path</url>
</mirror>
```

The value of the mirrorOf element must match the value of the repository/id element defined in the application POM file. In this case, the value of mirrorOf will be central, as follows:

```
<repository>
  <snapshots>
    <enabled>false</enabled>
  </snapshots>
  <id>central</id>
  <name>Central Repository</name>
  <url>http://repo.maven.apache.org/maven2</url>
</repository>
```

The Maven central repository has four mirrored repositories distributed in USA and Europe:

- The configuration for the mirrored repository at California, USA, is as follows:

```
<mirror>
  <id>Central</id>
  <url>http://repo1.maven.org/maven2</url>
  <mirrorOf>central</mirrorOf>
</mirror>
```

- The configuration for the mirrored repository at North Carolina, USA, is as follows:

```
<mirror>
  <id>ibiblio.org</id>
  <url>
    http://mirrors.ibiblio.org/pub/mirrors/maven2
  </url>
  <mirrorOf>central</mirrorOf>
</mirror>
```

- The configuration for the mirrored repository at United Kingdom is as follows:

```
<mirror>
  <id>uk.maven.org</id>
  <url>http://uk.maven.org/maven2</url>
  <mirrorOf>central</mirrorOf>
</mirror>
```

- The configuration for the mirrored repository at France is as follows:

```
<mirror>
  <id>antelink.com</id>
  <url>
    http://maven.antelink.com/content/repositories/central/
  </url>
  <mirrorOf>central</mirrorOf>
</mirror>
```

If Maven finds a corresponding mirrored repository for any given repository defined in the application POM file, it will start using the mirrored one instead of the primary.

The internal corporate repository

In a highly constrained, secured working environment, users won't be able
to connect to the Internet directly. At the same time, in a larger development
environment with hundreds of developers, if each developer tries to download
Maven artifacts from external repositories, this will create a great deal of the
inbound/outbound Internet traffic. This can be avoided by using an internal
corporate Maven repository. Each developer has to set the corporate repository as
a mirror in USER_HOME/settings.xml for all Maven repositories. To indicate that a
given mirror should be used for any of the repositories defined in application POM
files, the value of the mirrorOf configuration element must be set to *, as follows:

```
<mirror>
  <id>internal.mirror.mycompany.com</id>
  <url>
    http:// internal.mirror.mycompany.com/maven/
  </url>
  <mirrorOf>*</mirrorOf>
</mirror>
```

The following figure shows the use of an internal corporate Maven repository to
avoid a large amount of inbound/outbound Internet traffic:

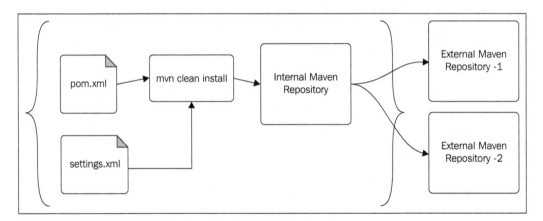

 In *Chapter 8, Maven Repository Management*, we will discuss
how to set up a Repository manager as a proxy.

Advanced mirror configurations

From Maven 2.0.9 onwards, Maven introduced some advanced filtering mechanisms for the `mirrorOf` element. The previous section used `*`, which, in fact, is for any repository. Further filtering can be done in the following manner:

```
<mirror>
  <id>internal.mirror.mycompany.com</id>
  <url>
    http://internal.mirror.mycompany.com/maven/
  </url>
  <mirrorOf>*,!central</mirrorOf>
</mirror>
```

The previous configuration says use the mirror for any repository except for the `central` repository.

The following configuration says use the mirror only for `repo1` and `repo2`:

```
<mirror>
  <id>internal.mirror.mycompany.com</id>
  <url>
    http://internal.mirror.mycompany.com/maven/
  </url>
  <mirrorOf>repo1,repo2</mirrorOf>
</mirror>
```

The following configuration says use the mirror for any repository other than the localhost or file-based repository. We'll be talking about file-based repositories as we proceed in this chapter.

```
<mirror>
  <id>internal.mirror.mycompany.com</id>
  <url>
    http://internal.mirror.mycompany.com/maven/
  </url>
  <mirrorOf>external:*</mirrorOf>
</mirror>
```

Deploying artifacts

To deploy artifacts into a Maven repository, we need to define a distributionManagement configuration element in the application POM file of the root Maven module. At the time of writing this book, Maven supports SSH, SFTP, FTP, and file-based artifact deployment. Let's have a look at how file-based artifact deployment works.

Deploying file-based artifacts

The following configuration will deploy the artifacts to the repository at /Users/ prabath/maven/deploy. This is one of the easiest and the quickest way of building a Maven repository, but this is not recommended for use in a large-scale development project. Use the mvn deploy command to deploy the artifacts into the configured repository.

```
<project>

  <modelVersion>4.0.0</modelVersion>
  <groupId>com.packt</groupId>
  <artifactId>jose</artifactId>
  <version>1.0.0</version>

  <distributionManagement>
    <repository>
      <id>local-file-repository</id>
      <name>Local File Repository</name>
      <url>file:///Users/prabath/maven/deploy</url>
    </repository>
  </distributionManagement>

  <dependencies>
    <dependency>
      <groupId>com.nimbusds</groupId>
      <artifactId>nimbus-jose-jwt</artifactId>
      <version>2.26</version>
    </dependency>
  </dependencies>

</project>
```

Deploying SSH-based artifacts

The following configuration will deploy the artifacts to the repository at USER_HOME/ maven/deploy of the server that has the IP address 192.168.1.4:

```
<project>

  <modelVersion>4.0.0</modelVersion>
  <groupId>com.packt</groupId>
  <artifactId>jose</artifactId>
  <version>1.0.0</version>

  <distributionManagement>
    <repository>
      <id>ssh-repository</id>
      <name>SSH Repository</name>
      <url>scpexe://192.168.1.4/maven/deploy</url>
    </repository>
  </distributionManagement>


  <build>
    <extensions>
      <extension>
        <groupId>org.apache.maven.wagon</groupId>
        <artifactId>wagon-ssh-external</artifactId>
        <version>1.0-beta-6</version>
      </extension>
    </extensions>
  </build>

  <dependencies>
    <dependency>
      <groupId>com.nimbusds</groupId>
      <artifactId>nimbus-jose-jwt</artifactId>
      <version>2.26</version>
    </dependency>
  </dependencies>

</project>
```

> The wagon-ssh-external JAR file is provided as a build extension in the previous application POM file. Extensions provide a list of artifacts that have to be used during a Maven build. These artifacts will be included into the build time class path.

To authenticate to the remote server, Maven provides two ways. One is based on the username and password. The other one is based on SSH authentication keys.

The following steps show how to configure username/password credentials against a Maven repository:

1. Add the following `<server>` configuration element to USER_HOME/.m2/ settings.xml under the `<servers>` parent element. The value of the id element must carry the value of the remote repository hostname.

```
<server>
  <id>192.168.1.4</id>
  <username>my_username</username>
  <password>my_password</password>
</server>
```

The password in the previous configuration can be encrypted by following the approach defined in the *Encrypting credentials in settings.xml* section of this chapter.

2. If the remote repository only supports SSH authentication keys, then we need to specify the location of the private key, as follows:

```
<server>
  <id>192.168.1.4</id>
  <username>my_username</username>
  <privateKey>/path/to/private/key</privateKey>
</server>
```

Deploying FTP-based artifacts

The following configuration will deploy the artifacts to the repository at USER_HOME/maven/deploy of the server having the IP address 192.168.1.4:

```
<project>

  <modelVersion>4.0.0</modelVersion>
  <groupId>com.packt</groupId>
  <artifactId>jose</artifactId>
  <version>1.0.0</version>

  <distributionManagement>
    <repository>
      <id>ftp-repository</id>
```

```
      <name>FTP Repository</name>
      <url>ftp://192.168.1.4/maven/deploy</url>
    </repository>
  </distributionManagement>

  <dependencies>
    <dependency>
      <groupId>com.nimbusds</groupId>
      <artifactId>nimbus-jose-jwt</artifactId>
      <version>2.26</version>
    </dependency>
  </dependencies>

  <build>
    <extensions>
      <extension>
        <groupId>org.apache.maven.wagon</groupId>
        <artifactId>wagon-ftp</artifactId>
        <version>1.0-beta-6</version>
      </extension>
    </extensions>
  </build>
</project>
```

To authenticate to the remote FTP server, we need to add the following `<server>` configuration element to USER_HOME/.m2/settings.xml under the `<servers>` parent element. The value of the id element must carry the value of the remote repository hostname.

```
<server>
  <id>192.168.1.4</id>
  <username>my_username</username>
  <password>my_password</password>
</server>
```

The password in the previous configuration can be encrypted by following the approach defined in the *Encrypting credentials in settings.xml* section of this chapter.

Enabling Maven logging

Everything does not work fine all the time. The connectivity to an external repository or a server can fail due to many reasons. Maven debugging helps you to nail down the root cause in such a situation. To run Maven with debug level logs enabled, use the following command:

```
$ mvn clean install -X
```

Maven 3.1.0 and higher versions use the SLF4J logging API. The following logging configuration available at `MAVEN_HOME/conf/logging/simplelogger.properties` can be used to alter the default behavior of Maven logging:

```
org.slf4j.simpleLogger.defaultLogLevel=info
org.slf4j.simpleLogger.showDateTime=false
org.slf4j.simpleLogger.showThreadName=false
org.slf4j.simpleLogger.showLogName=false
org.slf4j.simpleLogger.logFile=System.out
org.slf4j.simpleLogger.levelInBrackets=true
org.slf4j.simpleLogger.log.Sisu=info
org.slf4j.simpleLogger.warnLevelString=WARNING
```

By default, Maven publishes logs to the console itself. The following configuration shows how to direct it to a file by editing the `simplelogger.properties` file:

```
org.slf4j.simpleLogger.logFile=/Users/[user_name]/maven.log
```

Summary

In this chapter, we discussed how to configure Maven at three different levels: global, user, and project. The chapter also focused on introducing best practices while configuring Maven for optimal use. In the next chapter, we will discuss Maven build lifecycles and how to create custom lifecycles and lifecycle extensions.

4
Build Lifecycles

A Maven build lifecycle consists of a set of well-defined phases. Each phase groups a set of goals defined by Maven plugins and the lifecycle defines the order of execution. A Maven plugin is a collection of goals where each goal is responsible for performing a specific action. We'll be discussing Maven plugins in detail in *Chapter 5, Maven Plugins*.

In this chapter, the following topics will be covered:

- Standard lifecycles in Maven
- Lifecycle bindings
- Building custom lifecycles and lifecycle extensions

The following figure shows the relationship between Maven plugin goals and lifecycle phases:

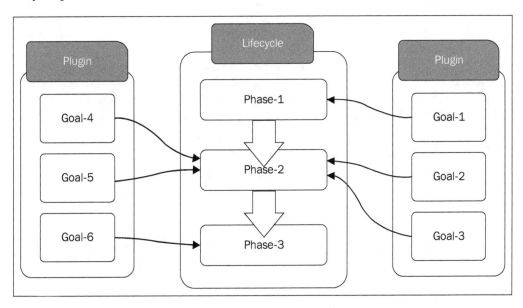

Let's take the simplest Maven build command that every Java developer is familiar with:

```
$ mvn clean install
```

What will this do? As a developer, how many times have you executed the previous command? Have you ever thought of what happens inside? If not, it's time to explore it now.

Standard lifecycles in Maven

Maven comes with three standard lifecycles: `default`, `clean`, and `site`. Each lifecycle defines its own set of phases.

The clean lifecycle

The `clean` lifecycle defines three phases: `pre-clean`, `clean`, and `post-clean`. A phase in a lifecycle is just an ordered placeholder in the build execution path. For example, the `clean` phase in the `clean` lifecycle cannot do anything on its own. In the Maven architecture, it has two key elements: nouns and verbs. Both nouns and verbs, which are related to a given project, are defined in the POM file. The name of the project, the name of the parent project, the dependencies, and the type of the packaging are nouns. Plugins bring verbs into the Maven build system, and they define what needs to be done during the build execution via its goals. A plugin is a group of goals. Each goal of a plugin can be executed on its own or can be registered as part of a phase in a Maven build lifecycle.

When you type `mvn clean`, it executes all the phases defined in the `clean` lifecycle up to and including the `clean` phase. Don't be confused; in this command, `clean` is not the name of the lifecycle, it's the name of a phase. It's only a coincidence that the name of the phase happens to be the name of the lifecycle. In Maven, you cannot simply execute a lifecycle by its name—it has to be the name of a phase. Maven will find the corresponding lifecycle and will execute it up to the given phase (including that phase).

When you type `mvn clean`, it cleans out project's working directory (by default, it's the `target` directory). This is done via the Maven `clean` plugin. To find more details about the Maven `clean` plugin, type the following command. It describes all the goals defined inside the `clean` plugin:

```
$ mvn help:describe -Dplugin=clean
```

Name: Maven Clean Plugin

Description: The Maven Clean Plugin is a plugin that removes files generated at build-time in a project's directory.

Group Id: org.apache.maven.plugins

Artifact Id: maven-clean-plugin

Version: 2.5

Goal Prefix: clean

This plugin has 2 goals.

clean:clean

Description: Goal, which cleans the build. This attempts to clean a project's working directory of the files that were generated at build-time. By default, it discovers and deletes the directories configured in project.build.directory, project.build.outputDirectory, project.build.testOutputDirectory, andproject.reporting.outputDirectory.Files outside the default may also be included in the deletion by configuring the filesets tag.

clean:help

Description: Display help information on maven-clean-plugin.Call

mvn clean:help -Ddetail=true -Dgoal=<goal-name> to display parameter details.

For more information, run 'mvn help:describe [...] -Ddetail'

> Everything in Maven is a plugin. Even the command we executed previously to get goal details of the `clean` plugin executes another plugin: the `help` plugin. The following command will describe the `help` plugin itself:
>
> ```
> $ mvn help:describe -Dplugin=help
> ```
>
> `describe` is a goal defined inside the `help` plugin.

The clean plugin has two goals defined in it: clean and help. As mentioned previously, each goal of a plugin can be executed on its own or can be registered as part of a phase in a Maven build lifecycle. A clean goal of the clean plugin can be executed on its own with the following command:

```
$ mvn clean:clean
```

The following figure shows the relationship between the Maven clean plugin goals and the clean lifecycle phases:

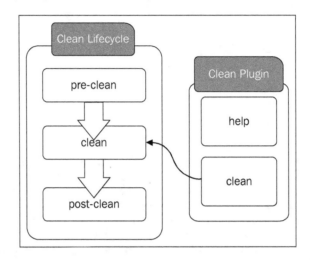

The first clean word in the previous command is the prefix of the clean plugin, while the second one is the name of the goal. When you type mvn clean, it's the same clean goal that gets executed. However, this time it gets executed through the clean phase of the clean lifecycle, and it also executes all the phases in the corresponding lifecycle up to the clean phase—not just the clean phase. The clean goal of the clean plugin is configured by default to get executed during the clean lifecycle. The plugin goal to lifecycle phase mapping can be provided through the application POM file. If not, it will be inherited from the super POM file. The super POM file, which defines the clean plugin by default, adds the plugin to the clean phase of the clean lifecycle. You cannot define the same phase in two different lifecycles.

The following code snippet shows how the clean goal of the Maven clean plugin is associated with the clean phase of the clean lifecycle:

```
<plugin>
  <artifactId>maven-clean-plugin</artifactId>
  <version>2.5</version>
  <executions>
    <execution>
      <id>default-clean</id>
```

```
      <phase>clean</phase>
      <goals>
        <goal>clean</goal>
      </goals>
    </execution>
  </executions>
</plugin>
```

The `pre-clean` and `post-clean` phases of the `clean` lifecycle do not have any plugin bindings. The objective of the `pre-clean` phase is to perform any operations prior to the cleaning task and the objective of the `post-clean` phase is to perform any operations after the cleaning task. If you need to associate any plugins with these two phases, you simply need to add them to the corresponding plugin configuration.

The default lifecycle

The `default` lifecycle in Maven defines 23 phases. When you run the command `mvn clean install`, it will execute all the phases from the `default` lifecycle up to and including the `install` phase. To be precise, Maven will first execute all the phases in `clean` lifecycle up to and including the `clean` phase, and will then execute the `default` lifecycle up to and including the `install` phase.

The phases in the `default` lifecycle do not have any associated plugin goals. The plugin bindings for each phase are defined by the corresponding packaging. If the type of packaging of your Maven project is JAR, then it will define its own set of plugins for each phase. If the packaging type is WAR, then it will have its own set of plugins. The following points summarize all the phases defined under the `default` lifecycle in their order of execution:

- `validate`: This phase validates the project POM file and makes sure all the necessary information related to carry out the build is available.

- `initialize`: This phase initializes the build by setting up the right directory structure and initializing properties.

- `generate-sources`: This phase generates any required source code.

- `process-sources`: This phase processes the generated source code. For example, there can be a plugin running in this phase to filter the source code based on some defined criteria.

- `generate-resources`: This phase generates any resources that need to be packaged with the final artifact.

- `process-resources`: This phase processes the generated resources. It copies the resources to their destination directories and makes them ready for packaging.

- `compile`: This phase compiles the source code.
- `process-classes`: This phase can be used to carry out any bytecode enhancements after the `compile` phase.
- `generate-test-sources`: This phase generates the required source code for tests.
- `process-test-sources`: This phase processes the generated test source code. For example, there can be a plugin running in this phase to filter the source code based on some defined criteria.
- `generate-test-resources`: This phase generates all the resources required to run tests.
- `process-test-resources`: This phase processes the generated test resources. It copies the resources to their destination directories and makes them ready for testing.
- `test-compile`: This phase compiles the source code for tests.
- `process-test-classes`: This phase can be used to carry out any bytecode enhancements after the `test-compile` phase.
- `test`: This phase executes tests using the appropriate unit test framework.
- `prepare-package`: This phase is useful in organizing the artifacts to be packaged.
- `package`: This phase packs the artifacts into a distributable format, for example, JAR or WAR.
- `pre-integration-test`: This phase performs the actions required (if any) before running integration tests. This may be used to start any external application servers and deploy the artifacts into different test environments.
- `integration-test`: This phase runs integration tests.
- `post-integration-test`: This phase can be used to perform any cleanup tasks after running the integration tests.
- `verify`: This phase verifies the validity of the package. The criteria to check the validity needs to be defined by the respective plugins.
- `install`: This phase installs the final artifact in the local repository.
- `deploy`: This phase deploys the final artifact to a remote repository.

 The packaging type of a given Maven project is defined under the `<packaging>` element in the `pom.xml` file. If the element is omitted, then Maven assumes it as `jar` packaging.

The following figure shows all the phases defined under the Maven default lifecycle and their order of execution:

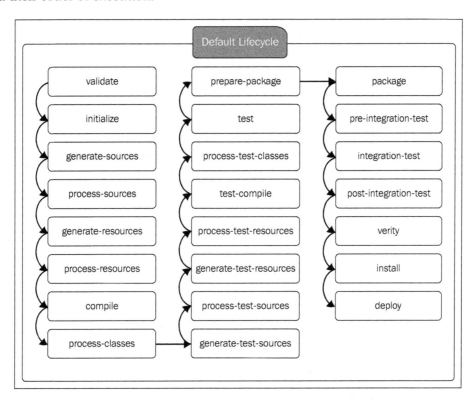

 More details about Maven lifecycles can be found at http://maven.apache.org/ref/3.2.3/maven-core/lifecycles.html.

Let's have a look at a concrete example. Run the following command against a Maven project having the `jar` packaging. If you do not have such a project you can download a sample Maven project from https://svn.wso2.org/repos/wso2/people/prabath/maven/chapter04/jose/.

```
$ mvn help:describe -Dcmd=deploy
```

Here we are using the Maven `help` plugin to find more details about the `deploy` phase corresponding to the `jar` packaging, and it will produce the following output:

```
It is a part of the lifecycle for the POM packaging 'jar'. This lifecycle
includes the following phases:

* validate: Not defined
```

```
* initialize: Not defined
* generate-sources: Not defined
* process-sources: Not defined
* generate-resources: Not defined
* process-resources: org.apache.maven.plugins:maven-resources-
  plugin:2.6:resources
* compile: org.apache.maven.plugins:maven-compiler-
  plugin:2.5.1:compile
* process-classes: Not defined
* generate-test-sources: Not defined
* process-test-sources: Not defined
* generate-test-resources: Not defined
* process-test-resources: org.apache.maven.plugins:maven-
  resources-plugin:2.6:testResources
* test-compile: org.apache.maven.plugins:maven-compiler-
  plugin:2.5.1:testCompile
* process-test-classes: Not defined
* test: org.apache.maven.plugins:maven-surefire-plugin:2.12.4:test
* prepare-package: Not defined
* package: org.apache.maven.plugins:maven-jar-plugin:2.4:jar
* pre-integration-test: Not defined
* integration-test: Not defined
* post-integration-test: Not defined
* verify: Not defined
* install: org.apache.maven.plugins:maven-install-
  plugin:2.4:install
* deploy: org.apache.maven.plugins:maven-deploy-plugin:2.7:deploy
```

The output lists out all the Maven plugins registered against different phases of the `default` lifecycle for the `jar` packaging. The `jar` goal of `maven-jar-plugin` is registered against the `package` phase, while the `install` goal of `maven-install-plugin` is registered in the `install` phase.

Let's run the previous command against a POM file having the `war` packaging. It produces the following output:

```
It is a part of the lifecycle for the POM packaging 'war'. This life
includes the following phases:
* validate: Not defined
* initialize: Not defined
* generate-sources: Not defined
* process-sources: Not defined
```

* generate-resources: Not defined
* process-resources: org.apache.maven.plugins:maven-resources-plugin:2.6:resources
* compile: org.apache.maven.plugins:maven-compiler-plugin:2.5.1:compile
* process-classes: Not defined
* generate-test-sources: Not defined
* process-test-sources: Not defined
* generate-test-resources: Not defined
* process-test-resources: org.apache.maven.plugins:maven-resources-plugin:2.6:testResources
* test-compile: org.apache.maven.plugins:maven-compiler-plugin:2.5.1:testCompile
* process-test-classes: Not defined
* test: org.apache.maven.plugins:maven-surefire-plugin:2.12.4:test
* prepare-package: Not defined
* package: org.apache.maven.plugins:maven-war-plugin:2.2:war
* pre-integration-test: Not defined
* integration-test: Not defined
* post-integration-test: Not defined
* verify: Not defined
* install: org.apache.maven.plugins:maven-install-plugin:2.4:install
* deploy: org.apache.maven.plugins:maven-deploy-plugin:2.7:deploy

Now if you look at the `package` phase, you will notice that we have a different plugin goal: `maven-war-plugin`.

Similarly to the `jar` and `war` packaging, each of the other packaging type defines its own bindings for the `default` lifecycle.

The site lifecycle

The `site` lifecycle is defined with four phases: `pre-site`, `site`, `post-site`, and `site-deploy`. The `site` lifecycle has no value without the Maven `site` plugin. The `site` plugin is used to generate static HTML content for a project. The generated HTML content will also include appropriate reports corresponding to the project. The `site` plugin defines eight goals and two of them are directly associated with the phases in the `site` lifecycle.

Let's run the following command against a POM file to describe the site goal:

```
$ mvn help:describe -Dcmd=site
```

As shown in the following output, the `site` goal of the `site` plugin is associated with the `site` phase, while the `deploy` goal of the `site` plugin is associated with the `site-deploy` phase:

```
[INFO] 'site' is a lifecycle with the following phases:
* pre-site: Not defined
* site: org.apache.maven.plugins:maven-site-plugin:3.3:site
* post-site: Not defined
* site-deploy: org.apache.maven.plugins:maven-site-plugin:3.3:deploy
```

The following figure shows the relationship between the Maven site plugin goals and the `site` lifecycle phases:

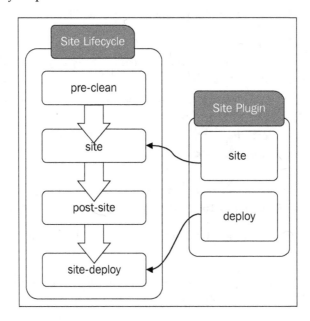

Lifecycle bindings

Under the discussion of the `default` lifecycle, we briefly touched upon the concept of lifecycle bindings. The `default` lifecycle is defined without any associated lifecycle bindings, while both the `clean` and `site` lifecycles are defined with bindings. The standard Maven lifecycles and their associated bindings are defined under the file `META-INF/plex/components.xml` of `MAVEN_HOME/lib/maven-core-3.2.3.jar`.

Here is the definition of the `default` lifecycle without the associated plugin bindings:

```
<component>
    <role>org.apache.maven.lifecycle.Lifecycle</role>
```

```
<implementation>org.apache.maven.lifecycle.Lifecycle
</implementation>
<role-hint>default</role-hint>
<configuration>
  <id>default</id>
  <phases>
    <phase>validate</phase>
    <phase>initialize</phase>
    <phase>generate-sources</phase>
    <phase>process-sources</phase>
    <phase>generate-resources</phase>
    <phase>process-resources</phase>
    <phase>compile</phase>
    <phase>process-classes</phase>
    <phase>generate-test-sources</phase>
    <phase>process-test-sources</phase>
    <phase>generate-test-resources</phase>
    <phase>process-test-resources</phase>
    <phase>test-compile</phase>
    <phase>process-test-classes</phase>
    <phase>test</phase>
    <phase>prepare-package</phase>
    <phase>package</phase>
    <phase>pre-integration-test</phase>
    <phase>integration-test</phase>
    <phase>post-integration-test</phase>
    <phase>verify</phase>
    <phase>install</phase>
    <phase>deploy</phase>
  </phases>
</configuration>
</component>
```

The `components.xml` file, which is also known as the component descriptor, describes the properties required by Maven to manage the lifecycle of a Maven project. The `role` element specifies the Java interface exposed by this lifecycle component and defines the type of the component. All the lifecycle components must have `org.apache.maven.lifecycle.Lifecycle` as role. The `implementation` tag specifies the concrete implementation of the interface. The identity of a component is defined by the combination of the `role` and the `role-hint` elements. The `role-hint` element is not a mandatory element; however, if we have multiple elements of the same type, then we must define a `role-hint` element. Corresponding to Maven lifecycles, the name of the lifecycle is set as the value of the `role-hint` element.

The clean lifecycle is defined with an associated plugin binding to the clean goal of maven-clean-plugin. The plugin binding is defined under the element default-phases. The code is as follows:

```
<component>
  <role>org.apache.maven.lifecycle.Lifecycle</role>
  <implementation>org.apache.maven.lifecycle.Lifecycle
  </implementation>
  <role-hint>clean</role-hint>
  <configuration>
    <id>clean</id>
    <phases>
      <phase>pre-clean</phase>
      <phase>clean</phase>
      <phase>post-clean</phase>
    </phases>
    <default-phases>
      <clean>
        org.apache.maven.plugins:maven-clean-plugin:2.4.1:clean
      </clean>
    </default-phases>
  </configuration>
</component>
```

The site lifecycle is defined with the associated plugin bindings to the site and the site-deploy goals of maven-site-plugin. The plugin bindings are defined under the element default-phases. The code is as follows:

```
<component>
  <role>org.apache.maven.lifecycle.Lifecycle</role>
  <implementation>org.apache.maven.lifecycle.Lifecycle
  </implementation>
  <role-hint>site</role-hint>
  <configuration>
    <id>site</id>
    <phases>
      <phase>pre-site</phase>
      <phase>site</phase>
      <phase>post-site</phase>
      <phase>site-deploy</phase>
    </phases>
    <default-phases>
      <site>
        org.apache.maven.plugins:maven-site-plugin:2.0.1:site
```

```
    </site>
    <site-deploy>
      org.apache.maven.plugins:maven-site-plugin:2.0.1:deploy
    </site-deploy>
  </default-phases>
 </configuration>
</component>
```

Finally, let's have a look at how the `jar` plugin binding for the `default` lifecycle is defined. The following `component` element defines a plugin binding to an existing lifecycle and the associated lifecycle is defined under the `configuration/lifecycles/lifecycle/id` element:

```
<component>
  <role>
    org.apache.maven.lifecycle.mapping.LifecycleMapping
  </role>
  <role-hint>jar</role-hint>
  <implementation>
    org.apache.maven.lifecycle.mapping.DefaultLifecycleMapping
  </implementation>
  <configuration>
    <lifecycles>
      <lifecycle>
        <id>default</id>
        <phases>
          <process-resources>
            org.apache.maven.plugins:maven-resources-
              plugin:2.4.3:resources
          </process-resources>
          <compile>
            org.apache.maven.plugins:maven-compiler-
              plugin:2.3.2:compile
          </compile>
          <process-test-resources>
            org.apache.maven.plugins:maven-resources-
              plugin:2.4.3:testResources
          </process-test-resources>
          <test-compile>
            org.apache.maven.plugins:maven-compiler-
              plugin:2.3.2:testCompile
          </test-compile>
          <test>
```

```
        org.apache.maven.plugins:maven-surefire-
          plugin:2.5:test
      </test>
      <package>
        org.apache.maven.plugins:maven-jar-
              plugin:2.3.1:jar
      </package>
      <install>
        org.apache.maven.plugins:maven-install-
          plugin:2.3.1:install
      </install>
      <deploy>
        org.apache.maven.plugins:maven-deploy-
          plugin:2.5:deploy
      </deploy>
    </phases>
  </lifecycle>
  </lifecycles>
  </configuration>
</component>
```

Building a custom lifecycle

A lifecycle defines a process. It defines an ordered set of phases that get executed one after the other. The Maven `default` lifecycle is sufficient to address most of the use cases in build management and automation. However, we might need to alter the behavior of certain phases. Defining a phase and altering a phase are two different things and they are done in two different ways. Accepting the `default` lifecycle but altering its default behavior has to be done with a proper plugin binding.

Lifecycle phases are dumb entities; they inherit the behavior from the associated plugins. The `jar` goal of `maven-jar-plugin` is associated with the `package` phase of the `default` lifecycle, for any artifact having the `jar` packaging. Similarly, we have a set of other plugins associated with the `package` phase for the `ear`, `war`, `pom`, `rar`, `par`, `ejb`, and `ejb3` packaging types. What if we need to introduce a new custom package type? How do we introduce it to the `package` phase of the `default` lifecycle?

Let's take a real-world example. Apache Axis2 is a Java-based open source project that is developed under **Apache Software Foundation (ASF)**. It provides a framework to build SOAP-based web services. The deployment unit of an Axis2 web service is a `.aar` file. The project provides a Maven plugin to package your Axis2 web services project as a `.aar` file: `axis2-aar-maven-plugin`. In *Chapter 5, Maven Plugins,* we will discuss building Maven plugins. For the time being, let's see how to alter the `default` lifecycle to accommodate the new `axis2-aar-maven-plugin`.

The Maven architecture is based on the **Inversion of Control (IoC)** architectural principal. You can read more about IoC in the article written by Martin Fowler at `http://martinfowler.com/articles/injection.html`. Maven uses Plexus as its IoC container. Plexus is similar to other IoC containers or dependency injection frameworks such as Spring. The `components.xml` file in Maven is the heart of the Plexus framework. We will discuss Plexus in *Chapter 5, Maven Plugins*.

To associate a plugin goal with an existing lifecycle, you need to define a lifecycle mapping in the `META-INF/plexus/components.xml` file of the corresponding plugin. The complete `components.xml` file of `axis2-aar-maven-plugin` is available at `http://svn.apache.org/repos/asf/axis/axis2/java/core/trunk/modules/tool/axis2-aar-maven-plugin/src/main/resources/META-INF/plexus/components.xml`.

The following code snippet shows how the plugin binding for the aar packaging type is defined, with the `axis2-aar-maven-plugin`:

```
<component-set>
  <component>
    <role>org.apache.maven.lifecycle.mapping.LifecycleMapping
    </role>
    <role-hint>aar</role-hint>
    <implementation>
      org.apache.maven.lifecycle.mapping.DefaultLifecycleMapping
    </implementation>
    <configuration>
      <lifecycles>
        <lifecycle>
          <id>default</id>
          <phases>
            <process-resources>
              org.apache.maven.plugins:maven-resources-
                plugin:resources
            </process-resources>
            <compile>
              org.apache.maven.plugins:maven-compiler-plugin:compile
            </compile>
            <process-test-resources>
              org.apache.maven.plugins:maven-resources-
                plugin:testResources
            </process-test-resources>
            <test-compile>
              org.apache.maven.plugins:maven-compiler-
                plugin:testCompile
            </test-compile>
```

```
        <test>
          org.apache.maven.plugins:maven-surefire-plugin:test
        </test>
        <package>
          org.apache.axis2:axis2-aar-maven-plugin:aar
        </package>
        <install>
          org.apache.maven.plugins:maven-install-plugin:install
        </install>
        <deploy>
          org.apache.maven.plugins:maven-deploy-plugin:deploy
        </deploy>
      </phases>
    </lifecycle>
   </lifecycles>
  </configuration>
 </component>
</component-set>
```

This configuration defines a customized behavior for the `default` lifecycle associated
with the `aar` packaging. When you define a custom lifecycle, you need to define plugin
goals for each and every phase explicitly; it won't inherit any default behavior once it's
kept undefined. If necessary, multiple plugin goals can be defined for a given phase,
each separated by a comma.

Let's have a quick look at another example. The following `maven-bundle-plugin`
that is available at `https://github.com/sonatype/sonatype-bundle-plugin/`
`blob/master/src/main/resources/META-INF/plexus/components.xml` defines
a custom behavior for the `package`, `install`, and `deploy` phases of the `default`
lifecycle for an artifact that has the `bundle` custom packaging:

```
<component-set>
  <components>
    <component>
      <role>
        org.apache.maven.lifecycle.mapping.LifecycleMapping
      </role>
      <role-hint>bundle</role-hint>
      <implementation>
        org.apache.maven.lifecycle.mapping.DefaultLifecycleMapping
      </implementation>
      <configuration>
        <lifecycles>
          <lifecycle>
```

```
        <id>default</id>
        <phases>
          <process-resources>
            org.apache.maven.plugins:maven-resources-
              plugin:resources
          </process-resources>
          <compile>
            org.apache.maven.plugins:maven-compiler-
              plugin:compile
          </compile>
          <process-test-resources>
            org.apache.maven.plugins:maven-resources-
              plugin:testResources
          </process-test-resources>
          <test-compile>
            org.apache.maven.plugins:maven-compiler-
              plugin:testCompile
          </test-compile>
          <test>
            org.apache.maven.plugins:maven-surefire-
              plugin:test
          </test>
          <package>
            org.apache.felix:maven-bundle-plugin:bundle
          </package>
          <install>
            org.apache.maven.plugins:maven-install-
              plugin:install,
            org.apache.felix:maven-bundle-plugin:install
          </install>
          <deploy>
            org.apache.maven.plugins:maven-deploy-
              plugin:deploy,
            org.apache.felix:maven-bundle-plugin:deploy
          </deploy>
        </phases>
      </lifecycle>
    </lifecycles>
  </configuration>
    </component>
  </components>
</component-set>
```

Plugins can introduce custom behaviors for existing lifecycle phases. How can we define our own lifecycle phases? Let's see how to write our own custom lifecycle with the following four phases:

- `get-code`
- `build-code`
- `run-tests`
- `notify`

The steps are as follows:

1. First, we need to define our custom lifecycle phases in a `components.xml`, shown in the following code. Inside the `default-phases` element, we associate plugin goals with each of the custom phase. Later, we'll see how to define goals within a plugin. The code is as follows:

```xml
<component-set>
  <components>
    <component>
      <role>org.apache.maven.lifecycle.Lifecycle</role>
      <role-hint>packt</role-hint>
      <implementation>
        org.apache.maven.lifecycle.Lifecycle
      </implementation>
      <configuration>
        <id>packt_lifecycle</id>
        <phases>
          <phase>get-code</phase>
          <phase>build-code</phase>
          <phase>run-tests</phase>
          <phase>notify</phase>
        </phases>
        <default-phases>
          <get-code>
            com.packt:com.packt.lifecycle.sample:get-code-goal
          </get-code>
          <build-code>
            com.packt:com.packt.lifecycle.sample:build-code-goal
          </build-code>
          <run-tests>
```

```
            com.packt:com.packt.lifecycle.sample:run-tests-goal
        </run-tests>
        <notify>
            com.packt:com.packt.lifecycle.sample:notify-goal
        </notify>
      </default-phases>
    </configuration>
  </component>
 </components>
</component-set>
```

2. Now we need to write a **Maven plain Old Java Object (MOJO)** , which
    extends from `org.apache.maven.plugin.AbstractMojo`. One MOJO can
    handle only one goal at a time, so we need to have four MOJOs — one for
    each goal. We'll discuss MOJOs and Maven plugins in depth in *Chapter 5,
    Maven Plugins*. The plugin goal supported by this class needs to be set as
    a Javadoc tag: `@goal get-code-goal`. The code is as follows:

```java
package com.packt.lifecycle.sample;

import org.apache.maven.plugin.AbstractMojo;
import org.apache.maven.plugin.MojoExecutionException;
import org.apache.maven.plugin.MojoFailureException;


/**
 * @goal get-code-goal
 * @requiresProject false
 */

public class GetCodeGoalMojo extends AbstractMojo {

public void execute() throws MojoExecutionException,
  MojoFailureException {

    System.out.println("get-code-goal");


  }
}
```

In the same way, you need to have three more classes, one for each goal,
and make sure that you have the right Javadoc tag in each class.

3. Once everything is ready, you can use the following POM file to build the plugin project. Here, the value of the `packaging` is set to `maven-plugin`, and then Maven knows how to build this project as a plugin. The code is as follows:

```
<project>
  <modelVersion>4.0.0</modelVersion>
  <groupId>com.packt</groupId>
  <artifactId>com.packt.lifecycle.sample</artifactId>
  <version>1.0.0</version>
  <packaging>maven-plugin</packaging>

  <dependencies>
    <dependency>
      <groupId>org.apache.maven</groupId>
      <artifactId>maven-plugin-api</artifactId>
      <version>2.0</version>
    </dependency>
  </dependencies>
</project>
```

The directory structure of the plugin project will be as follows:

```
|-pom.xml
|-src/main
        |-java/com/packt/lifecycle/sample/*.java
        |-resources/META-INF/plexus/components.xml
```

4. Now, we can build the project using `mvn clean install`. The plugin will get installed in the local Maven repository. The plugin that we created with a custom lifecycle is now ready for use by any Maven project. Let's create a simple Maven project with just the following POM file to consume this plugin:

```
<project>
  <modelVersion>4.0.0</modelVersion>
  <groupId>com.packt</groupId>
  <artifactId>com.packt.lifecycle.sample.project
  </artifactId>
  <version>1.0.0</version>
  <packaging>jar</packaging>
  <name>Custom Lifecycle Project</name>
  <build>
    <plugins>
      <plugin>
```

```
        <groupId>com.packt</groupId>
        <artifactId>com.packt.lifecycle.sample
        </artifactId>
        <version>1.0.0</version>
        <extensions>true</extensions>
      </plugin>
    </plugins>
  </build>
</project>
```

5. Now, you can execute the custom phase in the following manner against the previous POM file:

```
$ mvn notify
```

This will execute all the phases in the custom lifecycle up to and including the `notify` phase, and we will get the following output:

```
[INFO] -----------------------------------------------------------
[INFO] Building Custom Lifecycle Project 1.0.0
[INFO] -----------------------------------------------------------
[INFO]
[INFO] --- com.packt.lifecycle.sample:1.0.0:get-code-goal
  (default-get-code-goal) @ com.packt.lifecycle.sample.project
  ---get-code-goal

[INFO]
[INFO] --- com.packt.lifecycle.sample:1.0.0:build-code-goal
  (default-build-code-goal) @
  com.packt.lifecycle.sample.project ---build-code-goal

[INFO]
[INFO] --- com.packt.lifecycle.sample:1.0.0:run-tests-goal
(default-run-tests-goal) @ com.packt.lifecycle.sample.project
  ---run-tests-goal

[INFO]
[INFO] --- com.packt.lifecycle.sample:1.0.0:notify-goal
  (default-notify-goal) @ com.packt.lifecycle.sample.project

---notify-goal
```

The complete source code corresponding to the custom lifecycle project is available at `https://svn.wso2.org/repos/wso2/people/prabath/maven/chapter04/`.

Lifecycle extensions

The lifecycle extensions in Maven allow you to customize the standard build behavior. Let's have a look at the `org.apache.maven.AbstractMavenLifecycleParticipant` class. Your custom lifecycle extension should extend from the `AbstractMavenLifecycleParticipant` class, which provides the following three methods that you can override:

- `afterProjectsRead(MavenSession session)`: This method is invoked after all the MavenProject instances have been created. There will be one project instance for each POM file. In a large-scale build system, you have one parent POM and it points to multiple child POM files. This method can be used by an extension to manipulate the Maven projects prior to build execution.

- `afterSessionEnd(MavenSession session)`: This method is invoked after all Maven projects are built. An extension can use this method to cleanup any of the resources used during the build execution.

- `afterSessionStart(MavenSession session)`: This method is invoked after the `MavenSession` instance is created. An extension can use this method to inject execution properties, activate profiles and perform similar tasks that affect MavenProject instance construction.

Let's try out the following example:

```
package com.packt.lifecycle.ext;

import org.apache.maven.AbstractMavenLifecycleParticipant;
import org.apache.maven.MavenExecutionException;
import org.apache.maven.execution.MavenSession;
import org.codehaus.plexus.component.annotations.Component;

@Component(role = AbstractMavenLifecycleParticipant.class, hint
  ="packt")

public class PACKTLifeCycleExtension extends
  AbstractMavenLifecycleParticipant {

@Override
  public void afterProjectsRead(MavenSession session) {
    System.out.println("All MavenProject instances are created.");
    System.out.println("Offline building: " + session.isOffline());
  }

@Override
  public void afterSessionEnd(MavenSession session) throws
    MavenExecutionException {
```

```
      System.out.println("All Maven projects are built.");
   }
}
```

The previous code can be built with the following application POM file:

```xml
<project>
  <modelVersion>4.0.0</modelVersion>
  <groupId>com.packt</groupId>
  <artifactId>com.packt.lifecycle.ext</artifactId>
  <version>1.0.0</version>
  <packaging>jar</packaging>

  <dependencies>
    <dependency>
      <groupId>org.apache.maven</groupId>
      <artifactId>maven-compat</artifactId>
      <version>3.2.1</version>
    </dependency>
    <dependency>
      <groupId>org.apache.maven</groupId>
      <artifactId>maven-core</artifactId>
      <version>3.2.1</version>
    </dependency>
  </dependencies>

  <build>
    <plugins>
      <plugin>
        <groupId>org.codehaus.plexus</groupId>
        <artifactId>plexus-component-metadata</artifactId>
        <version>1.5.5</version>
        <executions>
          <execution>
            <goals>
              <goal>generate-metadata</goal>
              <goal>generate-test-metadata</goal>
            </goals>
          </execution>
        </executions>
      </plugin>
    </plugins>
  </build>
</project>
```

Here, in the POM file, we use the `plexus-component-metadata` plugin to generate the Plexus descriptor from the source tags and class annotations.

Once the extension project is built successfully with `mvn clean install`, we need to incorporate the extension to other Maven builds. You can do it in two ways: one is by adding it to the project POM as an extension, as shown in the following code:

```
<project>
  <modelVersion>4.0.0</modelVersion>
  <groupId>com.packt</groupId>
  <artifactId>
    com.packt.lifecycle.ext.sample.project
  </artifactId>
  <version>1.0.0</version>
  <packaging>jar</packaging>
  <name>Custom Lifecycle Extension Project</name>

  <build>
    <extensions>
      <extension>
        <groupId>com.packt</groupId>
        <artifactId>com.packt.lifecycle.ext</artifactId>
        <version>1.0.0</version>
      </extension>
    </extensions>
  </build>
</project>
```

Now, you can build the sample project with `mvn clean install`. It will produce the following output:

```
[INFO] Scanning for projects...
All Maven project instances are created.
Offline building: false


[INFO] ------------------------------------------------------------
[INFO] BUILD SUCCESS
[INFO] ------------------------------------------------------------
[INFO] Total time: 1.328 s
[INFO] Finished at: 2014-07-29T11:29:52+05:30
[INFO] Final Memory: 6M/81M
[INFO] ------------------------------------------------------------


All Maven projects are built.
```

If you want to execute this extension for all your Maven projects without changing each and every POM file, then you need to add the lifecycle extension JAR file to `MAVEN_HOME/lib/ext`.

The complete source code corresponding to the lifecycle extension project can be downloaded from `https://svn.wso2.org/repos/wso2/people/prabath/maven/chapter04/`.

Summary

In this chapter, we focused on Maven lifecycles and explained how the three standard lifecycles work and how we can customize them. Later in the chapter, we discussed how to define our own lifecycles and develop our own lifecycle extensions.

In the next chapter, we will discuss how to extend Maven's default behavior further via plugins.

5
Maven Plugins

The roots of Maven go back to the Jakarta Turbine project. It was started as an attempt to simplify the build process of Jakarta Turbine. The beauty of Maven is its design. It does not try to do everything itself, but rather delegate the work to a plugin framework. When you download Maven from its website, it's only the core framework and plugins are downloaded on demand. All the useful functionalities in the build process are developed as Maven plugins. You can also easily call Maven a plugin execution framework.

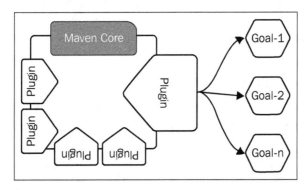

Maven plugins can be executed on their own or can be executed as a part of a Maven lifecycle. Maven lifecycles were discussed in *Chapter 4, Build Lifecycles*. Each plugin has its own set of goals. Let's see how to execute the clean goal of the Maven clean plugin, as follows. The clean goal will attempt to clean the working directory and the associated files created during the build:

```
$ mvn clean:clean
```

 Maven plugins can be self-executed as
mvn plugin-prefix-name:goal-name.

The same `clean` plugin can be executed via the `clean` lifecycle. The `clean` goal of the Maven `clean` plugin is associated with the `clean` phase of the `clean` lifecycle. One difference here is that when you execute a Maven plugin on its own, it only runs the goal specified in the command; however, when you run it as a part of a lifecycle, Maven executes all the plugins associated with the corresponding lifecycle up until the specified phase (including that phase). The command is as follows:

```
$ mvn clean
```

In this chapter, we will be discussing the following topics:

- Commonly used Maven plugins and their usage
- Plugin discovery and execution process
- Inversion of Control frameworks — Plexus and Google Guice (pronounced as juice)
- Custom Maven plugins

Common Maven plugins

Maven plugins are mostly developed under the Apache Maven project itself as well as under the Codehaus and Google Code projects. The next sections list out a set of commonly used Maven plugins and their usage.

The clean plugin

As discussed before, the `clean` plugin executes the `clean` goal of the Maven `clean` plugin to remove any of the working directories and other resources created during the build, as follows:

```
$ mvn clean:clean
```

The Maven `clean` plugin is also associated with the `clean` lifecycle. If you just execute mvn clean, the `clean` goal of the `clean` plugin will get executed.

You do not need to explicitly define the Maven `clean` plugin in your project POM file. Your project inherits it from the Maven super POM file. *Chapter 2, Demystifying Project Object Model*, discussed the Maven super POM file in detail. The following configuration in the super POM file associates the Maven `clean` plugin with all the Maven projects:

```
<plugin>
  <artifactId>maven-clean-plugin</artifactId>
  <version>2.5</version>
```

```
    <executions>
      <execution>
        <id>default-clean</id>
        <phase>clean</phase>
        <goals>
          <goal>clean</goal>
        </goals>
      </execution>
    </executions>
  </plugin>
```

 The Maven `default` lifecycle includes the phases: validate -> initialize -> generate-sources -> process-sources -> generate-resources -> process-resources -> compile -> process-classes -> generate-test-sources -> process-test-sources -> generate-test-resources -> process-test-resources -> test-compile -> process-test-classes -> test -> prepare-package -> package -> pre-integration-test -> integration-test -> post-integration-test -> verify -> install -> deploy.

By default, the `clean` goal of the `clean` plugin runs under the `clean` phase of the Maven `clean` lifecycle. If your project wants the `clean` plugin to run by default, then you can associate it with the `initialize` phase of the Maven `default` lifecycle. You can add the following configuration to your application POM file:

```
<project>
  [...]
  <build>
    <plugins>
      <plugin>
        <artifactId>maven-clean-plugin</artifactId>
        <version>2.5</version>
        <executions>
          <execution>
            <id>auto-clean</id>
            <phase>initialize</phase>
            <goals>
              <goal>clean</goal>
            </goals>
          </execution>
        </executions>
      </plugin>
    </plugins>
  </build>
  [...]
</project>
```

Now, the `clean` goal of the `clean` plugin will get executed when you execute any of the phases from the `initialize` phase in the Maven `default` lifecycle; no need to explicitly execute the `clean` phase of the `clean` lifecycle. For example, `mvn install` will run the `clean` goal in its `initialize` phase. This way, you can override the default behavior of the Maven `clean` plugin. A complete Maven sample project with the previous plugin configuration is available at `https://svn.wso2.org/repos/wso2/people/prabath/maven/chapter05/jose`.

The compiler plugin

The `compiler` plugin is used to compile the source code. This has two goals: `compile` and `testCompile`. The `compile` goal is bound to the `compile` phase of the Maven `default` lifecycle. When you type `mvn clean install`, Maven will execute all the phases in the `default` lifecycle up to and including the `install` phase, which also includes the `compile` phase. This in turn will run the `compile` goal of the `compiler` plugin.

The following command shows how to execute the `compile` goal of the `compiler` plugin by itself. This will simply compile your source code:

```
$ mvn compiler:compile
```

All the Maven projects inherit the `compiler` plugin from the super POM file. As shown in the following configuration, the super POM defines the `compiler` plugin. It associates the `testCompile` and `compile` goals with the `test-compile` and `compile` phases of the Maven `default` lifecycle:

```
<plugin>
  <artifactId>maven-compiler-plugin</artifactId>
  <version>3.1</version>
  <executions>
    <execution>
      <id>default-testCompile</id>
      <phase>test-compile</phase>
      <goals>
        <goal>testCompile</goal>
      </goals>
    </execution>
    <execution>
      <id>default-compile</id>
      <phase>compile</phase>
      <goals>
        <goal>compile</goal>
      </goals>
    </execution>
  </executions>
</plugin>
```

By default, the Maven `compiler` plugin assumes JDK 1.5 for both the `source` and `target` elements. JVM identifies the Java version of the source code via the `source` configuration parameter and the version of the compiled code via the `target` configuration parameter. If you want to break the assumption made by Maven and specify your own `source` and `target` versions, you need to override the `compiler` plugin configuration in your application POM file, as shown in the following code:

```
<project>
  [...]
    <build>
      [...]
        <plugins>
          <plugin>
            <groupId>org.apache.maven.plugins</groupId>
            <artifactId>maven-compiler-plugin</artifactId>
            <version>3.1</version>
            <configuration>
              <source>1.7</source>
              <target>1.7</target>
            </configuration>
          </plugin>
        </plugins>
      [...]
    </build>
  [...]
</project>
```

Not just the `source` and `target` elements, you can pass any argument to the `compiler` plugin under the `compilerArgument` element. This is more useful when the Maven `compiler` plugin does not have an element defined for the corresponding JVM argument. For example, the same `source` and `target` values can also be passed in the following manner:

```
<project>
  [...]
    <build>
      [...]
        <plugins>
          <plugin>
            <groupId>org.apache.maven.plugins</groupId>
            <artifactId>maven-compiler-plugin</artifactId>
            <version>3.1</version>
            <configuration>
              <compilerArgument>-source 1.7 -target
                .7</compilerArgument>
            </configuration>
          </plugin>
```

```
            </plugins>
        [...]
      </build>
    [...]
  </project>
```

The install plugin

The install plugin will deploy the final project artifacts into the local Maven repository defined under the localRepository element of MAVEN_HOME/conf/settings.xml. The default location is USER_HOME/.m2/repository. The install goal of the install plugin is bound to the install phase of the Maven default lifecycle. When you type mvn clean install, Maven will execute all phases in the default lifecycle up to and including the install phase.

The following command shows how to execute the install goal of the install plugin by itself:

$ mvn install:install

All Maven projects inherit the install plugin from the super POM file. As shown in the following configuration, the super POM defines the install plugin. It associates the install goal with the install phase of the Maven default lifecycle:

```
<plugin>
  <artifactId>maven-install-plugin</artifactId>
  <version>2.4</version>
  <executions>
    <execution>
      <id>default-install</id>
      <phase>install</phase>
      <goals>
        <goal>install</goal>
      </goals>
    </execution>
    <execution>
      <id>default-install-1</id>
      <phase>install</phase>
      <goals>
        <goal>install</goal>
      </goals>
    </execution>
  </executions>
</plugin>
```

The install goal of the install plugin does not have any configurations to be overridden at the project level.

The deploy plugin

The `deploy` plugin will deploy the final project artifacts into a remote Maven repository. The `deploy` goal of the `deploy` plugin is associated with the `deploy` phase of the `default` Maven lifecycle. To deploy an artifact via the `default` lifecycle, `mvn clean install` is not sufficient; it has to be `mvn clean deploy`. Any guesses why?

The `deploy` phase of the `default` Maven lifecycle comes after the `install` phase. Executing `mvn clean deploy` will execute all the phases of the `default` Maven lifecycle up to and including the `deploy` phase, which also includes the `install` phase. The following command shows how to execute the `deploy` goal of the `deploy` plugin by itself:

```
$ mvn deploy:deploy
```

All the Maven projects inherit the `deploy` plugin from the super POM file. As shown in the following configuration, the super POM defines the `deploy` plugin. It associates the `deploy` goal with the `deploy` phase of the Maven `default` lifecycle:

```
<plugin>
  <artifactId>maven-deploy-plugin</artifactId>
  <version>2.7</version>
  <executions>
    <execution>
      <id>default-deploy</id>
      <phase>deploy</phase>
      <goals>
        <goal>deploy</goal>
      </goals>
    </execution>
  </executions>
</plugin>
```

Before executing either `mvn deploy:deploy` or `mvn deploy`, you need to set up the remote Maven repository details in your project POM file, under the `distributionManagement` section, as follows. We will discuss Maven repositories in detail in *Chapter 8, Maven Repository Management*:

```
[...]
  <distributionManagement>
    <repository>
      <id>wso2-maven2-repository</id>
      <name>WSO2 Maven2 Repository</name>
      <url>scp://dist.wso2.org/home/httpd/dist.wso2.org/
        maven2/</url>
    </repository>
  </distributionManagement>
[...]
```

In this example, Maven connects to the remote repository via `scp`. **Secure Copy (scp)** defines a way of securely transferring files between two nodes in a computer network, which is built on top of the popular SSH. To authenticate to the remote server, Maven provides two ways. One is based on the username and password. The other one is based on SSH authentication keys. To configure username/password credential against the Maven repository, we need to add the following `<server>` configuration element to `USER_HOME/.m2/settings.xml` under the `<servers>` parent element. The value of the `id` element must carry the value of the remote repository hostname:

```
<server>
  <id>dist.wso2.org</id>
  <username>my_username</username>
  <password>my_password</password>
</server>
```

If the remote repository only supports SSH authentication keys, then we need to specify the location of the private key, as follows:

```
<server>
  <id>dist.wso2.org</id>
  <username>my_username</username>
  <privateKey>/path/to/private/key</privateKey>
</server>
```

The `deploy` goal of the `deploy` plugin does not have any configurations to be overridden at the project level.

The surefire plugin

The `surefire` plugin will run the unit tests associated with the project. The `test` goal of the `surefire` plugin is bound to the `test` phase of the `default` Maven lifecycle. When you type `mvn clean install`, Maven will execute all the phases in the `default` lifecycle up to and including the `install` phase, which also includes the `test` phase.

The following command shows how to execute the `test` goal of the `surefire` plugin by itself:

```
$ mvn surefire:test
```

All the Maven projects inherit the `surefire` plugin from the super POM file. As shown in the following configuration, the super POM defines the `surefire` plugin. It associates the `test` goal with the `test` phase of the Maven `default` lifecycle:

```
<plugin>
  <artifactId>maven-surefire-plugin</artifactId>
```

```
      <version>2.12.4</version>
      <executions>
        <execution>
          <id>default-test</id>
          <phase>test</phase>
          <goals>
            <goal>test</goal>
          </goals>
        </execution>
        <execution>
          <id>default-test-1</id>
          <phase>test</phase>
          <goals>
            <goal>test</goal>
          </goals>
        </execution>
      </executions>
    </plugin>
```

As the `surefire` plugin is defined in the super POM file, you do not need to add it explicitly to your application POM file. However, you need to add a dependency to `junit`, shown as follows:

```
<dependencies>
  [...]
    <dependency>
      <groupId>junit</groupId>
      <artifactId>junit</artifactId>
      <version>4.8.1</version>
      <scope>test</scope>
    </dependency>
  [...]
</dependencies>
```

The `surefire` plugin is not just coupled to JUnit; it can also be used with other testing frameworks as well. If you are using TestNG, then you need to add a dependency to `testng`, shown as follows:

```
<dependencies>
  [...]
    <dependency>
      <groupId>org.testng</groupId>
      <artifactId>testng</artifactId>
      <version>6.3.1</version>
```

```
        <scope>test</scope>
      </dependency>
    [...]
  </dependencies>
```

The `surefire` plugin introduces a concept called test providers. You can specify a test provider within the plugin itself; if not, it will be derived from the dependency JAR file. For example, if you want to use the `junit47` provider, then within the plugin configuration, you can specify it as shown in the following configuration. The `surefire` plugin supports, by default, four test providers, which are `surefire-junit3`, `surefire-junit4`, `surefire-junit47`, and `surefire-testng`:

```
<plugins>
  [...]
    <plugin>
      <groupId>org.apache.maven.plugins</groupId>
      <artifactId>maven-surefire-plugin</artifactId>
      <version>2.17</version>
      <dependencies>
        <dependency>
          <groupId>org.apache.maven.surefire</groupId>
          <artifactId>surefire-junit47</artifactId>
          <version>2.17</version>
        </dependency>
      </dependencies>
    </plugin>
  [...]
</plugins>
```

As all the Maven projects inherit the `surefire` plugin from the super POM file, you do not override its configuration in the application POM file unless it's an absolute necessity. One reason for this could be to override the default test provider selection algorithm.

The site plugin

The `site` plugin generates static HTML web content for the project, including the reports configured in a project. This defines eight goals, where each goal runs in one of the four phases defined in the Maven site lifecycle: `pre-site`, `site`, `post-site`, and `site-deploy`. The eight goals are:

- `site:site`: This goal generates a site for a single Maven project

- `site:deploy`: This goal deploys the generated site via the Wagon-supported protocol to the site URL specified in the `<distributionManagement>` section of the POM file

- `site:run`: This goal starts the site with the Jetty web server

- `site:stage`: This goal generates a site in a local staging or mock directory based on the site URL specified in the `<distributionManagement>` section of the POM file

- `site:stage-deploy`: This goal deploys the generated site to a staging or mock directory to the site URL specified in the `<distributionManagement>` section of the POM file

- `site:attach-descriptor`: This goal adds the site descriptor (`site.xml`) to the list of files to be installed/deployed

- `site:jar`: This goal bundles the site output into a JAR file so that it can be deployed to a repository

- `site:effective-site`: This goal calculates the effective site descriptor after inheritance and interpolation of `site.xml`

All the Maven projects inherit the `site` plugin from the super POM file. As shown in the following configuration, the super POM defines the `site` plugin. It associates the `site` and `deploy` goals with the `site` and `site-deploy` phases of the Maven `default` lifecycle:

```
<plugin>
  <artifactId>maven-site-plugin</artifactId>
  <version>3.3</version>
  <executions>
    <execution>
      <id>default-site</id>
      <phase>site</phase>
      <goals>
        <goal>site</goal>
      </goals>
      <configuration>
        <outputDirectory>
        PROJECT_HOME/target/site</outputDirectory>
        <reportPlugins>
          <reportPlugin>
            <groupId>org.apache.maven.plugins</groupId>
            <artifactId>
              maven-project-info-reports-plugin
            </artifactId>
          </reportPlugin>
        </reportPlugins>
      </configuration>
    </execution>
    <execution>
```

```
        <id>default-deploy</id>
        <phase>site-deploy</phase>
        <goals>
          <goal>deploy</goal>
        </goals>
        <configuration>
          <outputDirectory>
          PROJECT_HOME/target/site</outputDirectory>
          <reportPlugins>
            <reportPlugin>
              <groupId>org.apache.maven.plugins</groupId>
              <artifactId>
                maven-project-info-reports-plugin
              </artifactId>
            </reportPlugin>
          </reportPlugins>
        </configuration>
      </execution>
    </executions>
    <configuration>
      <outputDirectory>
      PROJECT_HOME/target/site</outputDirectory>
      <reportPlugins>
        <reportPlugin>
          <groupId>org.apache.maven.plugins</groupId>
          <artifactId>
            maven-project-info-reports-plugin
          </artifactId>
        </reportPlugin>
      </reportPlugins>
    </configuration>
  </plugin>
```

As defined in the previous configuration, when you run mvn site or mvn site:site, the resultant HTML web content will be created inside the target/site directory under the project home. The site goal of the site plugin only generates the HTML web content; to deploy it, you need to use the deploy goal. To deploy the generated website to a remote application server, you need to specify the remote machine details under the distributionManagement section of your application POM file, as follows:

```
<project>
  ...
  <distributionManagement>
    <site>
      <id>mycompany.com</id>
```

```
            <url>scp://mycompany/www/docs/project/</url>
        </site>
    </distributionManagement>
    ...
</project>
```

To configure credentials to connect to the remote computer, you need to add the following `<server>` configuration element to `USER_HOME/.m2/settings.xml` under the `<servers>` parent element:

```
<server>
  <id>mycompany.com</id>
  <username>my_username</username>
  <password>my_password</password>
</server>
```

The generated site or the web content can be deployed to the remote location by executing the `deploy` goal of the Maven `site` plugin, as follows:

```
$ mvn site:deploy
```

In most of the cases, you do not need to override the `site` plugin configuration.

The jar plugin

The `jar` plugin creates a JAR file from your Maven project. The `jar` goal of the `jar` plugin is bound to the `package` phase of the Maven `default` lifecycle. When you type `mvn clean install`, Maven will execute all the phases in the `default` lifecycle up to and including the `install` phase, which also includes the `package` phase.

The following command shows how to execute the `jar` goal of the `jar` plugin by itself:

```
$ mvn jar:jar
```

All the Maven projects inherit the `jar` plugin from the super POM file. As shown in the following configuration, the super POM defines the `jar` plugin. It associates the `jar` goal with the `package` phase of the Maven `default` lifecycle:

```
<plugin>
  <artifactId>maven-jar-plugin</artifactId>
  <version>2.4</version>
  <executions>
    <execution>
      <id>default-jar</id>
      <phase>package</phase>
      <goals>
```

```
        <goal>jar</goal>
      </goals>
    </execution>
    <execution>
      <id>default-jar-1</id>
      <phase>package</phase>
      <goals>
        <goal>jar</goal>
      </goals>
    </execution>
  </executions>
</plugin>
```

In most of the cases, you do not need to override the `jar` plugin configuration, except in a case, where you need to create a self-executable `jar` file.

 Details on how to create a self-executable JAR file with `maven-jar-plugin` can be found at `http://maven.apache.org/shared/maven-archiver/examples/classpath.html`.

The source plugin

The `source` plugin creates a JAR file with the project source code. It defines five goals: `aggregate`, `jar`, `test-jar`, `jar-no-fork`, and `test-jar-no-fork`. All these five goals of the `source` plugin will run under the `package` phase of the `default` lifecycle.

Unlike any of the plugins we discussed before, if you want to execute the `source` plugin with the Maven `default` lifecycle, it has to be defined in the project POM file, shown as follows. The super POM file does not define the `source` plugin; it has to be within your Maven project itself:

```
<project>
...
  <build>
    <plugins>
      <plugin>
        <groupId>org.apache.maven.plugins</groupId>
        <artifactId>maven-source-plugin</artifactId>
        <version>2.3</version>
        <configuration>
          <outputDirectory>
            /absolute/path/to/the/output/directory
          </outputDirectory>
```

```
        <finalName>filename-of-generated-jar-file</finalName>
        <attach>false</attach>
      </configuration>
    </plugin>
  </plugins>
</build>
...
</project>
```

What is the difference between the `jar` and `source` plugins? Both create JAR files; however, the `jar` plugin creates a JAR file from the binary artifact, while the `source` plugin creates a JAR file from the source code. Small-scale open source projects use this approach to distribute the corresponding source code along with the binary artifacts.

The resources plugin

The `resources` plugin copies the resources associated with the main project as well as the tests to the project output directory. The `resources` goal of the `resources` plugin copies the main resources into the main output directory, and it runs under the `process-resources` phase of the Maven `default` lifecycle. The `testResources` goal copies all the resources associated with the tests to the test output directory, and runs under the `process-test-resources` phase of the Maven `default` lifecycle. The `copyResources` goal can be configured to copy any resource to the project output directory, and this is not bound to any of the phases in the Maven `default` lifecycle.

All the Maven projects inherit the `resources` plugin from the super POM file. As shown in the following configuration, the super POM defines the `resources` plugin. It associates `resources` and `testResources` goals with the `process-resources` and `process-test-resources` phases of the Maven `default` lifecycle. When you type `mvn clean install`, Maven will execute all the phases in the `default` lifecycle up to and including the `install` phase, which also includes the `process-resources` and `process-test-resources` phases:

```
<plugin>
  <artifactId>maven-resources-plugin</artifactId>
  <version>2.6</version>
  <executions>
    <execution>
      <id>default-resources</id>
      <phase>process-resources</phase>
      <goals>
        <goal>resources</goal>
      </goals>
```

```
      </execution>
      <execution>
        <id>default-testResources</id>
        <phase>process-test-resources</phase>
        <goals>
          <goal>testResources</goal>
        </goals>
      </execution>
      <execution>
        <id>default-resources-1</id>
        <phase>process-resources</phase>
        <goals>
          <goal>resources</goal>
        </goals>
      </execution>
      <execution>
        <id>default-testResources-1</id>
        <phase>process-test-resources</phase>
        <goals>
          <goal>testResources</goal>
        </goals>
      </execution>
    </executions>
  </plugin>
```

In most of the cases, you do not need to override the `resources` plugin configuration, unless you have a specific need to filter `resources`.

 More details about resource filtering with `maven-resources-plugin` can be found at `http://maven.apache.org/plugins/maven-resources-plugin/examples/filter.html`.

The release plugin

Releasing a project requires a lot of repetitive tasks. The objective of the Maven `release` plugin is to automate them. The `release` plugin defines the following eight goals, which are executed in two stages, which are preparing the release and performing the release:

- `release:clean`: This goal cleans up after a release preparation

- `release:prepare`: This goal prepares for a release in **Software Configuration Management (SCM)**

- `release:prepare-with-pom`: This goal prepares for a release in SCM and generates release POMs by fully resolving the dependencies
- `release:rollback`: This goal rolls back to a previous release
- `release:perform`: This goal performs a release from SCM
- `release:stage`: This goal performs a release from SCM into a staging folder/repository
- `release:branch`: This goal creates a branch of the current project with all versions updated
- `release:update-versions`: This goal updates the versions in POM(s)

The preparation stage will complete the following tasks with the `release:prepare` goal:

- Verify that all the changes in the source code are committed.
- Make sure that there are no SNAPSHOT dependencies. During the project development phase we use SNAPSHOT dependencies; however, at the time of the release, all the dependencies should be changed to a released version.
- The version of the project POM file will be changed from SNAPSHOT to a concrete version number.
- The SCM information in the project POM file will be changed to include the final destination of the tag.
- Execute all the tests against the modified POM files.
- Commit the modified POM files to SCM and tag the code with the version name.
- Change the version in POM files in the trunk to a SNAPSHOT version and commit the modified POM files to the trunk.

Finally, the release will be performed with the `release:perform` goal. This will check out the code from the `release` tag in the SCM and run a set of predefined goals: `site` and `deploy-site`.

The `maven-release-plugin` is not defined in the super POM file; it should be explicitly defined in your application POM file. The `releaseProfiles` configuration element defines the profiles to be released and the `goals` configuration element defines the plugin goals to be executed during `release:perform`, as follows:

```
<plugin>
  <artifactId>maven-release-plugin</artifactId>
  <version>2.5</version>
  <configuration>
```

```
      <releaseProfiles>release</releaseProfiles>
      <goals>deploy assembly:single</goals>
    </configuration>
  </plugin>
```

Plugin discovery and execution

To associate a plugin with your Maven project, either you have to define it explicitly from your application POM file, or you should inherit from a parent POM or the super POM file. Let's have a look at the Maven `jar` plugin. The `jar` plugin is defined by the super POM file, and all the Maven projects inherit it. To define a plugin (which is not inherited from the POM hierarchy) or associate a plugin with your Maven project, you must add the plugin configuration under the `build/plugins/plugin` element. In this way, you can associate any number of plugins with your project, shown as follows:

```
<project>
...
  <build>
    <plugins>
      <plugin>
        <artifactId>maven-jar-plugin</artifactId>
        <version>2.4</version>
        <executions>
          <execution>
            <id>default-jar</id>
            <phase>package</phase>
            <goals>
              <goal>jar</goal>
            </goals>
          </execution>
          <execution>
            <id>default-jar-1</id>
            <phase>package</phase>
            <goals>
              <goal>jar</goal>
            </goals>
          </execution>
        </executions>
      </plugin>
    </plugins>
  </build>
...
</project>
```

In the Maven execution environment, what matters is not just your application POM file but the effective POM file. The effective POM file is constructed by the project POM file, any parent POM files, and the super POM file.

A Maven plugin can be executed in two ways: via a lifecycle or directly invoking a plugin goal. If it is via a lifecycle, then there are plugin goals associated with different phases of the lifecycle. When each phase gets executed, all the plugin goals will also get executed only if the effective POM file of the project has defined the corresponding plugins under its plugins configuration. The same applies even when you try to invoke a plugin goal directly (for example, `mvn jar:jar`), the goal will be executed only if the corresponding plugin is associated with the project.

In either way, once Maven decides to execute a plugin goal, how does it find the plugin?

Similar to any other dependency in Maven, a plugin is also uniquely identified by three coordinates: `groupId`, `artifactId`, and `version`. However, for plugins, you do not need to explicitly specify `groupId`. Maven assumes two `groupIds` by default: `org.apache.maven.plugins` and `org.codehaus.mojo`. First, it will try to locate the plugin from `USER_HOME/.m2/repository/org/apache/maven/plugins`, and if this fails, it will go for `USER_HOME/.m2/repository/org/codehaus/mojo`.

In the previous sample plugin configuration, you do not find `groupId`. Maven loads the `jar` plugin from `USER_HOME/.m2/repository/org/apache/maven/plugins/maven-jar-plugin`.

Maven also lets you add your own plugin groups, and they can be included in the plugin discovery. You can do it by updating `USER_HOME/.m2/settings.xml` or `MAVEN_HOME/conf/settings.xml`, as shown in the following manner:

```
<pluginGroups>
  <pluginGroup>com.packt.plugins</pluginGroup>
</pluginGroups>
```

Maven will always give the first priority to the previous configuration and then start looking for the well-known `groupId` elements: `org.apache.maven.plugins` and `org.codehaus.mojo`.

Let's have a look at some of the sample plugin configurations used in some popular open source projects.

Apache Felix provides a `bundle` plugin for Maven, which creates an OSGi bundle out of a Maven project. Another open source project, WSO2 Carbon, uses this `bundle` plugin in its development. You can find a sample POM file, which consumes the plugin at `https://svn.wso2.org/repos/wso2/carbon/platform/branches/turing/service-stubs/org.wso2.carbon.qpid.stub/4.2.0/pom.xml`. This is a custom plugin, which does not fall into any of `groupIds` known to Maven by default. In this case, anyone who uses the plugin must qualify the plugin with `groupId`, or else must add the corresponding `groupId` to the `pluginGroups` configuration element, as discussed earlier.

The following code shows the plugin configuration from the WSO2 Carbon project:

```
<plugin>
  <groupId>org.apache.felix</groupId>
  <artifactId>maven-bundle-plugin</artifactId>
  <extensions>true</extensions>
  <configuration>
    <instructions>
      <Bundle-SymbolicName>
      ${project.artifactId}</Bundle-SymbolicName>
      <Bundle-Name>${project.artifactId}</Bundle-Name>
      <Carbon-Component>UIBundle</Carbon-Component>
      <Import-Package>
        org.apache.axis2.*;
          version="${axis2.osgi.version.range}",
        org.apache.axiom.*;
          version="${axiom.osgi.version.range}",
        *;resolution:=optional
      </Import-Package>
      <Export-Package>
        org.wso2.carbon.qpid.stub.*;
          version=»${carbon.platform.package.export.version}»,
      </Export-Package>
    </instructions>
  </configuration>
</plugin>
```

Plugin management

If you look at the previous configuration carefully, you do not see a version for the `bundle` plugin. This is where the `pluginManagement` element comes into play. With the `pluginManagement` configuration element, you can avoid repetitive usage of the plugin version. Once you define a plugin under `pluginManagement`, all the child POM files will inherit that configuration.

WSO2 Carbon project defines all the plugins used by its child projects under the `pluginManagement` section of `https://svn.wso2.org/repos/wso2/carbon/platform/branches/turing/parent/pom.xml`, and all the projects inherit it. A truncated part of the configuration is as follows:

```
<pluginManagement>
  <plugin>
    <groupId>org.apache.felix</groupId>
    <artifactId>maven-bundle-plugin</artifactId>
    <version>2.3.5</version>
    <extensions>true</extensions>
  </plugin>
</pluginManagement>
```

 We'll discuss more about plugin management in *Chapter 9, Best Practices*.

Plugin repositories

Maven downloads plugins on demand when it cannot find a plugin in its local repository. By default, Maven looks for any plugin that is not available locally in the Maven plugin repository defined by the super POM file (this is the default behavior; you can also define plugin repositories in the application POM file). The following code snippet shows how to define plugin repositories:

```
<pluginRepositories>
  <pluginRepository>
    <id>central</id>
    <name>Maven Plugin Repository</name>
    <url>http://repo1.maven.org/maven2</url>
    <layout>default</layout>
    <snapshots>
      <enabled>false</enabled>
    </snapshots>
    <releases>
      <updatePolicy>never</updatePolicy>
    </releases>
  </pluginRepository>
</pluginRepositories>
```

If you develop a custom plugin, just like the Apache Felix `bundle` plugin, you must make it available for the rest via a plugin repository, and any other consumer of this plugin, such as the WSO2 Carbon project, must define the corresponding plugin repository in its POM file or in a parent POM file.

We'll discuss more about plugin repositories in *Chapter 8, Maven Repository Management*.

The WSO2 Carbon project defines two plugin repositories in its parent POM file at `https://svn.wso2.org/repos/wso2/carbon/platform/branches/turing/parent/pom.xml` and the Apache Felix `bundle` plugin is available at `http://dist.wso2.org/maven2/org/apache/felix/maven-bundle-plugin/`.

The following configuration is part of the WSO2 Carbon project `parent/pom.xml`, which defines the two plugin repositories:

```
<pluginRepositories>
  <pluginRepository>
    <id>wso2-maven2-repository-1</id>
    <url>http://dist.wso2.org/maven2</url>
  </pluginRepository>
  <pluginRepository>
    <id>wso2-maven2-repository-2</id>
    <url>http://dist.wso2.org/snapshots/maven2</url>
  </pluginRepository>
</pluginRepositories>
```

Plugin as an extension

If you look at the definition of the Apache Felix `bundle` plugin, you might have noticed the `extensions` configuration element, which is set to `true`, shown as follows:

```
<plugin>
  <groupId>org.apache.felix</groupId>
  <artifactId>maven-bundle-plugin</artifactId>
  <extensions>true</extensions>
</plugin>
```

As we discussed before, the goal of the `bundle` plugin is to build an OSGi bundle from a Maven project. In other words, the Apache Felix `bundle` plugin introduces a new packaging type with an existing file extension, `jar`. If you look at the POM file of the WSO2 Carbon project, which consumes the `bundle` plugin, you can see the packaging of the project is set to `bundle` (`https://svn.wso2.org/repos/wso2/carbon/platform/branches/turing/service-stubs/org.wso2.carbon.qpid.stub/4.2.0/pom.xml`), as follows:

```
<packaging>bundle</packaging>
```

If you associate a plugin with your project, which introduces a new packaging type or a customized lifecycle, then you must set the value of the `extensions` configuration element to `true`. Once that is done, the Maven engine will go further and will look for the `components.xml` file inside `META-INF/plexus` of the corresponding `jar` plugin.

Plexus

Most of you might be familiar with Spring but not Plexus. Plexus provides an **Inversion of Control (IoC)** or a **Dependency Injection (DI)** framework similar to Spring. If you are new to the concept of Dependency Injection, it's highly recommended that you go through the article by Martin Fowler, *Inversion of Control Containers and the Dependency Injection pattern* at `http://martinfowler.com/articles/injection.html`.

Forget about Maven for a bit; let's see how to implement Dependency Injection with Plexus with the following steps:

1. First, we need to define our own Java interface for our business service as follows. There can be more than one implementation of this service:

    ```
    package com.packt.di;
    public interface MessagingService {

        public void sendMessage(String recipient, String message);
    }
    ```

2. Let's write a couple of implementations for the previous interface. The `SMSMessagingService` class will text the message to the recipient while the `EmailMessagingService` class will email the message, shown as follows:

    ```
    package com.packt.di;

    public class SMSMessagingService implements MessagingService {

        @Override
        public void sendMessage(String recipient, String message)
        {
            System.out.println("SMS sent to : "+recipient);
        }
    }


    package com.packt.di;
    ```

```
public class EmailMessagingService implements
  MessagingService {

  @Override
  public void sendMessage(String recipient,
    String message)
  {
    System.out.println("Email sent to : "+recipient);
  }
}
```

3. Now we have multiple implementations of the same `MessagingService` interface. The Plexus DI framework lets you define each implementation in a configuration file (`components.xml`) and pick whatever you need in the runtime, as follows:

```
<component-set>
  <components>
    <component>
      <role>com.packt.di.MessagingService</role>
      <role-hint>sms</role-hint>
      <implementation>
      com.packt.di.SMSMessagingService
      </implementation>
    </component>
    <component>
      <role>com.packt.di.MessagingService</role>
      <role-hint>email</role-hint>
      <implementation>
      com.packt.di.EmailMessagingService
      </implementation>
    </component>
  </components>
</component-set>
```

4. Let's write a client application that loads different implementations of the `MessagingService` interface via Plexus. Make sure that you have the previous `components.xml` file inside the `src/main/resources/META-INF/plexus` directory inside your client project. Also, make sure that you get all the Plexus `jar` dependencies from `https://svn.wso2.org/repos/wso2/people/prabath/maven/chapter05/plexus/lib`, and add them to your Java class path before running the client code:

```
package com.packt.di;

import org.codehaus.plexus.DefaultPlexusContainer;
```

```
import org.codehaus.plexus.PlexusContainer;

public class MessageSender {

  public static void main(String[] args) {

    PlexusContainer container = null;
    MessagingService msgService = null;

    try {
      container = new DefaultPlexusContainer();
      // send SMS
      msgService = (MessagingService)
      container.lookup(MessagingService.class, "sms");
      msgService.sendMessage("+94718096732", "Welcome to
        Plexus");

      // send Email
      msgService = (MessagingService)
      container.lookup(MessagingService.class, "email");
      msgService.sendMessage("prabath@apache.org", "Welcome to
        Plexus");
    } catch (Exception e) {

      e.printStackTrace();

    } finally {

    if (container != null) {
      container.dispose();
    }
   }
  }
 }
}
```

The `role-hint` configuration element in the `components.xml` file helps to identify different implementations of the same interface uniquely. The fully qualified name of the interface is set as the value of the `role` element. In runtime, the lookup is done by both the `role` and `role-hint` elements. If there is only one implementation, then we do not need the `role-hint` element and the lookup can be done only by the value of `role`.

The previous code produces the following output:

```
SMS sent to :+94718096732
Email sent to :prabath@apache.org
```

In practice, each implementation of the service interface can come from different JAR files, and the client application does not need to have any dependency to the implementation classes at the build time. In runtime, the implementation classes will be injected into the system by the Plexus framework.

The complete Java project used here can be downloaded from `https://svn.wso2.org/repos/wso2/people/prabath/maven/chapter05/plexus`.

Maven and Dependency Injection

When Maven kicked off in 2002, it strongly looked for an IoC or a DI framework. As we discussed before, Maven provides a build framework while the actual work is done by the components and plugins developed on top of it. That's part of the Maven's design philosophy, and this raised the need to have some kind of a component framework to bring in plugins and other extensions.

By 2002, Spring was not that popular and Apache Avalon was the only IoC framework out there. However, the initial set of Maven committers, who also had a strong influence on Plexus, decided to use it as the IoC container for Maven.

Plexus did exactly what Maven wanted to have. However, it uses its own custom DI mechanism. In November 2009, the Java community standardized DI via JSR 330 (`https://www.jcp.org/en/jsr/detail?id=330`). Maven 3.0 onwards started supporting JSR 330 via Google Guice (`https://github.com/google/guice`). Then again, the components that were written using Plexus APIs could still coexist with JSR 330 compliant components and plugins.

To know more about Maven and Google Guice, refer to *From Plexus to Guice (#1): Why Guice?* at `http://blog.sonatype.com/2010/01/from-plexus-to-guice-1-why-guice`.

Google Guice

Google Guice is a lightweight DI framework that has support for JSR 330. Guice was initially developed by Google under the leadership of Bob Lee. He currently works as the CTO of Square and was the lead of JSR 330.

Let's rewrite the same example we did with Plexus in Guice, to be JSR 330 compliant, as follows:

1. First, we need to define our own Java interface for our business service as follows. There can be more than one implementations of this service:

```
package com.packt.di;

public interface MessagingService {
  public void sendMessage(String recipient, String message);
}
```

2. Let's write couple of implementations for the previous interface. The SMSMessagingService class will text the message to the recipient, while the EmailMessagingService class will email the message, shown as follows:

```
package com.packt.di;

public class SMSMessagingService implements
MessagingService{

  @Override
  public void sendMessage(String recipient,
    String message)
  {
    System.out.println("SMS sent to : "+recipient);
  }

}
```

```
package com.packt.di;

public class EmailMessagingService implements
MessagingService{

  @Override
  public void sendMessage(String recipient,
    String message)
  {
    System.out.println("Email sent to : "+recipient);
  }
}
```

3. Now, we need to write a `GuiceMessageSender` class, which will dynamically pick the `MessagingService` implementation to send the message, shown as follows. The Guice framework will inject the implementation class instance into the method that has the `Inject` annotation:

```
package com.packt.di;

import javax.inject.Inject;

public class GuiceMessageSender {

  private MessagingService messagingService;

  @Inject
  public void setService(MessagingService
    messagingService)
  {
    this.messagingService = messagingService;
  }

  public void sendMessage(String recipient, String
    message)
  {
    messagingService.sendMessage(recipient, message);
  }
}
```

4. Now, we need to write a class extending the `AbstractModule` class of the `com.google.inject` package, which will bind an implementation class to the interface, as follows:

```
package com.packt.di;

import com.google.inject.AbstractModule;

public class GuiceInjector extends AbstractModule {
  @Override
  protected void configure() {
    bind(MessagingService.class).
      to(SMSMessagingService.class);
  }
}
```

5. Finally, the `GuiceClientApplication` class will send the message using an instance of the `GuiceMessageSender` class, as follows. You can download all the dependency JARs from https://svn.wso2.org/repos/wso2/people/prabath/maven/chapter05/guice/lib:

```
package com.packt.di;

import com.google.inject.Guice;
import com.google.inject.Injector;
```

```
public class GuiceClientApplication {

  public static void main(String[] args) {
    Injector injector;
    GuiceMessageSender messageSender;

    injector = Guice.createInjector(new GuiceInjector());
    messageSender = injector.
      getInstance(GuiceMessageSender.class);
    messageSender.sendMessage("+94718096732", "Welcome to
      Plexus");
  }
}
```

The complete Java project used here can be downloaded from `https://svn.wso2.org/repos/wso2/people/prabath/maven/chapter05/guice`.

Developing custom plugins

A greater part of this chapter is already spent on providing all the necessary background knowledge to start Maven custom plugin development. Under this section, let's see how to build your own Maven custom plugin from scratch. There are so many Maven plugins out there, and most of the time, you can find a plugin to do whatever you want. Let's start by defining a use case for our custom plugin. Say, you want to write a plugin to send an email to a given recipient once the build is completed.

Maven plain Old Java Object (MOJO) is at the heart of a Maven plugin. A Maven plugin is a collection of goals, and each goal is implemented via a MOJO. In other words, a Maven plugin is a collection of MOJOs. To create a custom plugin, proceed with the following steps:

1. The first step in writing a custom plugin is to identify the goals of the plugin, and then represent (and implement) each of them with a MOJO. In our case, we have a single goal, that is, to send an email once the build is completed.

    We will write our own `EmailMojo` class that extends the `AbstractMojo` class of the `org.apache.maven.plugin` package. This class must have the `Mojo` annotation, and the value of the `name` attribute represents the goal name. In your custom plugin, if you have multiple goals, then for each goal, you need to have a MOJO and override the `execute()` method. The code is as follows:

    ```
    package com.packt.plugins;

    import org.apache.maven.plugin.AbstractMojo;
    ```

```
import org.apache.maven.plugin.MojoExecutionException;
import org.apache.maven.plugins.annotations.Mojo;

@Mojo( name = "mail")
public class EmailMojo extends AbstractMojo
{
  public void execute() throws MojoExecutionException
  {
    getLog().info( "Sending Email…" );
  }
}
```

2. For the time being, let's not worry about the email sending logic. Once you
   have implemented your business logic inside the `execute()` method of your
   MOJO, next we need to package this as a plugin so that the Maven plugin
   execution framework can identify and execute it.

   You can use `maven-plugin-plugin` to generate the metadata related to your
   custom plugin. The following POM file associates `maven-plugin-plugin` with
   your custom plugin project. Also, we need to have two dependencies: one for
   `maven-plugin-api` and the other one for `maven-plugin-annotations`.

```
<project>

  <modelVersion>4.0.0</modelVersion>
  <groupId>com.packt.plugins</groupId>
  <artifactId>mail-maven-plugin</artifactId>
  <version>1.0.0</version>
  <packaging>maven-plugin</packaging>
  <name>PACKT Maven Plugin Project</name>

  <dependencies>
    <dependency>
      <groupId>org.apache.maven</groupId>
      <artifactId>maven-plugin-api</artifactId>
      <version>2.0</version>
    </dependency>
    <dependency>
      <groupId>org.apache.maven.plugin-tools</groupId>
      <artifactId>maven-plugin-annotations</artifactId>
      <version>3.2</version>
      <scope>provided</scope>
    </dependency>
  </dependencies>
```

```
<build>
  <plugins>
    <plugin>
      <groupId>org.apache.maven.plugins</groupId>
      <artifactId>maven-plugin-plugin</artifactId>
      <version>3.2</version>
      <configuration>
        <skipErrorNoDescriptorsFound>
          true
        </skipErrorNoDescriptorsFound>
      </configuration>
      <executions>
        <execution>
          <id>mojo-descriptor</id>
          <goals>
            <goal>descriptor</goal>
          </goals>
        </execution>
      </executions>
    </plugin>
  </plugins>
</build>
</project>
```

3. Make sure that your project structure looks similar to the following structure, and then build the project with `mvn clean install`:

```
|-src/main/
|         |-java/org/java/com/packt/plugins
|              |-EmailMojo.java
|-pom.xml
```

4. The previous step will produce the `mail-maven-plugin-1.0.0.jar` file inside the `target` directory of your Maven project. Extract the JAR file with following command:

```
$ jar -xvf  mail-maven-plugin-1.0.0.jar
```

5. The extracted JAR file will have the following directory structure, with the generated metadata files. Only the key/important files are shown here:

```
|-com/packt/plugins/EmailMojo.class
|-META-INF
     |-maven/plugin.xml
```

6. Let's have a look at the `plugin.xml` file first, which is as follows. A `mojo` element will be generated for each MOJO in the plugin project, having the annotation `Mojo`. All the child elements defined under the `mojo` element are derived from the annotations. If there is no annotation, the default value is set. We will discuss the key attributes in the `plugin.xml` file later in this chapter.

```xml
<plugin>
  <name>PACKT Maven Plugin Project</name>
  <description></description>
  <groupId>com.packt.plugins</groupId>
  <artifactId>mail-maven-plugin</artifactId>
  <version>1.0.0</version>
  <goalPrefix>mail</goalPrefix>
  <isolatedRealm>false</isolatedRealm>
  <inheritedByDefault>true</inheritedByDefault>
  <mojos>
    <mojo>
      <goal>mail</goal>
      <requiresDirectInvocation>false
      </requiresDirectInvocation>
      <requiresProject>true</requiresProject>
      <requiresReports>false</requiresReports>
      <aggregator>false</aggregator>
      <requiresOnline>false</requiresOnline>
      <inheritedByDefault>true</inheritedByDefault>
      <implementation>com.packt.plugins.EmailMojo
      </implementation>
      <language>java</language>
      <instantiationStrategy>per-lookup
      </instantiationStrategy>
      <executionStrategy>once-per-session
      </executionStrategy>
      <threadSafe>false</threadSafe>
      <parameters/>
    </mojo>
  </mojos>
  <dependencies>
    <dependency>
      <groupId>org.apache.maven</groupId>
      <artifactId>maven-plugin-api</artifactId>
      <type>jar</type>
      <version>2.0</version>
    </dependency>
  </dependencies>
</plugin>
```

7. The following Mojo annotation of the `EmailMojo` class will generate exactly the same configuration as shown in the previous step:

```
@Mojo(name = "mail", requiresDirectInvocation = false,
   requiresProject = true, requiresReports = false,
   aggregator = true, requiresOnline = true,
   inheritByDefault = true, instantiationStrategy =
   InstantiationStrategy.PER_LOOKUP, executionStrategy =
   "once-per-session", threadSafe = false)
```

Before moving any further, let's have a look at the definition of each configuration element used in the previous `Mojo` annotation:

Elements	Explanation
name	Every MOJO has a goal. The `name` attribute represents the goal name.
requiresDirectInvocation	A given plugin can be invoked in two ways. The first is by direct invocation where you invoke the plugin as `mvn plugin-name:goal-name`. The second way of invoking a plugin is as part of a Maven lifecycle, where you execute a lifecycle phase, and being part of a lifecycle phase, plugin goals also get executed. If you set `requiresDirectInvocation` to `true`, then you cannot associate the plugin with a lifecycle.
requiresProject	If `requiresProject` is set to `true`, this means you cannot execute the Maven plugin without a Maven project. It must be executed against a Maven POM file.
requiresReports	If your plugin depends on a set of reports, the goal of your plugin is to aggregate, or summarize a set of reports, then you must set the value of `requiresReports` to `true`.
aggregator	If you set the value of `aggregator` to `true`, the corresponding goal of your plugin will get executed only once during the complete build lifecycle. In other words, it won't run for each project build. In our case, we want to send an email when the complete Maven build is executed and not for each project; in this case, we must set the value of the `aggregator` to true.

Elements	Explanation
requiresOnline	If you set the value of requiresOnline to true, the corresponding goal of your plugin will only get executed when you are performing an online build. In our case, we have to set requiresOnline to true, because you need to be online to send an email.
instantiationStrategy	This is related to Plexus. If the value of instantiationStrategy is set to per-lookup, then a new instance of the corresponding MOJO will be created each time Maven looks up from Plexus. Other possible values are keep-alive, singleton, and poolable.
executionStrategy	This attribute will be deprecated in the future. It informs Maven when and how to execute a MOJO. The possible values are once-per-session and always.
threadSafe	Once the value of threadSafe is set to true, MOJO will execute in a thread-safe manner during parallel builds.
inheritByDefault	If the value of inheritByDefault is set to true, then any plugin goal associated with a Maven project will be inherited by all its child projects.

Another important element in the generated plugin.xml file is goalPrefix. If nothing is explicitly mentioned in maven-plugin-plugin, the value of goalPrefix is derived by the naming convention of the plugin artifactId. In our case, the artifactId of the plugin is mail-maven-plugin and the value before the first hyphen is taken as the goalPrefix. Maven uses goalPrefix to invoke a plugin goal in the following manner:

```
$ mvn goalPrefix:goal
```

In our case, our custom plugin can be executed as follows, where the first mail word is the goalPrefix, while the second one is the goal name:

```
$ mvn mail:mail
```

If you want to override the value of the `goalPrefix` without following the naming convention, then you need to explicitly give a value to the `goalPrefix` configuration element of `maven-plugin-plugin` in the POM file of the custom Maven plugin project, as follows:

```
<configuration>
  <goalPrefix>email</goalPrefix>
</configuration>
```

8. All set. Now we need to execute our custom plugin. To execute the Maven plugin without a Maven project (to consume it), you need to set the value of the `requiresProject` annotation attribute to `false`.

   In our case, we have not set this attribute in our MOJO, so the default value is set, which is `true`. To execute the Maven plugin without a project (you do not need to have a POM file), you need to set the value of `requiresProject` to `false` and rebuild the plugin project, as follows:

```
@Mojo( name = "mail", requiresProject=false)
public class EmailMojo extends AbstractMojo
{
}
```

9. Now try to execute the plugin goal in the following manner:

   ```
   $ mvn mail:mail
   ```

   This will result in an error. Any guesses why? This is related to how Maven looks up for plugins. When you execute a plugin by its `goalPrefix`, we do not specify its `groupId`, so the Maven engine will look for it in the local Maven repository (and then in the remote repository) assuming its `groupId` to be one of the default `groupIds`. As this is a custom plugin with our own `groupId`, the Maven engine won't find it. The error is as follows:

   ```
   [ERROR] No plugin found for prefix 'mail' in the current
     project and in the plugin groups [org.apache.maven.plugins,
     org.codehaus.mojo] available from the repositories [local
     (/Users/prabath/.m2/repository), Central
     (http://repo1.maven.org/maven2)] -> [Help 1]
   ```

10. To help Maven to locate the `groupId` plugin, add the following configuration element to `USER_HOME/.m2/settings.xml` under `<pluginGroups>`:

    ```
    <pluginGroup>com.packt.plugins</pluginGroup>
    ```

11. Now try to execute the plugin goal once again:

    ```
    $ mvn mail:mail
    ```

This will now produce the following output:

```
[INFO] --- mail-maven-plugin:1.0.0:mail (default-cli) @ mail-
  maven-plugin ---
[INFO] Sending Email...
```

Associating a plugin with a lifecycle

A plugin can be executed on its own or as a part of a Maven lifecycle. In the previous section, we went through the former, and now let's see how to associate our custom plugin with the Maven default lifecycle. The Maven default lifecycle has 23 phases, and let's see how to engage our custom plugin to the post-integration-test phase. We only want to send the email if everything up to the post-integration-test phase is successful.

> The Maven default lifecycle includes the phases: validate -> initialize -> generate-sources -> process-sources -> generate-resources -> process-resources -> compile -> process-classes -> generate-test-sources -> process-test-sources -> generate-test-resources -> process-test-resources -> test-compile -> process-test-classes -> test -> prepare-package -> package -> pre-integration-test -> integration-test -> post-integration-test -> verify -> install -> deploy.

Proceed with the following steps:

1. First, you need to create a Maven project to consume the custom plugin that we just developed. Create a project with the following sample POM file, which associates the mail-maven-plugin with the project:

```
<project>
  <modelVersion>4.0.0</modelVersion>
  <groupId>com.packt.plugins</groupId>
  <artifactId>plugin-consumer</artifactId>
  <version>1.0.0</version>
  <packaging>jar</packaging>
  <name>PACKT Maven Plugin Consumer Project</name>

  <build>
    <plugins>
      <plugin>
        <groupId>com.packt.plugins</groupId>
```

```
      <artifactId>mail-maven-plugin</artifactId>
      <version>1.0.0</version>
      <executions>
        <execution>
          <id>post-integration-mail</id>
          <phase>post-integration-test</phase>
          <goals>
            <goal>mail</goal>
          </goals>
        </execution>
      </executions>
    </plugin>
  </plugins>
</build>
</project>
```

Inside the `execution` element of the plugin configuration, we associate the corresponding plugin goal with a lifecycle phase.

2. Just type `mvn clean install` against the previous POM file. It will execute all the phases in the Maven `default` lifecycle up to and including the `install` phase, which also includes the `post-integration-test` phase. The `mail` goal of the plugin will get executed during the `post-integration-test` phase and will result in the following output:

```
[INFO] --- maven-jar-plugin:2.4:jar (default-jar-1) @ plugin-
  consumer ---
[INFO]
[INFO] --- mail-maven-plugin:1.0.0:mail (post-integration-
  mail) @ plugin-consumer ---
[INFO] Sending Email.
```

This is only one way of associating a plugin with a lifecycle phase. Here, the responsibility is with the consumer application to define the phase. The other way is that the plugin itself declares the phase it wants to execute in. To do this, you need to add the `Execute` annotation to your MOJO class, shown as follows:

```
@Mojo( name = "mail", requiresProject=false)
@Execute (phase=LifecyclePhase.POST_INTEGRATION_TEST)
public class EmailMojo extends AbstractMojo
{
}
```

Now, in the POM file of your plugin consumer project, you do not need to define a phase for the plugin. The configuration is as follows:

```
<project>
  <modelVersion>4.0.0</modelVersion>
  <groupId>com.packt.plugins</groupId>
  <artifactId>plugin-consumer</artifactId>
  <version>1.0.0</version>
  <packaging>jar</packaging>
  <name>PACKT Maven Plugin Consumer Project</name>

  <build>
    <plugins>
      <plugin>
        <groupId>com.packt.plugins</groupId>
        <artifactId>mail-maven-plugin</artifactId>
        <version>1.0.0</version>
      </plugin>
    </plugins>
  </build>
</project>
```

The plugin execution order

When a plugin gets executed through a lifecycle phase, the order of execution is governed by the lifecycle itself. If there are multiple plugin goals associated with the same phase, then the order of execution is governed by the order you define the plugins in your application POM file.

Inside the execute method

The business logic of a Maven plugin is implemented inside the execute method. The execute method is the only abstract method defined in the org.apache.maven. plugin.AbstractMojo class. The following Java code shows how to get the details about the current Maven project going through the build. Notice that the instance variable of the MavenProject type is annotated with the Component annotation:

```
package com.packt.plugins;

import org.apache.maven.plugin.AbstractMojo;
import org.apache.maven.plugin.MojoExecutionException;
import org.apache.maven.plugins.annotations.Component;
import org.apache.maven.plugins.annotations.Mojo;
```

```
import org.apache.maven.project.MavenProject;

@Mojo(name = "mail")
public class EmailMojo extends AbstractMojo {

  @Component
  private MavenProject project;

  public void execute() throws MojoExecutionException {
    getLog().info("Artifact Id " + project.getArtifactId());
    getLog().info("Version " + project.getVersion());
    getLog().info("Packaging " + project.getPackaging());
  }
}
```

The previous code is required to have the following three dependencies:

```
<dependency>
  <groupId>org.apache.maven</groupId>
  <artifactId>maven-plugin-api</artifactId>
  <version>2.0</version>
</dependency>
<dependency>
  <groupId>org.apache.maven.plugin-tools</groupId>
  <artifactId>maven-plugin-annotations</artifactId>
  <version>3.2</version>
  <scope>provided</scope>
</dependency>
<dependency>
  <groupId>org.apache.maven</groupId>
  <artifactId>maven-core</artifactId>
  <version>3.2.1</version>
</dependency>
```

In the example use case, we took to develop the custom plugin; we need to figure out the list of recipients who we want to send the emails. Also, we might need to get connection parameters related to the mail server. The following code example shows you how to read plugin configuration details from a MOJO:

```
@Mojo(name = "mail")
public class EmailMojo extends AbstractMojo {

  @Component
  private MavenProject project;
```

```
public void execute() throws MojoExecutionException {

    // get all the build plugins associated with the
    // project under the build.
    List<Plugin> plugins = project.getBuildPlugins();

    if (plugins != null && plugins.size() > 0) {
      for (Iterator<Plugin> iterator = plugins.iterator();
      iterator.hasNext();) {
        Plugin plugin = iterator.next();
        // iterate till we find mail-maven-plugin.
        if ("mail-maven-plugin".equals(plugin.getArtifactId()))
        {
          getLog().info(plugin.getConfiguration().toString());
          break;
        }
      }
    }
  }
}
```

For the email plugin we developed, the required configuration can be defined inside the plugin definition, shown as follows. This should go into the POM file of the plugin consumer application. Under the configuration element of the corresponding plugin, you can define your own XML element to carry out the configuration required by your custom plugin:

```xml
<build>
  <plugins>
    <plugin>
      <groupId>com.packt.plugins</groupId>
      <artifactId>mail-maven-plugin</artifactId>
      <version>1.0.0</version>
      <configuration>
        <emailList>
          prabath@wso2.com,
          prabath@apache.org</emailList>
        <mailServer>mail.google.com</mailServer>
        <password>password</password>
      </configuration>
      <executions>
        <execution>
          <id>post-integration-mail</id>
          <phase>post-integration-test</phase>
          <goals>
```

```
            <goal>mail</goal>
          </goals
        </execution>
      </executions>
    </plugin>
  </plugins>
</build>
```

When you run the plugin with the previous configuration, it will result in the following output. The MOJO implementation can parse the XML element and get the required values:

```
[INFO] <?xml version="1.0" encoding="UTF-8"?>
<configuration>
  <emailList>prabath@wso2.com,prabath@apache.org</emailList>
  <mailServer>mail.google.com</mailServer>
  <password>password</password>
</configuration>
```

The complete source code related to the `mail` Maven plugin is available at `https://svn.wso2.org/repos/wso2/people/prabath/maven/chapter05/mail-plugin`, and the plugin consumer code is available at `https://svn.wso2.org/repos/wso2/people/prabath/maven/chapter05/plugin-consumer`.

Summary

In this chapter, we focused on Maven plugins. Maven only provides a build framework while the Maven plugins perform the actual tasks. Maven has a large rich set of plugins, and the chances are very low that you have to write your own custom plugin. The chapter covered some of the most used Maven plugins and later explained how to develop your own custom Maven plugin.

In the next chapter, we will focus on Maven assemblies. There we will discuss the Maven assembly plugin, assembly descriptor, and filters.

6
Maven Assemblies

Maven provides an extensible architecture via plugins and lifecycles. Archive types such as `.jar`, `.war`, `.ear`, and many more are supported by plugins and associated lifecycles. The JAR plugin creates an artifact with the `.jar` extension and the relevant metadata, according to the JAR specification. The JAR file is, in fact, a ZIP file with the optional `META-INF` directory. You can find more details about the JAR specification from `http://docs.oracle.com/javase/7/docs/technotes/guides/jar/jar.html`.

The JAR file aggregates a set of class files to build a single distribution unit. The WAR file aggregates a set of JAR files, Java classes, JSPs, images, and many more resources into a single distribution unit that can be deployed in a Java EE application server. However, when you build a product, you might need to aggregate many JAR files from different places, WAR files, README files, LICENSE files, and many more into a single ZIP file. To build such an archive, we can use the Maven `assembly` plugin.

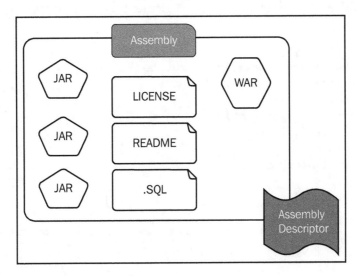

In this chapter, we will discuss the following topics:

- The Maven `assembly` plugin
- The `assembly` descriptor
- Artifact/resource filters
- An end-to-end example to build a custom distribution archive

The Maven `assembly` plugin produces a custom archive, which adheres to a user-defined layout. This custom archive is also known as the Maven assembly. In other words, it's a distribution unit, which is built according to a custom layout.

The assembly plugin

Let's have a quick look at a real-world example, which uses the `assembly` plugin.

WSO2 Identity Server (WSO2 IS) is an open source identity and entitlement management product distributed under the Apache 2.0 license as a ZIP file. The ZIP distribution is assembled using the Maven `assembly` plugin. Let's have a look at the root POM file of the `distribution` module of WSO2 IS, which builds the Identity Server distribution, available at `https://svn.wso2.org/repos/wso2/carbon/platform/branches/turing/products/is/5.0.0/modules/distribution/pom.xml`.

First, pay attention to the `plugins` section of the POM file. Here, you can see that `maven-assembly-plugin` is associated with the project. Inside the plugin configuration, you can define any number of executions with the `execution` element, which is a child element of the `executions` element. The configuration is as follows:

```
<plugin>
  <groupId>org.apache.maven.plugins</groupId>
  <artifactId>maven-assembly-plugin</artifactId>
  <executions>
    <execution>
      <id>copy_components</id>
      <phase>test</phase>
      <goals>
        <goal>attached</goal>
      </goals>
      <configuration>
        <filters>
          <filter>${basedir}/src/assembly/filter.properties
          </filter>
        </filters>
```

```
        <descriptors>
          <descriptor>src/assembly/dist.xml</descriptor>
        </descriptors>
      </configuration>
    </execution>
    <execution>
      <id>dist</id>
      <phase>package</phase>
      <goals>
        <goal>attached</goal>
      </goals>
      <configuration>
        <filters>
          <filter>${basedir}/src/assembly/filter.properties
          </filter>
        </filters>
        <descriptors>
          <descriptor>src/assembly/bin.xml</descriptor>
          <descriptor>src/assembly/src.xml</descriptor>
          <descriptor>src/assembly/docs.xml</descriptor>
        </descriptors>
      </configuration>
    </execution>
  </executions>
</plugin>
```

If you look at the first execution element, it associates the attached goal of the assembly plugin with the test phase of the default lifecycle. In the same manner, the second execution element associates the attached goal with the package phase of the default lifecycle.

> The Maven default lifecycle includes: validate -> initialize -> generate-sources -> process-sources -> generate-resources -> process-resources -> compile -> process-classes -> generate-test-sources -> process-test-sources -> generate-test-resources -> process-test-resources -> test-compile -> process-test-classes -> test -> prepare-package -> package -> pre-integration-test -> integration-test -> post-integration-test -> verify -> install -> deploy.

Everything inside the `configuration` element is plugin specific. In this case, the Maven `assembly` plugin knows how to process the `filters` and `descriptors` elements.

In this particular example, only the `attached` goal of the `assembly` plugin is used. The `assembly` plugin introduces eight goals; however, six of them are deprecated, including the `attached` goal. It is not recommended that you use any of the deprecated goals. Later, we'll see how to use the `single` goal of the `assembly` plugin instead of the deprecated `attached` goal. The following lists out the six deprecated goals of the `assembly` plugin. If you are using any of them, you should migrate your project to use the `single` goal, except for the last one, the `directory-unpack` goal. For this, you need to use the `unpack` goal of the Maven `dependency` plugin.

- `assembly:assembly`
- `assembly:attached`
- `assembly:directory`
- `assembly:unpack`
- `assembly:directory-single`
- `assembly:directory-inline`

 More details about the Maven `assembly` plugin and its goals can be found at `http://maven.apache.org/plugins/maven-assembly-plugin/plugin-info.html`.

The assembly descriptor

The `assembly` descriptor is an XML-based configuration, which defines how to build an assembly and how its content should be structured.

If we go back to our example, the `attached` goal of the `assembly` plugin creates a binary distribution according to the `assembly` descriptor, both in the `test` and `package` phases of the `default` Maven lifecycle. The `assembly` descriptors for each phase can be specified under the `descriptors` element. As in this particular example, there can be multiple `descriptor` elements defined under the `descriptors` parent element. For the `package` phase, it has the following three assembly descriptors:

```
<descriptors>
  <descriptor>src/assembly/bin.xml</descriptor>
  <descriptor>src/assembly/src.xml</descriptor>
  <descriptor>src/assembly/docs.xml</descriptor>
</descriptors>
```

Each `descriptor` element instructs the `assembly` plugin where to load the descriptor, and each `descriptor` file will be executed sequentially in the defined order.

Let's have a look at the `src/assembly/bin.xml` file, shown as follows. The file path is given relative to the root POM file under the `distribution` module. You can find the complete `bin.xml` file at `https://svn.wso2.org/repos/wso2/carbon/platform/branches/turing/products/is/5.0.0/modules/distribution/src/assembly/bin.xml`:

```
<assembly>
  <formats>
    <format>zip</format>
  </formats>
```

The value of the `format` element specifies the ultimate type of the artifact to be produced. It can be `zip`, `tar`, `tar.gz`, `tar.bz2`, `jar`, `dir`, or `war`. You can use the same assembly descriptor to create multiple formats. In this case, you can include multiple `format` elements under the `formats` parent element.

> Even though you can specify the format of the assembly in the `assembly` descriptor, it is recommended that you do this via the plugin configuration itself. In the plugin configuration, you can define different formats for your assembly shown as follows. The benefit here is that you can have multiple Maven profiles to build different archive types. We will be talking about Maven profiles in *Chapter 9, Best Practices*:
>
> ```
> <configuration>
>   <formats>
>     <format>zip</format>
>   </formats>
> </configuration>
> ```

```
<includeBaseDirectory>false</includeBaseDirectory>
```

When the value of the `includeBaseDirectory` element is set to `false`, the artifact will be created with no base directory. If this is set to `true`, which is the default value, the artifact will be created under a base directory. You can specify a value for the base directory under the `baseDirectory` element. In most of the cases, the value of `includeBaseDirectory` is set to `false` so that the final distribution unit directly packs all the artifacts right under it, without having another root directory.

```
<fileSets>
  <fileSet>
    <directory>target/wso2carbon-core-4.2.0</directory>
    <outputDirectory>wso2is-${pom.version}</outputDirectory>
    <excludes>
      <exclude>**/*.sh</exclude>
```

Each `fileSet` element under the `fileSets` parent element specifies the set of files to be assembled to build the final archive. The first `fileSet` element instructs to copy all the content from the `directory` (which is `target/wso2carbon-core-4.2.0`) to the output directory specified under the `outputDirectory` configuration element, excluding all the files defined under each `exclude` element. If no exclusions are defined, then all the content inside `directory` will be copied to the `outputDirectory`. In this particular case, the value of `${pom.version}` will be replaced the by `version` of the artifact, which is defined in the `pom.xml` file under the `distribution` module.

The `exclude` element instructs not to copy any file that has the `.sh` extension from anywhere inside `target/wso2carbon-core-4.2.0` to the `outputDirectory`.

```
<exclude>**/wso2server.bat</exclude>
<exclude>**/axis2services/sample01.aar</exclude>
```

The `exclude` element instructs not to copy the `sample01.aar` file inside a directory called `axis2services` from anywhere inside `target/wso2carbon-core-4.2.0` to `outputDirectory`.

```
<exclude>**/axis2services/Echo.aar</exclude>
<exclude>**/axis2services/Version.aar</exclude>
<exclude>**/pom.xml</exclude>
<exclude>**/version.txt</exclude>
<exclude>**/README*</exclude>
<exclude>**/carbon.xml</exclude>
<exclude>**/axis2/*</exclude>
<exclude>**/LICENSE.txt</exclude>
<exclude>**/INSTALL.txt</exclude>
<exclude>**/release-notes.html</exclude>
<exclude>**/claim-config.xml</exclude>
<exclude>**/log4j.properties</exclude>
<exclude>**/registry.xml</exclude>
      </excludes>
  </fileSet>
  <fileSet>
    <directory>../p2-profile-gen/target/wso2carbon-core-
    4.2.0/repository/conf/identity
    </directory>
    <outputDirectory>wso2is-${pom.version}/repository/
    conf/identity
    </outputDirectory>
    <includes>
      <include>**/*.xml</include>
    </includes>
```

The `include` element instructs to copy only the files that have the `.xml` extension from anywhere inside the `../p2-profile-gen/target/wso2carbon-core-4.2.0/repository/conf/identity` directory to the `outputDirectory`. If no include element is defined, everything will be included.

```
</fileSet>
<fileSet>
  <directory>../p2-profile-gen/target/wso2carbon-core-
  4.2.0/repository/resources/security/ldif
  </directory>
  <outputDirectory>wso2is-${pom.version}/repository/
  resources/security/ldif
  </outputDirectory>
  <includes>
    <include>identityPerson.ldif</include>
    <include>scimPerson.ldif</include>
    <include>wso2Person.ldif</include>
  </includes>
```

The `include` element instructs to copy only the files having specific names from anywhere inside the `../p2-profile-gen/target/wso2carbon-core/4.2.0/repository/resources/security/ldif` directory to the `outputDirectory`.

```
</fileSet>
<fileSet>
  <directory>../p2-profile-gen/target/wso2carbon-core-
  4.2.0/repository/deployment/server/webapps
  </directory>
  <outputDirectory>${pom.artifactId}-${pom.version}
  /repository/deployment/server/webapps
  </outputDirectory>
  <includes>
    <include>oauth2.war</include>
  </includes>
```

The `include` element instructs to copy only the WAR file with the name `oauth2.war` from anywhere inside the `../p2-profile-gen/target/wso2carbon-core/4.2.0/repository/resources/deployment/server/webappas` directory to the `outputDirectory`.

```
</fileSet>
<fileSet>
  <directory>../p2-profile-gen/target/wso2carbon-core-
  4.2.0/repository/deployment/server/webapps
  </directory>
```

```
<outputDirectory>${pom.artifactId}-${pom.version}
/repository/deployment/server/webapps
</outputDirectory>
<includes>
  <include>authenticationendpoint.war</include>
</includes>
</fileSet>
<fileSet>
<directory>../styles/service/src/main/resources
/web/styles/css
</directory>
<outputDirectory>${pom.artifactId}-${pom.version}
/resources/allthemes/Default/admin
</outputDirectory>
<includes>
  <include>**/**.css</include>
</includes>
```

The include element instructs to copy any file with the .css extension from anywhere inside the ../styles/service/src/main/resources/web/styles/css directory to the outputDirectory.

```
</fileSet>
<fileSet>
<directory>../p2-profile-gen/target/WSO2-CARBON-PATCH-
4.2.0-0006
</directory>
<outputDirectory>wso2is-
${pom.version}/repository/components/patches/
</outputDirectory>
<includes>
  <include>**/patch0006/*.*</include>
</includes>
```

The include element instructs to copy all the files inside the patch006 directory from anywhere inside the ../p2-profile-gen/target/WSO2-CARBON-PATCH-4.2.0-0006 directory to the outputDirectory.

```
</fileSet>
</fileSets>
<files>
```

The `file` element is very similar to the `fileSet` element in terms of the key functionality. Both can be used to control the content of the assembly.

 The `file` element should be used when you are fully aware of the exact source file location, while the `fileSet` element is much more flexible to pick files from a source based on a defined pattern.

The `fileMode` element in the following snippet defines a set of permissions to be attached to the copied file. The permissions are defined as per the four-digit octal notation. You can read more about the four-digit octal notation from `http://en.wikipedia.org/wiki/File_system_permissions#Octal_notation_ and_additional_permissions`:

```
<file>
    <source>../p2-profile-gen/target/WSO2-CARBON-PATCH-
    ${carbon.kernel.version}-
    0006/lib/org.wso2.ciphertool-1.0.0-wso2v2.jar
    </source>
    <outputDirectory>${pom.artifactId}-${pom.version}/lib/
    </outputDirectory>
    <filtered>true</filtered>
    <fileMode>644</fileMode>
    </file>
<files>
</assembly>
```

There are three `descriptor` elements defined under the `assembly` plugin for the `package` phase. The one we just discussed earlier will create the binary distribution, while the `src/assembly/src.xml` and `src/assembly/docs.xml` files will create the source distribution and the documentation distribution, respectively.

Let's also look at the `assembly` descriptor defined for the `test` phase:

```
<descriptors>
  <descriptor>src/assembly/dist.xml</descriptor>
</descriptors>
```

This is quite short and only includes the configuration required to build the initial distribution of WSO2 Identity Server. Even though this project does this at the `test` phase, it seems like it has no value in doing this. In this case, it seems like `maven-antrun-plugin`, which is also associated with the `package` phase but prior to the definition of the `assembly` plugin, needs the ZIP file distribution. Ideally, you should not have the `assembly` plugin run at the `test` phase unless there is a very strong reason. You might need the distribution ready to run the integration tests; however, the integration tests should be executed in the `integration-test` phase, which comes after the `package` phase. In most of the cases, the `assembly` plugin is associated with the `package` phase of the Maven `default` lifecycle.

```xml
<assembly>
  <formats>
    <format>zip</format>
  </formats>
  <includeBaseDirectory>false</includeBaseDirectory>
  <fileSets>
    <!-- Copying p2 profile and osgi bundles-->
    <fileSet>
      <directory>../p2-profile-gen/target/wso2carbon-core-
      4.2.0/repository/components
      </directory>
      <outputDirectory>wso2is-${pom.version}/repository/components
      </outputDirectory>
      <excludes>
        <exclude>**/eclipse.ini</exclude>
        <exclude>**/*.lock</exclude>
        <exclude>**/.data</exclude>
        <exclude>**/.settings</exclude>
      </excludes>
    </fileSet>
  </fileSets>
  <dependencySets>
    <dependencySet>
      <outputDirectory>wso2is-${pom.version}/repository/
      deployment/client/modules
      </outputDirectory>
      <includes>
        <include>org.apache.rampart:rampart:mar</include>
      </includes>
    </dependencySet>
  </dependencySets>
</assembly>
```

This configuration introduces a new element that we have not seen before: dependencySet. The dependencySet element lets you include/exclude project dependencies to/from the final assembly that we are building. In the previous example, it adds the rampart module into the outputDirectory. The value of the include element should be in the groupdId:artifactId:type[:classifier][:version] format. Maven will look for this artifact with the defined coordinates in its local Maven repository first, and if found, it will copy the artifact to the outputDirectory element.

Unlike the fileSet or file configuration, dependencySet does not define a concrete path to pick and copy the dependency from. Maven finds artifacts via the defined coordinates. If you want to include a dependency just by its groupId and the artifactId, then you can follow the groupdId:artifactId pattern. The particular artifact should be defined in the POM file, which has the assembly plugin defined under the dependencies section. You can find the following dependency definition for the rampart module in the POM file under the distribution module. If two versions of the same dependency are being defined in the same POM file (rather unlikely), then the last in the order will be copied.

```
<dependency>
   <groupId>org.apache.rampart</groupId>
   <artifactId>rampart</artifactId>
   <type>mar</type>
   <version>1.6.1-wso2v12</version>
</dependency>
```

You can also include a dependency by its groupId, artifactId, and type elements, as shown in the following configuration. Then, you can follow the groupdId:artifactId:type[:classifier] pattern. This is the exact pattern followed in the previous example:

```
<includes>
   <include>org.apache.rampart:rampart:mar</include>
</includes>
```

If you want to be more precise, you can also include the version in the pattern. Then, it will look like this:

```
<includes>
   <include>org.apache.rampart:rampart:mar:1.6.1-wso2v12
   </include>
</includes>
```

Most of the time, we talk about four Maven coordinates; however, to be precise there are five. A Maven artifact can be uniquely identified by these five coordinates: `groupdId:artifactId:type[:class ifier]:version`. We have already discussed about the four main coordinates, but not about the classifier. This is very rarely used; it can be quite useful in a scenario where we build an artifact out of the same POM file but with multiple target environments. We will discuss `classifiers` in detail in *Chapter 9, Best Practices*.

The previous example only covered a very little subset of the `assembly` descriptor. You can find all available configuration options at `http://maven.apache.org/plugins/maven-assembly-plugin/assembly.html`, which is a quite exhausting list.

It is a best practice or a convention to include all the assembly `descriptor` files inside a directory called `assembly`, though it is not mandatory.

Let's have a look at another real-world example with Apache Axis2. Axis2 is an open source project released under the Apache 2.0 license. Axis2 has three types of distributions: a binary distribution as a ZIP file, a WAR file distribution, and a source distribution as a ZIP file. The binary ZIP distribution of Axis2 can be run on its own, while the WAR distribution must be deployed in a Java EE application server.

All three Axis2 distributions are created from the POM file inside the `distribution` module, which can be found at `http://svn.apache.org/repos/asf/axis/axis2/java/core/trunk/modules/distribution/pom.xml`. This POM file associates the `single` goal of the Maven `assembly` plugin with the project, which initiates the process of creating the final distribution artifacts. The assembly configuration points to three different `assembly` descriptors: one for the ZIP distribution, another for the WAR distribution, and a third one for the source code distribution.

```
<plugin>
  <groupId>org.apache.maven.plugins</groupId>
  <artifactId>maven-assembly-plugin</artifactId>
  <executions>
    <execution>
      <id>distribution-package</id>
      <phase>package</phase>
      <goals>
        <goal>single</goal>
      </goals>
      <configuration>
        <finalName>axis2-${project.version}</finalName>
```

```
    <descriptors>
      <descriptor>src/main/assembly/war-assembly.xml
      </descriptor>
      <descriptor>src/main/assembly/src-assembly.xml
      </descriptor>
      <descriptor>src/main/assembly/bin-assembly.xml
      </descriptor>
    </descriptors>
  </configuration>
 </execution>
 </executions>
</plugin>
```

Let's have a look at the `bin-assembly.xml` file, which is the `assembly` descriptor that builds the ZIP distribution:

```
<assembly>
  <id>bin</id>
  <includeBaseDirectory>true</includeBaseDirectory>
  <baseDirectory>axis2-${version}</baseDirectory>
  <formats>
    <!--<format>tar.gz</format>
    //uncomment,if tar.gz archive needed-->
    <format>zip</format>
  </formats>
```

This is exactly what we discussed earlier and exactly what we wanted to avoid due to the same reason as in the comment. If we want to build a `tar.gz` distribution, then we need to modify the file. Instead of doing this, we should have moved the `format` configuration element out of the `assembly` descriptor to the plugin configuration defined in the `pom.xml` file. Then, you can define multiple profiles and configure the archive type based on the profile.

```
<fileSets>
</fileSets>
<dependencySets>
  <dependencySet>
    <useProjectArtifact>false</useProjectArtifact>
```

The `useProjectArtifact` configuration element instructs the plugin whether or not to include the artifact produced in this project build into the `dependencySet` element. By setting the value to `false`, we avoid it.

```
    <outputDirectory>lib</outputDirectory>
    <includes>
      <include>*:*:jar</include>
```

```
    </includes>
    <excludes>
      <exclude>org.apache.geronimo.specs:
      geronimo-activation_1.1_spec:jar
      </exclude>
    </excludes>
</dependencySet>
<dependencySet>
    <useProjectArtifact>false</useProjectArtifact>
    <outputDirectory>lib/endorsed</outputDirectory>
    <includes>
      <include>javax.xml.bind:jaxb-api:jar</include>
    </includes>
</dependencySet>
<dependencySet>
    <useProjectArtifact>false</useProjectArtifact>
    <includes>
      <include>org.apache.axis2:axis2-webapp</include>
    </includes>
</includes>
```

The includes and excludes configuration elements will make sure that all the JAR files defined under the dependencies section of the distribution/pom. xml file will be included in the assembly, except the JAR files defined under the excludes configuration element. If you do not have any include elements, all the dependencies defined in the POM file will be included in the assembly, except what is defined under the excludes section.

```
<unpack>true</unpack>
```

Once the unpack configuration element is set to true, all the dependencies defined under the include elements will be unpacked to the outputDirectory. The plugin is capable of unpacking the jar, zip, tar.gz, and tar.bz2 archives. The unpackOptions configuration element, can be used to filter out the content of the dependencies getting unpacked. According to the following configuration, only the files defined under the include elements under the unpackOptions element will be included; the rest will be ignored and won't be included in the assembly. In this particular case, axis2-webapp is a WAR file and the distributions/pom.xml file has a dependency to it. This web app will be exploded, and then all the files inside the WEB-INF/classes and axis2-web directories will be copied into the webapp directory of the ZIP distribution along with the WEB-INF/web.xml file:

```
<outputDirectory>webapp</outputDirectory>
<unpackOptions>
    <includes>
      <include>WEB-INF/classes/**/*</include>
      <include>WEB-INF/web.xml</include>
      <include>axis2-web/**/*</include>
```

```
      </includes>
      </unpackOptions>
    </dependencySet>
  </dependencySets>
</assembly>
```

Now, let's have a look at `war-assembly.xml`, which is the assembly descriptor that builds the WAR distribution. There is nothing new in this configuration, except the `outputFileNameMapping` configuration element. As the value of the `format` element is set to `zip`, this `assembly` descriptor will produce an archive file conforming to the ZIP file specification. The value of the `outputFileNameMapping` configuration element gets applied to all the dependencies. The default value is parameterized, that is, `${artifactId}-${version}${classifier?}.${extension}`. In this case, it's hardcoded to `axis2.war`, so the `axis2-webapp` artifact will be copied to `outputDirectory` as `axis2.war`. As there is no value defined for the `outputDirectory` element, the files will be copied to the root location.

```
<assembly>
  <id>war</id>
  <includeBaseDirectory>false</includeBaseDirectory>
  <formats>
    <format>zip</format>
  </formats>
  <dependencySets>
    <dependencySet>
      <useProjectArtifact>false</useProjectArtifact>
      <includes>
        <include>org.apache.axis2:axis2-webapp</include>
      </includes>
      <outputFileNameMapping>axis2.war</outputFileNameMapping>
    </dependencySet>
  </dependencySets>
  <fileSets>
    <fileSet>
      <directory>../..</directory>
      <outputDirectory></outputDirectory>
      <includes>
        <include>LICENSE.txt</include>
        <include>NOTICE.txt</include>
        <include>README.txt</include>
        <include>release-notes.html</include>
      </includes>
    <filtered>true</filtered>
    </fileSet>
    </fileSets>
</assembly>
```

Artifact/resource filtering

We had a `filters` configuration, defined for the `assembly` plugin in the first example with WSO2 Identity Server. This instructs the `assembly` plugin to apply the filter criteria defined in the provided filter or the set of filters for the files being copied to the final archive file. If you want to apply the filters to a given file, then you should set the value of the `filtered` element to `true`. The following configuration shows how to define a filter criteria with a property file:

```
<filters>
  <filter>${basedir}/src/assembly/filter.properties</filter>
</filters>
```

Let's have a look at the `${basedir}/src/assembly/filter.properties` file. This file defines a set of name/value pairs. The name is a special placeholder, which should be enclosed between `${` and `}` in the file to be filtered, and during the filtering process, it will be replaced by the value. Say for example, the value `${product.name}` in the original file will be replaced with `WSO2 Identity Server` after the filtering process:

```
product.name=WSO2 Identity Server
product.key=IS
product.version=5.0.0
hotdeployment=true
hotupdate=true
default.server.role=IdentityServer
```

Assembly help

As discussed before, the `assembly` plugin currently has only two active goals: `single` and `help`; all the others are deprecated. As we witnessed in the previous example, the `single` goal is responsible for creating the archive with all sort of other configurations.

The following command shows how to execute the `help` goal of the `assembly` plugin. This has to be executed from a directory that has a POM file:

```
$ mvn assembly:help -Ddetail=true
```

If you see the following error when you run this command, you might not have the latest version. Update the plugin version to 2.4.1 or higher:

```
[ERROR] Could not find goal 'help' in plugin
org.apache.maven.plugins:maven-assembly-plugin:2.2-beta-2 among
available goals assembly, attach-assembly-descriptor, attach-
component-descriptor, attached, directory-inline, directory,
directory-single, single, unpack -> [Help 1]
```

A runnable, standalone Maven project

As we covered a lot of ground-related information to the Maven `assembly` plugin, let's see how to build a complete end-to-end runnable, standalone project with the `assembly` plugin. You can find the complete sample at `https://svn.wso2.org/repos/wso2/people/prabath/maven/chapter06`. Proceed with the following steps:

1. First, create a directory structure in the following manner:

    ```
    |-pom.xml
    |-modules
        |- json-parser
            |- src/main/java/com/packt/json/JSONParser.java
            |- pom.xml
        |- distribution
            |- src/main/assembly/dist.xml
            |- pom.xml
    ```

2. `JSONParser.java` is a simple Java class, which reads a JSON file and prints to the console, shown as follows:

    ```java
    package com.packt.json;

    import java.io.File;
    import java.io.FileReader;
    import org.json.simple.JSONObject;

    public class JSONParser {

      public static void main(String[] args) {

      FileReader fileReader;
      JSONObject json;
      org.json.simple.parser.JSONParser parser;
      parser = new org.json.simple.parser.JSONParser();

      try {
        if (args == null || args.length == 0 || args[0] ==
        null || !new File(args[0]).exists()){
        System.out.println("No valid JSON file provided");
        }else{
          fileReader = new FileReader(new File(args[0]));
          json = (JSONObject) parser.parse(fileReader);
          if (json != null) {
            System.out.println(json.toJSONString());
          }
        }
      } catch (Exception e) {
        e.printStackTrace();}
      }
    }
    ```

3. Now, we can create a POM file under `modules/json-parser` to build our JAR file, as follows:

```
<project>
  <modelVersion>4.0.0</modelVersion>
  <groupId>com.packt</groupId>
  <artifactId>json-parser</artifactId>
  <version>1.0.0</version>
  <packaging>jar</packaging>
  <name>PACKT JSON Parser</name>
  <dependencies>
    <dependency>
      <groupId>com.googlecode.json-simple
      </groupId>
      <artifactId>json-simple</artifactId>
      <version>1.1</version>
    </dependency>
  </dependencies>
</project>
```

4. Once we are done with the `json-parser` module, the next step is to create the `distribution` module. The `distribution` module will have a POM file and an `assembly` descriptor. Let's first create the POM file under `modules/distribution`, shown as follows. This will associate two plugins with the project: `maven-assembly-plugin` and `maven-jar-plugin`. Both the plugins get executed in the `package` phase of the Maven `default` lifecycle. As `maven-assembly-plugin` is defined prior to `maven-jar-plugin`, it will get executed first:

```
<project>
  <modelVersion>4.0.0</modelVersion>
  <groupId>com.packt</groupId>
  <artifactId>json-parser-dist</artifactId>
  <version>1.0.0</version>
  <packaging>jar</packaging>
  <name>PACKT JSON Parser Distribution</name>
  <dependencies>
<!--
Under the dependencies section we have to specify all the
dependent jars that must be assembled into the final
artifact. In this case we have two jar files. The first one
is the external dependency that we used to parse the JSON
file and the second one includes the class we wrote.
-->
    <dependency>
      <groupId>com.googlecode.json-simple</groupId>
```

```xml
        <artifactId>json-simple</artifactId>
        <version>1.1</version>
    </dependency>
    <dependency>
        <groupId>com.packt</groupId>
        <artifactId>json-parser</artifactId>
        <version>1.0.0</version>
    </dependency>
  </dependencies>
  <build>
    <plugins>
      <plugin>
        <groupId>org.apache.maven.plugins</groupId>
        <artifactId>maven-assembly-plugin</artifactId>
        <executions>
          <execution>
            <id>distribution-package</id>
            <phase>package</phase>
            <goals>
              <goal>single</goal>
            </goals>
            <configuration>
              <finalName>json-parser</finalName>
              <descriptors>
                <descriptor>src/main/assembly/dist.xml
                </descriptor>
              </descriptors>
            </configuration>
          </execution>
        </executions>
      </plugin>
<!--
```

Even though the maven-jar-plugin is inherited from the super POM, here we have redefined it because we need to add some extra configurations. Since we need to make our final archive executable, we need to define the class to be executable in the jar manifest. Here we have set com.packt.json.JSONParser as our main class. Also - classpath is set to the lib directory. If you look at the assembly descriptor used in the assembly plugin, you will notice that, the dependent jar files are copied into the lib directory. The manifest configuration in the maven-jar-plugin will result in the following manifest file (META-INF/MANIFEST.MF).

```
Manifest-Version: 1.0
Archiver-Version: Plexus Archiver
Created-By: Apache Maven
Built-By: prabath
Build-Jdk: 1.6.0_65
Main-Class: com.packt.json.JSONParser
Class-Path: lib/json-simple-1.1.jar lib/json-parser-1.0.0.jar
-->
```

```xml
        <plugin>
          <groupId>org.apache.maven.plugins</groupId>
          <artifactId>maven-jar-plugin</artifactId>
          <version>2.3.1</version>
          <configuration>
            <archive>
              <manifest>
                <addClasspath>true</addClasspath>
                <classpathPrefix>lib/</classpathPrefix>
                <mainClass>com.packt.json.JSONParser
                </mainClass>
              </manifest>
            </archive>
          </configuration>
        </plugin>
      </plugins>
    </build>
</project>
```

5. The following configuration shows the `assembly` descriptor (`module/ distribution/ src/main/assembly/dist.xml`), corresponding to the `assembly` plugin defined in the previous step:

```xml
<assembly>
  <id>bin</id>
  <formats>
    <format>zip</format>
  </formats>
  <dependencySets>
    <dependencySet>
      <useProjectArtifact>false</useProjectArtifact>
      <outputDirectory>lib</outputDirectory>
      <unpack>false</unpack>
    </dependencySet>
  </dependencySets>
  <fileSets>
```

```
<fileSet>
  <directory>${project.build.directory}</directory>
  <outputDirectory></outputDirectory>
  <includes>
    <include>*.jar</include>
  </includes>
</fileSet>
</fileSets>
</assembly>
```

6. Now, we are done with the `distribution` module too. The next step is to create the root POM file, which aggregates both the `json-parser` and `distribution` modules, as follows:

```
<project>
  <modelVersion>4.0.0</modelVersion>
  <groupId>com.packt</groupId>
  <artifactId>json-parser-aggregator</artifactId>
  <version>1.0.0</version>
  <packaging>pom</packaging>
  <name>PACKT JSON Parser Aggregator</name>
  <modules>
    <module>modules/json-parser</module>
    <module>modules/distribution</module>
  </modules>
</project>
```

7. We are all set to build the project. From the root directory, type `mvn clean install`. This will produce the `json-parser-bin.zip` archive inside `modules/distribution/target`. The output is shown as follows:

```
[INFO] ------------------------------------------------------
[INFO] Reactor Summary:
[INFO]
[INFO] PACKT JSON Parser............... SUCCESS [  1.790 s]
[INFO] PACKT JSON Parser Distribution.. SUCCESS [  0.986 s]
[INFO] PACKT JSON Parser Aggregator.... SUCCESS [  0.014 s]
[INFO] ------------------------------------------------------
[INFO] BUILD SUCCESS
[INFO] ------------------------------------------------------
```

8. Go to `modules/distribution/target` and unzip `json-parser-bin.zip`.

9. To run the parser, type the following command, which will produce the `No valid JSON file provided` output:

```
$ java -jar json-parser/json-parser-dist-1.0.0.jar
```

10. Run the parser again with the following valid JSON file. You need to pass the path to the JSON file as an argument, as shown:

```
$ java -jar json-parser/json-parser-dist-1.0.0.jar
myjsonfile.json
```

The following is the content of the JSON file:

```
{
  "bookName"   : "Mastering Maven", "publisher" : "PACKT"
}
```

Summary

In this chapter, we focused on the Maven `assembly` plugin. The `assembly` plugin provides a way of building custom archive files and aggregating many other custom configurations and resources. Most of the Java-based products out there use the `assembly` plugin to build the final distribution artifacts. These can be binary distributions, source code distributions, or even documentation distributions. The chapter covered real-world examples on how to use the Maven `assembly` plugin in detail and finally concluded with an end-to-end sample Maven project.

In the next chapter, we will discuss Maven archetypes. Maven archetypes provide a way of reducing repetitive work when building Maven projects.

7
Maven Archetypes

The word archetype has roots in Greek literature. It's derived from two Greek words, *archein* and *typos*. The word archein means original or old, while typos means patterns. Therefore, the word archetype itself means original patterns. The famous psychologist, Carl Gustav Jung introduced the archetype concept in psychology. Jung, argued that there are twelve different archetypes that represent human motivation, and he further divided them into three categories: the ego, the soul, and the self. The innocent, regular guy, hero, and caregiver fall under the ego type. The explorer, rebel, lover, and creator fall under the soul type. The self type includes jester, sage, magician, and ruler. The concept behind Maven archetypes does not deviate a lot from what Jung explained in psychology. The following figure shows the relationship between a Maven project, a project archetype and projects generated from an archetype:

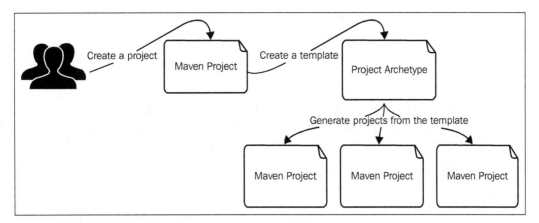

When we create a Java project, we need to structure it in different ways based on the type of the project. If it's a Java EE web application, then we need to have a WEB-INF directory and a web.xml file. If it's a Maven plugin project, we need to have a Mojo class that extends from org.apache.maven.plugin.AbstractMojo. As each type of project has its own predefined structure, why would everyone have to build the same structure again and again? Why not start with a template? Each project can have its own template, and the developers can extend the template to suite their requirements. Maven archetypes address this concern. Each archetype is a project template.

A list of Maven archetypes can be found at
http://maven-repository.com/archetypes.

In this chapter, we will discuss the following topics:

- The Maven archetype plugin
- The most used archetypes
- Developing a custom archetype from scratch

Archetype quickstart

Maven's archetype itself is a plugin. The generate goal of the archetype plugin is used to generate a Maven project from an archetype. Let's start with a simple example:

```
$ mvn archetype:generate -DgroupId=com.packt.samples
                         -DartifactId=com.packt.samples.archetype
                         -Dversion=1.0.0
                         -DinteractiveMode=false
```

This command will invoke the generate goal of the Maven archetype plugin to create a simple Java project. You will see that the following project structure is created with a sample POM file. The name of the root or the base directory is derived from the value of the artifactId parameter:

```
com.packt.samples.archetype
            |-pom.xml
            |-src
            |-main/java/com/packt/samples/App.java
            |-test/java/com/packt/samples/AppTest.java
```

The sample POM file will only have a dependency to the junit JAR file, with test as scope:

```
<project>
  <modelVersion>4.0.0</modelVersion>
  <groupId>com.packt.samples</groupId>
  <artifactId>com.packt.samples.archetype</artifactId>
  <packaging>jar</packaging>
  <version>1.0.0</version>
  <name>com.packt.samples.archetype</name>
  <url>http://maven.apache.org</url>
  <dependencies>
    <dependency>
      <groupId>junit</groupId>
      <artifactId>junit</artifactId>
      <version>3.8.1</version>
      <scope>test</scope>
    </dependency>
  </dependencies>
</project>
```

The generated App.java class will have the following template code. The name of the package is derived from the provided groupId parameter. If we want to have a different value as the package name, then we need to pass that value in the command itself as -Dpackage=com.packt.samples.application:

```
package com.packt.samples;

/**
 * Hello world!
 *
 */
public class App
{
  public static void main( String[] args )
    {
      System.out.println( "Hello World!" );
    }
}
```

This is the simplest way to get started with a Maven project. In the previous example, we used the non-interactive mode, by setting interactiveMode=false. This will force the plugin to use whatever the values we passed in the command itself, along with the default values.

To invoke the plugin in the interactive mode, just type `mvn archetype:generate`. This will prompt for user inputs as the plugin proceeds with its execution. The very first one is to ask for a filter or a number for the type of the archetype. The filter can be specified in the format of `[groupdId:]artifactId`, as follows:

```
Choose a number or apply filter (format: [groupId:]artifactId, case
    sensitive contains): 471:
```

When you type the filter criteria, for example, `org.apache.maven.archetypes:maven-archetype-quickstart`, the plugin will display the number associated with it, as follows:

```
Choose a number or apply filter (format: [groupId:]artifactId, case
    sensitive contains): 471: org.apache.maven.archetypes:maven-
    archetype-quickstart


Choose archetype:
1: remote -> org.apache.maven.archetypes:maven-archetype-quickstart
   (An archetype which contains a sample Maven project.)


Choose a number or apply filter (format: [groupId:]artifactId, case
    sensitive contains): 1:
```

In this case, there is only one archetype, which matches the filter, and the number associated with it is 1. If you just press *Enter* against the last line in the previous output, or just type 1, the plugin will start to proceed with the `org.apache.maven.archetypes:maven-archetype-quickstart` archetype.

Something you might have already noticed is that as soon as you type `mvn archetype:generate`, the plugin will display a long list of Maven archetypes supported by the plugin, and each archetype has a number associated with it. You can avoid this long list by specifying a filter criterion with the command itself, which is shown as follows:

```
$ mvn archetype:generate
    -Dfilter=org.apache.maven.archetypes:maven-archetype-quickstart


Choose archetype:
1: remote -> org.apache.maven.archetypes:maven-archetype-quickstart
   (An archetype that contains a sample Maven project.)


Choose a number or apply filter (format: [groupId:]artifactId, case
    sensitive contains): 1:
```

The batch mode

The `archetype` plugin can operate in the batch mode either by setting the `interactiveMode` argument to `false` or passing `-B` as an argument. When operating in the batch mode, you need to clearly specify which archetype you are going to use with the arguments: `archetypeGroupId`, `archetypeArtifactId`, and `archetypeVersion`. Also, you need to clearly identify the resultant artifact with the `groupId`, `artifactId`, `version`, and `package` arguments, as follows:

```
$ mvn archetype:generate -B
                -DarchetypeGroupId=org.apache.maven.archetypes
                -DarchetypeArtifactId=maven-archetype-quickstart
                -DarchetypeVersion=1.0
                -DgroupId=com.packt.samples
                -DartifactId=com.packt.samples.archetype
                -Dversion=1.0.0
                -Dpackage=com.packt.samples.archetype
```

Any inquisitive mind should be having a very valid question by now.

In the non-interactive mode, we did not type any filter or provide any Maven coordinates for the archetype in the very first example. So, how does the plugin know about the archetype? When no archetype is specified, the plugin goes with the default one, which is `org.apache.maven.archetypes:maven-archetype-quickstart`.

Archetype catalogues

How does the plugin find all the archetypes available in the system? When you just type `mvn archetype:generate`, a list of archetypes is displayed by the plugin for user selection. The complete list is around 1100, and only the first 10 are shown here:

```
1: remote -> br.com.ingenieux:elasticbeanstalk-service-webapp-
   archetype (A Maven Archetype Encompassing RestAssured, Jetty,
   Jackson, Guice and Jersey for Publishing JAX-RS-based Services on
   AWS' Elastic Beanstalk Service)
2: remote -> br.com.ingenieux:elasticbeanstalk-wrapper-webapp-
   archetype (A Maven Archetype Wrapping Existing war files on AWS'
   Elastic Beanstalk Service)
3: remote -> br.com.otavio.vraptor.archetypes:vraptor-archetype-blank
   (A simple project to start with VRaptor 4)
4: remote -> br.gov.frameworkdemoiselle.archetypes:demoiselle-html-
   rest (Archetype for web applications (HTML + REST) using Demoiselle
   Framework)
```

```
5: remote -> br.gov.frameworkdemoiselle.archetypes:demoiselle-jsf-jpa
   (Archetype for web applications (JSF + JPA) using Demoiselle
   Framework)
6: remote -> br.gov.frameworkdemoiselle.archetypes:demoiselle-minimal
   (Basic archetype for generic applications using Demoiselle
   Framework)
7: remote -> br.gov.frameworkdemoiselle.archetypes:demoiselle-vaadin-
   jpa (Archetype for Vaadin web applications)
8: remote -> ch.sbb.maven.archetypes:iib9-maven-projects (IBM
   Integration Bus 9 Maven Project Structure)
9: remote -> ch.sbb.maven.archetypes:wmb7-maven-projects (WebSphere
   Message Broker 7 Maven Project Structure)
10: remote -> co.ntier:spring-mvc-archetype (An extremely simple
    Spring MVC archetype, configured with NO XML.)
```

Going back to the original question, how does the plugin find these details about different archetypes?

The `archetype` plugin maintains the details about different archetypes in an internal catalogue, which comes with the plugin itself. The archetype catalogue is simply an XML file. The following configuration shows the internal catalogue of the `archetype` plugin:

```xml
<archetype-catalog>

<!-- Internal archetype catalog listing archetypes from the Apache
Maven project. -->

  <archetypes>
    <archetype>
      <groupId>org.apache.maven.archetypes</groupId>
      <artifactId>maven-archetype-archetype</artifactId>
      <version>1.0</version>
      <description>An archetype that contains a sample
        archetype.</description>
    </archetype>
    <archetype>
      <groupId>org.apache.maven.archetypes</groupId>
      <artifactId>maven-archetype-j2ee-simple</artifactId>
      <version>1.0</version>
      <description>An archetype that contains a simplified sample
        J2EE application.</description>
    </archetype>
    <archetype>
      <groupId>org.apache.maven.archetypes</groupId>
```

```
      <artifactId>maven-archetype-plugin</artifactId>
      <version>1.2</version>
      <description>An archetype that contains a sample Maven
         plugin.</description>
   </archetype>
   <archetype>
      <groupId>org.apache.maven.archetypes</groupId>
      <artifactId>maven-archetype-plugin-site</artifactId>
      <version>1.1</version>
      <description>An archetype that contains a sample Maven plugin
         site. This archetype can be layered upon an existing Maven
         plugin project.</description>
   </archetype>
   <archetype>
      <groupId>org.apache.maven.archetypes</groupId>
      <artifactId>maven-archetype-portlet</artifactId>
      <version>1.0.1</version>
      <description>An archetype that contains a sample JSR-268
         Portlet.</description>
   </archetype>
   <archetype>
      <groupId>org.apache.maven.archetypes</groupId>
      <artifactId>maven-archetype-profiles</artifactId>
      <version>1.0-alpha-4</version>
      <description></description>
   </archetype>
   <archetype>
      <groupId>org.apache.maven.archetypes</groupId>
      <artifactId>maven-archetype-quickstart</artifactId>
      <version>1.1</version>
      <description>An archetype that contains a sample Maven
         project.</description>
   </archetype>
   <archetype>
      <groupId>org.apache.maven.archetypes</groupId>
      <artifactId>maven-archetype-site</artifactId>
      <version>1.1</version>
      <description>An archetype that contains a sample Maven site,
         which demonstrates some of the supported document types like
         APT, XDoc, and FML and demonstrates how to i18n your site.
         This archetype can be layered upon an existing Maven
         project.</description>
   </archetype>
   <archetype>
      <groupId>org.apache.maven.archetypes</groupId>
```

```
      <artifactId>maven-archetype-site-simple</artifactId>
      <version>1.1</version>
      <description>An archetype that contains a sample Maven
         site.</description>
   </archetype>
   <archetype>
      <groupId>org.apache.maven.archetypes</groupId>
      <artifactId>maven-archetype-webapp</artifactId>
      <version>1.0</version>
      <description>An archetype that contains a sample Maven Webapp
         project.</description>
   </archetype>
 </archetypes>
</archetype-catalog>
```

In addition to the internal catalogue, you can also maintain a `local` archetype catalogue. This is available at `USER_HOME/.m2/archetype-catalog.xml`, and by default, it's an empty file.

There is also a remote catalogue, which is available at `http://repo1.maven.org/maven2/archetype-catalog.xml`. By default, the `archetype` plugin will load all the available archetypes from the `local` and `remote` catalogues. If we go back to the archetype list displayed by the plugin, when you type `mvn archetype:generate`, by looking at the each entry, we can determine whether a given archetype is loaded from the `internal`, `local`, or `remote` catalogue.

For example, the following archetype is loaded from the remote catalogue:

```
1: remote -> br.com.ingenieux:elasticbeanstalk-service-webapp-
   archetype (A Maven Archetype Encompassing RestAssured, Jetty,
   Jackson, Guice and Jersey for Publishing JAX-RS-based Services on
   AWS' Elastic Beanstalk Service)
```

If you want to enable the `archetype` plugin to list all the archetypes from the internal catalogue, you need to use the following command:

```
$ mvn archetype:generate -DarchetypeCatalog=internal
```

To list all the archetypes from the `local` catalogue, you need to use the following command:

```
$ mvn archetype:generate -DarchetypeCatalog=local
```

To list all the archetypes from the `internal`, `local`, and `remote` catalogues, you need to use the following command:

```
$ mvn archetype:generate -DarchetypeCatalog=internal,local,remote
```

Building an archetype catalogue

In addition to the `internal`, `local`, and `remote` catalogues, you can also build your own catalogue. Say you have developed your own set of Maven archetypes and need to build a catalogue out of them, so it can be shared with others by publicly hosting it. Once you have built the archetypes, they will be available in your `local` Maven repository. The following command will crawl through the `local` Maven repository and build an archetype catalogue from all the archetypes available there. Here, we use the `crawl` goal of the archetype plugin:

```
$ mvn archetype:crawl -DcatalogFile=my-catalog.xml
```

Public archetype catalogues

People who develop archetypes for their projects will list them in publicly hosted archetype catalogues. The following points list some of the publicly available Maven archetype catalogues:

- Fuse: The archetype catalogue can be found at `http://repo.fusesource.com/nexus/content/groups/public/archetype-catalog.xml`

- Java.net: The archetype catalogue can be found at `http://download.java.net/maven/2/archetype-catalog.xml`

- Cocoon: The archetype catalogue can be found at `http://cocoon.apache.org/archetype-catalog.xml`

- MyFaces: The archetype catalogue can be found at `http://myfaces.apache.org/archetype-catalog.xml`

- Apache Synapse: The archetype catalogue can be found at `http://synapse.apache.org/archetype-catalog.xml`

Let's take Apache Synapse as an example. Synapse is an open source Apache project that builds an **Enterprise Service Bus** (**ESB**). The following command will use the Apache Synapse archetype to generate a Maven project:

```
$ mvn archetype:generate
                -DgroupId=com.packt.samples
                -DartifactId=com.packt.samples.synapse
                -Dversion=1.0.0
                -Dpackage=com.packt.samples.synapse.application
                -DarchetypeCatalog=http://synapse.apache.org
                -DarchetypeGroupId=org.apache.synapse
                -DarchetypeArtifactId=synapse-package-archetype
                -DarchetypeVersion=2.0.0
                -DinteractiveMode=false
```

The previous command will produce the following directory structure. If you look at the `pom.xml` file, you will notice that it contains all necessary instructions along with the required dependencies to build the Synapse project:

```
com.packt.samples.synapse
                        |-pom.xml
                        |-src/main/assembly/bin.xml
                        |-conf/log4j.properties
                        |-repository/conf
                                        |-axis2.xml
                                        |-synapse.xml
```

Let's have look at the previous Maven command we used to build the project with the Synapse archetype. The most important argument is `archetypeCatalog`. The value of the `archetypeCatalog` argument can point directly to an `archetype-catalog.xml` file or to a directory, which contains an `archetype-catalog.xml` file. The following configuration shows the `archetype-catalog.xml` file corresponding to the Synapse archetype. It has only a single archetype but with two different versions:

```xml
<archetype-catalog>
  <archetypes>
    <archetype>
      <groupId>org.apache.synapse</groupId>
      <artifactId>synapse-package-archetype</artifactId>
      <version>1.3</version>
      <repository>http://repo1.maven.org/maven2</repository>
      <description>Create a Synapse 1.3 custom package</description>
    </archetype>
    <archetype>
      <groupId>org.apache.synapse</groupId>
      <artifactId>synapse-package-archetype</artifactId>
      <version>2.0.0</version>
      <repository>
        http://people.apache.org/repo/m2-snapshot-repository
      </repository>
      <description>Create a Synapse 2.0.0 custom
        package</description>
    </archetype>
  </archetypes>
</archetype-catalog>
```

The value of the `archetypeCatalog` parameter can be a comma-separated list, where each item points to an `archetype-catalog.xml` file or to a directory, which contains `archetype-catalog.xml`. The default value is `remote,local`, where the archetypes are loaded from the `local` repository and the remote repository. If you want to load an `archetype-catalog.xml` file from the local filesystem, then you need to prefix the absolute path to the file with `file://`. The value `local` is just a shortcut for `file://~/.m2/archetype-catalog.xml`.

In the previous Maven command, we used the `archetype` plugin in the non-interactive mode, so we have to be very specific with the archetype we need to generate the Maven project. This is done with the following three arguments. The value of these three arguments must match the corresponding elements defined in the associated `archetype-catalog.xml` file:

```
-DarchetypeGroupId=org.apache.synapse
-DarchetypeArtifactId=synapse-package-archetype
-DarchetypeVersion=2.0.0
```

The anatomy of archetype-catalog.xml

We already went through couple of sample `archetypes-catalog.xml` files and their usage. The XML schema of the `archetypes-catalog.xml` file is available at `http://maven.apache.org/xsd/archetype-catalog-1.0.0.xsd`. The following configuration shows an `archetypes-catalog.xml` file skeleton with all the key elements:

```
<archetype-catalog>
  <archetypes>
    <archetype>
      <groupId></groupId>
      <artifactId></artifactId>
      <version></version>
      <repository></repository>
      <description></description>
    </archetype>
    ...
  </archetypes>
</archetype-catalog>
```

The `archetypes` parent element can hold one or more archetype child elements. Each `archetype` element should uniquely identify the Maven artifact corresponding to the archetype. This is done using `groupId`, `artifactId`, and `version` of the artifact. These three elements carry exactly the same meaning that we discussed under Maven coordinates. The `description` element can be used to describe the archetype. The value of the description element will appear against the archetype, when it is listed by the `archetype` plugin. For example, the following output is generated according to the pattern, `groupId:artifactId (description)` from the `archetypes-catalog.xml` file, when you type `mvn archetype:generate`:

```
Choose archetype:
1: remote -> org.apache.maven.archetypes:maven-archetype-quickstart
   (An archetype that contains a sample Maven project.)
```

Each `archetype` child element can carry a value for the `repository` element. This instructs the `archetype` plugin on where to find the corresponding artifact. When no value is specified, the artifact is loaded from the repository where the catalogue comes from.

The archetype plugin goals

So far in this chapter, we have only discussed the `generate` and `crawl` goals of the `archetype` plugin. The following goals are associated with the `archetype` plugin:

- `archetype:generate`: The `generate` goal creates a Maven project corresponding to the selected archetype. This accepts the `archetypeGroupId`, `archetypeArtifactId`, `archetypeVersion`, `filter`, `interactiveMode`, `archetypeCatalog`, and `baseDir` arguments. We have already discussed almost all of these arguments in detail.

- `archetype:update-local-catalog`: The `update-local-catalog` goal has to be executed against a Maven archetype project. This will update the `local` archetype catalogue with the new archetype. The `local` archetype catalogue is available at `~/.m2/archetype-catalog.xml`. We'll use the `update-local-catalog` goal later in this chapter when we create our own Maven archetype.

- `archetype:jar`: The `jar` goal has to be executed against a Maven archetype project, and it will create a JAR file out of it. This accepts the `archetypeDirectory` argument, and this contains classes, the `finalName` argument, the name of the JAR file to be generated, and the `outputDirectory` argument, which is the location the final output is copied. We'll use the `jar` goal later in this chapter when we create our own Maven archetype.

- `archetype:crawl`: The `crawl` goal crawls through a local- or a filesystem-based Maven repository (not remote or via HTTP) and creates an archetype catalogue file. This accepts `catalogFile` as an input parameter, which is the name of the catalogue file to be created. By default, this crawls through the `local` Maven repository, and to override the location, we need to pass the corresponding repository URL with the `repository` parameter.

- `archetype:create-from-project`: The `create-from-project` goal creates an archetype project from an existing project. If you compare this with the `generate` goal, `generate` creates a new Maven project from scratch corresponding to the selected archetype, while `create-from-project` creates a Maven archetype project from an existing project. In other words, `create-from-project` generates a template out of an existing Maven project. We'll discuss the `create-from-project` goal later in this chapter when we create our own Maven archetype.

- `archetype:integration-test`: The `integration-test` goal will execute the integration tests associated with the Maven archetype project. We'll discuss the `integration-test` goal later in this chapter when we create our own Maven archetype.

- `archetype:help`: The `help` goal will display the manual associated with the `archetype` plugin listing out all available goals. If you want to get a detailed description of all the goals, then use the `-Ddetail=true` parameter along with the command. It is also possible to get the help for a given goal. For example, the following command will display the help associated with the `generate` goal:

```
$ mvn archetype:help -Ddetail=true -Dgoal=generate
```

Maven plugins with the archetype plugin

In *Chapter 5*, *Maven Plugins*, we discussed in detail how to develop Maven plugins. However, in all of those cases, we started from scratch, building everything from the project structure to everything by hand. Now, we will look at how to create a Maven plugin project with the `archetype` plugin. Here, we use the `maven-archetype-plugin`:

```
$ mvn archetype:generate
                -DgroupId=com.packt.samples
                -DartifactId=com.packt.samples.plugins.myplugin
                -DarchetypeGroupId=org.apache.maven.archetypes
                -DarchetypeArtifactId=maven-archetype-plugin
                -DinteractiveMode=false
```

The previous command will produce the following directory structure and the source code. If you look at the pom.xml file, you will notice that it contains all necessary instructions along with the required dependencies that are needed to build the Maven plugin project:

```
com.packt.samples.plugins.myplugin
                |-pom.xml
                |-src
                    |-main/java/com/packt/samples/MyMojo.java
                    |-it/settings.xml
                        |-simple-it/pom.xml
                        |-simple-it/verify.groovy
```

Let's have a look at the generated MyMojo.java file. This class is a template plugin class, which extends from org.apache.maven.plugin.AbstractMojo. This is a good example that demonstrates the capability of Maven archetypes to generate Java code templates and is also the most used use case of archetypes. Whenever your project has extension points (such as handlers), you can create an archetype to build them, and this will surely make the life of programmers extremely comfortable:

```java
package com.packt.samples;

import org.apache.maven.plugin.AbstractMojo;
import org.apache.maven.plugin.MojoExecutionException;

import org.apache.maven.plugins.annotations.LifecyclePhase;
import org.apache.maven.plugins.annotations.Mojo;
import org.apache.maven.plugins.annotations.Parameter;
import org.apache.maven.plugins.annotations.ResolutionScope;

import java.io.File;
import java.io.FileWriter;
import java.io.IOException;

/**
 * Goal, which touches a timestamp file.
 *
 * @deprecated - Don't use!
 */
@Mojo(name="touch",defaultPhase =LifecyclePhase.PROCESS_SOURCES)
public class MyMojo extends AbstractMojo
{
  /**
    * Location of the file.
```

```
*/
@Parameter(defaultValue="${project.build.directory}",
   property = "outputDir", required = true )
private File outputDirectory;

public void execute() throws MojoExecutionException
{
   //add your code here.
}
}
```

Java EE web applications with the archetype plugin

If you want to start with a Java EE web application, you can simply use the maven-archetype-webapp archetype to generate the Maven project skeleton, which is shown as follows:

```
$ mvn archetype:generate -B
                    -DgroupId=com.packt.samples
                    -DartifactId=my-webapp
                    -Dpackage=com.packt.samples.webapp
                    -Dversion=1.0.0
                    -DarchetypeGroupId=org.apache.maven.archetypes
                    -DarchetypeArtifactId=maven-archetype-webapp
                    -DarchetypeVersion=1.0
```

The preceding command will produce the following directory structure. One issue here is that it does not have the java directory just after src/main. If you want to add any Java code, you need to make sure that you first create an src/main/java directory and create your Java package under it. Otherwise, with the default configuration settings, Maven won't pick your classes for compilation. By default, Maven looks for the source code inside src/main/java:

```
my-webapp
   |-pom.xml
   |-src/main/webapp
                 |-index.jsp
                 |-WEB-INF/web.xml
   |- src/main/resources
```

The `maven-archetype-webapp` archetype is not the only archetype to generate a Java EE project using the `archetype` plugin. Codehaus, a collaborative environment to build open source projects, also provides a few archetypes to generate web applications. The following example uses the `webapp-javaee6` archetype from Codehaus:

```
$ mvn archetype:generate -B
                -DgroupId=com.packt.samples
                -DartifactId=my-webapp
                -Dpackage=com.packt.samples.webapp
                -Dversion=1.0.0
                -DarchetypeGroupId=org.codehaus.mojo.archetypes
                -DarchetypeArtifactId=webapp-javaee6
                -DarchetypeVersion=1.3
```

The preceding command will produce the following directory structure. This overcomes one of the issues in the `maven-archetype-webapp` archetype and creates the `src/main/java` and `src/test/java` directories. The only issue here is that it does not create the `src/main/webapp/WEB-INF` directory and you need to create it manually:

```
my-webapp
     |-pom.xml
     |-src/main/webapp/index.jsp
     |-src/main/java/com/packt/samples/webapp/
     |-src/test/java/com/packt/samples/webapp/
```

Deploying web applications to a remote Apache Tomcat server

Now we have created a template web application either using the `maven-archetype-webapp` or `webapp-javaee6` archetype. Let's see how to deploy this web application into a remote Apache Tomcat application server from Maven itself. Most developers would prefer doing this rather over manual copying. To deploy the web application, perform the following steps:

This assumes you have already installed Apache Tomcat in your environment. If not, you can download Tomcat 7.x distribution from `http://tomcat.apache.org/download-70.cgi` and set it up.

1. As we are going to deploy the web application to a remote Tomcat server, we need to have a valid user account that has the privilege of deploying a web application. Add the following entries to the TOMCAT_HOME/conf/tomcat-users.xml file under the tomcat-users root element. This will create a user with the name admin and the password password, having the manager-gui and manager-script roles.

```
<role rolename="manager-gui"/>
<role rolename="manager-script"/>
<user username="admin" password="password" roles="manager-
  gui,manager-script"/>
```

2. Now, we need to configure Maven to talk to the remote Tomcat server. Add the following configuration to USER_HOME/.m2/settings.xml under the servers element, as follows:

```
<server>
  <id>apache-tomcat</id>
  <username>admin</username>
  <password>password</password>
</server>
```

3. Go inside the root directory of the template web application we generated before (my-webapp) and then add tomcat7-maven-plugin to it. The complete pom.xml file should look like this:

```
<project >
  <modelVersion>4.0.0</modelVersion>
  <groupId>com.packt.samples</groupId>
  <artifactId>my-webapp</artifactId>
  <packaging>war</packaging>
  <version>1.0.0</version>
  <name>my-webapp Maven Webapp</name>
  <url>http://maven.apache.org</url>

  <dependencies>
    <dependency>
      <groupId>junit</groupId>
      <artifactId>junit</artifactId>
      <version>3.8.1</version>
      <scope>test</scope>
    </dependency>
  </dependencies>

  <build>
    <finalName>my-webapp</finalName>
```

```
<plugins>
  <plugin>
    <groupId>org.apache.tomcat.maven</groupId>
    <artifactId>tomcat7-maven-plugin</artifactId>
    <version>2.2</version>
    <configuration>
      <url>http://localhost:8080/manager/text</url>
      <server>apache-tomcat</server>
      <path>/my-webapp</path>
    </configuration>
  </plugin>
</plugins>
</build>
</project>
```

4. Use the following Maven command to build and deploy the template web application into the Tomcat server. Once it is deployed, you can access it via `http://localhost:8080/my-webapp/`:

```
$ mvn clean install tomcat7:deploy
```

5. To redeploy, use the following command:

```
$ mvn clean install tomcat7:redeploy
```

6. To undeploy, use the following command:

```
$ mvn clean install tomcat7:undeploy
```

Android mobile applications with the archetype plugin

If you are an Android application developer who wants to start with a skeleton Android project, you can use the `android-quickstart` archetype developed by akquinet, which is shown in the following code:

```
$ mvn archetype:generate -B
          -DarchetypeGroupId=de.akquinet.android.archetypes
          -DarchetypeArtifactId=android-quickstart
          -DarchetypeVersion=1.0.4
          -DgroupId=com.packt.samples
          -DartifactId=my-android-app
          -Dversion=1.0.0
```

This command produces the following skeleton project:

```
my-android-app
    |-pom.xml
    |-AndroidManifest.xml
    |-android.properties
    |-src/main/java/com/packt/samples/HelloAndroidActivity.java
    |-res/drawable-hdpi/icon.png
    |-res/drawable-ldpi/icon.png
    |-res/drawable-mdpi/icon.png
    |-res/layout/main.xml
    |-res/values/strings.xml
    |-assets
```

To build the Android skeleton project, run the following Maven command from the `my-android-app` directory:

```
$ mvn clean install -Dandroid.sdk.path=/path/to/android/sdk
```

The previous command looks straightforward, but based on your Android SDK version, you might encounter certain issues. Some of the possible issues and solutions are as follows:

- You will see the following error if you pass an invalid value to the `android.sdk.path` argument:

```
[ERROR] Failed to execute goal
  com.jayway.maven.plugins.android.generation2:maven-android-
  plugin:2.8.3:generate-sources (default-generate-sources) on
  project my-android-app: Execution default-generate-sources
  of goal com.jayway.maven.plugins.android.generation2:maven-
  android-plugin:2.8.3:generate-sources failed: Path
  "/Users/prabath/Downloads/adt-bundle-mac-x86_64-
  20140702/platforms" is not a directory.
```

  The path should point to the Android `sdk` directory, and right under it, you should find the `platforms` directory. By setting `android.sdk.path` to the correct path, you can avoid this error.

- By default, the `android-quickstart` archetype assumes the Android platform to be 7. You will see the following error if the Android platform installed in your local machine is different from this:

```
[ERROR] Failed to execute goal com.jayway.maven.plugins.android.
generation2:maven-android-
  plugin:2.8.3:generate-sources (default-generate-sources) on
  project my-android-app: Execution default-generate-sources
  of goal com.jayway.maven.plugins.android.generation2:maven-
  android-plugin:2.8.3:generate-sources failed: Invalid SDK:
  Platform/API level 7 not available.
```

To fix this, open the `pom.xml` file and set the right platform version with `<sdk><platform>20</platform></sdk>`.

- By default, the `android-quickstart` archetype assumes that the `aapt` tool is available under `sdk/platform-tools` directory. However, with the latest `sdk`, it has been moved to `sdk/build-tools/android-4.4W`, and you will get the following error:

```
[ERROR] Failed to execute goal
   com.jayway.maven.plugins.android.generation2:maven-android-
   plugin:2.8.3:generate-sources (default-generate-sources) on
   project my-android-app: Execution default-generate-sources
   of goal com.jayway.maven.plugins.android.generation2:maven-
   android-plugin:2.8.3:generate-sources failed: Could not find
   tool 'aapt'.
```

To fix the error, you need to update the `maven-android-plugin` version and `artifactId`.

Open up the `pom.xml` file inside the `my-android-app` directory and find the following plugin configuration. Change `artifactId` to `android-maven-plugin` and version to `4.0.0-rc.1`, which is shown as follows:

```
<plugin>
  <groupId>
    com.jayway.maven.plugins.android.generation2
  </groupId>
  <artifactId>android-maven-plugin</artifactId>
  <version>4.0.0-rc.1</version>
  <configuration></configuration>
  <extensions>true</extensions>
</plugin>
```

Once the build is completed, `android-maven-plugin` will produce the `my-android-app-1.0.0.apk` and `my-android-app-1.0.0.jar` artifacts inside the `target` directory.

To deploy the skeleton Android application (apk) to the connected device, use the following Maven command:

```
$ mvn android:deploy -Dandroid.sdk.path=/path/to/android/sdk
```

EJB archives with the archetype plugin

Here, we will discuss how to create a Maven **Enterprise JavaBeans (EJB)** project using the `ejb-javaee6` archetype developed by Codehaus, which is a collaborative environment for building open source projects:

```
$ mvn archetype:generate -B
                -DgroupId=com.packt.samples
                -DartifactId=my-ejbapp
                -Dpackage=com.packt.samples.ejbapp
                -Dversion=1.0.0
                -DarchetypeGroupId=org.codehaus.mojo.archetypes
                -DarchetypeArtifactId=ejb-javaee6
                -DarchetypeVersion=1.5
```

The previous command produces the following skeleton project. You can create your EJB classes inside `src/main/java/com/packt/samples/ejbapp/`:

```
my-ejbapp
        |-pom.xml
        |-src/main/java/com/packt/samples/ejbapp/
        |-src/main/resources/META-INF/MANIFEST.MF
```

If you look at the following `pom.xml` file inside `my-ejbapp`, you will notice that `maven-ejb-plugin` is used internally to produce the EJB artifact:

```xml
<plugin>
   <groupId>org.apache.maven.plugins</groupId>
   <artifactId>maven-ejb-plugin</artifactId>
   <version>2.3</version>
   <configuration>
     <ejbVersion>3.1</ejbVersion>
   </configuration>
</plugin>
```

Even though we highlighted `ejb-javaee6`, it is not the best out there for generating a Maven EJB project. The template produced by the `ejb-javaee6` archetype is very basic. Oracle WebLogic has developed a better EJB archetype, `basic-webapp-ejb`. The following example shows how to use the `basic-webapp-ejb` archetype:

```
$ mvn archetype:generate -B
        -DarchetypeGroupId=com.oracle.weblogic.archetype
        -DarchetypeArtifactId=basic-webapp-ejb
        -DarchetypeVersion=12.1.3-0-0
        -DgroupId=com.packt.samples
```

```
-DartifactId=my-ejbapp
-Dpackage=com.packt.samples.ejbapp
-Dversion=1.0.0
```

Prior to executing the previous command, there is more homework to be done. The `basic-webapp-ejb` archetype is not available in any public Maven repositories. First, you need to download the WebLogic distribution from `http://www.oracle.com/webfolder/technetwork/tutorials/obe/java/wls_12c_netbeans_install/wls_12c_netbeans_install.html` and then install it locally by performing the instructions in the `README.txt` file. Once the installation is completed, the `basic-webapp-ejb` archetype and `weblogic-maven-plugin` can be installed into the local Maven repository, as follows:

1. Go to `wls12130/wlserver/server/lib` and execute the following command. This will build the plugin JAR file using the WebLogic JarBuilder tool.

    ```
    $ java -jar wljarbuilder.jar -profile weblogic-maven-plugin
    ```

2. The previous command created the `weblogic-maven-plugin.jar` file. Now we need to extract it to get the `pom.xml` file. From `wls12130/wlserver/server/lib`, execute the following command:

    ```
    $ jar xvf weblogic-maven-plugin.jar
    ```

3. Now we need to copy the `pom.xml` file to `wls12130/wlserver/server/lib`. From `wls12130/wlserver/server/lib`, execute the following command:

    ```
    $ cp META-INF/maven/com.oracle.weblogic/weblogic-maven-plugin/pom.xml .
    ```

4. Now we can install `weblogic-maven-plugin.jar` into the `local` Maven repository. From `wls12130/wlserver/server/lib`, execute the following command:

    ```
    $ mvn install:install-file -Dfile=weblogic-maven-plugin.jar -DpomFile=pom.xml
    ```

5. In addition to the plugin, we also need to install the `basic-webapp-ejb` archetype. To do this, go to `wls12130/oracle_common/plugins/maven/com/oracle/maven/oracle-maven-sync/12.1.3` and execute the following two commands. Note that `oracle_common` is a hidden directory. If you are using a different version of WebLogic instead of 12.1.3, use the number associated with your version:

    ```
    $ mvn install:install-file -DpomFile=oracle-maven-sync-12.1.3.pom -Dfile=oracle-maven-sync-12.1.3.jar
    $ mvn com.oracle.maven:oracle-maven-sync:push -Doracle-maven-sync.oracleHome=/Users/prabath/Downloads/wls12130 -Doracle-maven-sync.testingOnly=false
    ```

Once we are done with these steps, you can execute the following command to generate the EJB template project using the WebLogic `basic-webapp-ejb` archetype. Make sure that you have the right version for `archetypeVersion`. This should match the archetype version that comes with your WebLogic distribution:

```
$ mvn archetype:generate -B
        -DarchetypeGroupId=com.oracle.weblogic.archetype
        -DarchetypeArtifactId=basic-webapp-ejb
        -DarchetypeVersion=12.1.3-0-0
        -DgroupId=com.packt.samples
        -DartifactId=my-ejbapp
        -Dpackage=com.packt.samples.ejbapp
        -Dversion=1.0.0
```

This command produces the following skeleton project:

```
my-ejbapp
  |-pom.xml
  |-src/main/java/com/packt/samples/ejbapp
                            |-entity/Account.java
                            |-service/AccountBean.java
                            |-service/AccountManager.java
                            |-service/AccountManagerImpl.java
                            |-interceptor/LogInterceptor.java
                            |-interceptor/OnDeposit.java
  |-src/main/resources/META-INF/persistence.xml
  |-src/main/scripts
  |-src/main/webapp/WEB-INF/web.xml
  |-src/main/webapp/WEB-INF/beans.xml
  |-src/main/webapp/css/bootstrap.css
  |-src/main/webapp/index.xhtml
  |-src/main/webapp/template.xhtml
```

To package the EJB archive, execute the following command from the `my-ejbapp` directory. This will produce `basicWebappEjb.war` inside the `target` directory. Now you can deploy this WAR file into your Java EE application server, which supports EJB:

```
$ mvn package
```

JIRA plugins with the archetype plugin

JIRA is an issue-tracking system developed by Atlassian. It is quite popular among many open source projects. One of the extension points in JIRA is its plugins. Here, we will see how to generate a skeleton JIRA plugin using `jira-plugin-archetype` developed by Atlassian:

```
$ mvn archetype:generate -B
        -DarchetypeGroupId=com.atlassian.maven.archetypes
        -DarchetypeArtifactId=jira-plugin-archetype
        -DarchetypeVersion=3.0.6
        -DgroupId=com.packt.samples
        -DartifactId=my-jira-plugin
        -Dpackage=com.packt.samples.jira
        -Dversion=1.0.0
        -DarchetypeRepository=
    http://repo.jfrog.org/artifactory/libs-releases/
```

This command will produce the following project template:

```
my-jira-plugin
        |-pom.xml
        |-README
        |-LICENSE
        |-src/main/java/com/packt/samples/jira/MyPlugin.java
        |-src/main/resources/atlassian-plugin.xml
        |- src/test/java/com/packt/samples/jira/MyPluginTest.java
        |-src/test/java/it/MyPluginTest.java
        |-src/test/resources/TEST_RESOURCES_README
        |-src/test/xml/TEST_XML_RESOURCES_README
```

Spring MVC applications with the archetype plugin

Spring **Model View Controller** (**MVC**) is a web application framework developed under the Spring framework, which is an open source application framework and an inversion of control container. Here, we will see how to generate a template Spring MVC application using the `spring-mvc-quickstart` archetype.

 To know more about the Spring MVC framework, refer to http://docs.spring.io/spring/docs/current/ spring-framework-reference/html/mvc.html.

Currently, the `spring-mvc-quickstart` archetype is not available in any of the public Maven repositories, so we have to download it from GitHub and build from the source, as follows:

```
$ git clone https://github.com/kolorobot/spring-mvc-quickstart-
archetype.git
$ cd spring-mvc-quickstart-archetype
$ mvn clean install
```

Once the archetype is built from the source and is available in the `local` Maven repository, you can execute the following command to generate the template Spring MVC application:

```
$ mvn archetype:generate -B
          -DarchetypeGroupId=com.github.spring-mvc-archetypes
          -DarchetypeArtifactId=spring-mvc-quickstart
          -DarchetypeVersion=1.0.0-SNAPSHOT
          -DgroupId=com.packt.samples
          -DartifactId=my-spring-app
          -Dpackage=com.packt.samples.spring
          -Dversion=1.0.0
```

This will produce the following project template:

```
my-spring-app
          |-pom.xml
          |-src/main/java/com/packt/samples/spring/Application.java
          |-src/main/webapp/WEB-INF/views
          |-src/main/webapp/resources
          |-src/main/resources
          |-src/test/java/com/packt/samples/spring
          |-src/test/resources
```

Let's see how to run the template Spring MVC application with the embedded Tomcat via Maven itself. Embedded Tomcat can be launched via the `run` goal of the `tomcat7` plugin, which is shown in the following code. Once the server is up, you can browse through to the web application via `http://localhost:8080/my-spring-app`.

```
$ mvn test tomcat7:run
```

> More details about the `tomcat7` plugin is available at
> `http://tomcat.apache.org/maven-plugin-trunk/tomcat7-maven-plugin/`.

Building a custom archetype

So far in this chapter, we have discussed several applications of Maven archetypes. It's high time now to build our own custom archetype. Let's see how to develop a Maven archetype for an Apache Axis2 module/handler. Let's start with a simple Maven project:

```
$ mvn archetype:generate
            -DgroupId=com.packt.axis2
            -DartifactId=com.packt.axis2.archetype.handler
            -Dversion=1.0.0
            -Dpackage=com.packt.axis2.archetype.handler
            -DinteractiveMode=false
```

This command will generate the following directory structure:

```
com.packt.axis2.archetype.handler
            |-pom.xml
            |-src
            |-main/java/com/packt/axis2/archetype/
            handler/App.java
            |-test/java/com/packt/axis2/archetype/
            handler/AppTest.java
```

Before creating the archetype, first we need to build the project template. In this case, the project template itself is an Axis2 module/handler. Let's see how to improve the simple Maven project generated from the maven-archetype-quickstart archetype into an Axis2 handler by performing the following steps:

1. First, we need to edit the generated pom.xml file and add all of the required dependencies there. We also need two plugins to build the Axis2 module archive file. The value of packaging is changed to mar. After the modifications, pom.xml will look as follows:

    ```xml
    <project>
      <modelVersion>4.0.0</modelVersion>
      <groupId>com.packt.axis2</groupId>
      <artifactId>com.packt.axis2.archetype.handler
      </artifactId>
      <packaging>mar</packaging>
      <version>1.0.0</version>
      <name>com.packt.axis2.archetype.handler</name>
      <url>http://maven.apache.org</url>
      <dependencies>
        <dependency>
          <groupId>junit</groupId>
    ```

```xml
          <artifactId>junit</artifactId>
          <version>3.8.1</version>
          <scope>test</scope>
      </dependency>
      <dependency>
          <groupId>org.apache.axis2</groupId>
          <artifactId>axis2</artifactId>
          <version>1.6.2</version>
      </dependency>
      <dependency>
          <groupId>org.apache.neethi</groupId>
          <artifactId>neethi</artifactId>
          <version>2.0.2</version>
      </dependency>
  </dependencies>

  <build>
    <plugins>
      <plugin>
        <groupId>org.apache.axis2</groupId>
          <artifactId>axis2-mar-maven-plugin</artifactId>
          <version>1.2</version>
          <extensions>true</extensions>
          <configuration>
            <includeDependencies>false</includeDependencies>
            <moduleXmlFile>module.xml</moduleXmlFile>
          </configuration>
      </plugin>
      <plugin>
        <groupId>org.codehaus.mojo</groupId>
          <artifactId>build-helper-maven-
            plugin</artifactId>
          <version>1.0</version>
            <executions>
              <execution>
                <id>aar</id>
                <phase>package</phase>
                <goals>
                  <goal>attach-artifact</goal>
                </goals>
                <configuration>
                  <artifacts>
                    <artifact>
                      <file>
                        target/${project.artifactId}-
                          ${project.version}.mar
                      </file>
```

```
              <type>jar</type>
            </artifact>
          </artifacts>
        </configuration>
      </execution>
    </executions>
  </plugin>
  </plugins>
  </build>
</project>
```

2. Now we can create the skeleton for the Axis2 handler. All Axis2 handlers must extend from the `org.apache.axis2.engine.Handler` class. Here, we will rename the generated `App.java` file to `SampleAxis2Handler.java` and modify its code, as shown here:

```java
package com.packt.axis2.archetype.handler;

import org.apache.axis2.AxisFault;
import org.apache.axis2.context.MessageContext;
import org.apache.axis2.description.HandlerDescription;
import org.apache.axis2.description.Parameter;
import org.apache.axis2.engine.Handler;

public class SampleAxis2Handler implements Handler {

  private HandlerDescription handlerDesc;

  @Override
  public void cleanup() {
    // TODO Auto-generated method stub
  }

  @Override
  public void flowComplete(MessageContext arg0) {
    // TODO Auto-generated method stub
  }

  @Override
  public HandlerDescription getHandlerDesc() {
    return handlerDesc;
  }
```

```java
    @Override
    public String getName() {
      return "SampleAxis2Handler";
    }

    @Override
    public Parameter getParameter(String name) {
      return this.handlerDesc.getParameter(name);
    }

    @Override
    public void init(HandlerDescription handlerDesc) {
      this.handlerDesc = handlerDesc;
    }

    @Override
    public InvocationResponse invoke(MessageContext
      msgContext) throws AxisFault {
      return InvocationResponse.CONTINUE;
    }

  }
```

3. Rename the generated `AppTest.java` file to `SampleAxis2HandlerTest.java` and modify its code, as shown here:

```java
package com.packt.axis2.archetype.handler;

import junit.framework.Test;
import junit.framework.TestCase;
import junit.framework.TestSuite;

/**
  * Unit test for SampleAxis2Handler.
*/
public class SampleAxis2HandlerTest extends TestCase
{
  /**
    * Create the test case
    *
    * @param testName name of the test case
  */
    public SampleAxis2HandlerTest( String testName )
    {
      super( testName );
    }
```

```
/**
 * @return the suite of tests being tested
 */
public static Test suite()
{
  return new TestSuite(SampleAxis2HandlerTest.class );
}

/**
 * Rigourous Test :-)
 */
public void testHandler()
{
  assertTrue( true );
}

}
```

4. Now we need to write a template Axis2 module class as follows. This will go under src/main/java/com/packt/axis2/archetype/module. You might need to create the archetype/module directory, as it's not there by default:

```
package com.packt.axis2.archetype.module;

import org.apache.axis2.AxisFault;
import org.apache.axis2.context.ConfigurationContext;
import org.apache.axis2.description.AxisDescription;
import org.apache.axis2.description.AxisModule;
import org.apache.axis2.modules.Module;
import org.apache.neethi.Assertion;
import org.apache.neethi.Policy;

public class SampleAxis2Module implements Module {

  @Override
  public void applyPolicy(Policy arg0, AxisDescription
    arg1) throws AxisFault {
    // TODO Auto-generated method stub
  }

  @Override
  public boolean canSupportAssertion(Assertion arg0) {
    // TODO Auto-generated method stub
    return false;
  }
```

```java
@Override
public void engageNotify(AxisDescription arg0) throws
  AxisFault {
  // TODO Auto-generated method stub
}

@Override
public void init(ConfigurationContext arg0, AxisModule
  arg1) throws AxisFault {
  // TODO Auto-generated method stub
}

@Override
public void shutdown(ConfigurationContext arg0) throws
  AxisFault {
  // TODO Auto-generated method stub
}

}
```

5. Create a file called `module.xml` inside the `root` directory (at the same level of the `pom.xml` file), as shown here:

```xml
<module name="sample-axis2-module"
  class="com.packt.axis2.archetype.module.
    SampleAxis2Module">
  <Description>Sample Axis2 Module</Description>
  <OutFlow>
    <handler
      name="SampleOutHandler"
      class="com.packt.axis2.archetype.handler.
        SampleAxis2Handler">
      <order phase="samplephase" />
    </handler>
  </OutFlow>
  <InFlow>
    <handler
      name="SampleInHandler"
      class="com.packt.axis2.archetype.hanlder.
        SampleAxis2Handler">
      <order phase="samplephase" />
    </handler>
  </InFlow>
  <OutFaultFlow>
    <handler
```

```
        name="SampleOutFaultHandler"
          class="com.packt.axis2.archetype.hanlder.
            SampleAxis2Handler">
        <order phase="samplephase" />
      </handler>
    </OutFaultFlow >
    <InFaultFlow>
      <handler
        name="SampleInFaultHandler"
          class="com.packt.axis2.archetype.hanlder.
            SampleAxis2Handler">
        <order phase="samplephase" />
      </handler>
    </InFaultFlow >

  </module>
```

6. With all these modifications, you should now see the following
    directory structure:

```
com.packt.axis2.archetype.hanlder
        |-pom.xml
        |-module.xml
        |-src
            |-main/java/com/packt/axis2/archetype/
            handler/SampleAxis2Handler.java
            |-main/java/com/packt/axis2/archetype/
             module/SampleAxis2Module.java
            |-test/java/com/packt/axis2/archetype/
            handler/SampleAxis2HandlerTest.java
```

7. If everything went fine, you should be able to build the project
    successfully with `mvn clean install`. Inside the `target` directory,
    you will see the resultant module archive, `com.packt.axis2.archetype.`
    `handler-1.0.0.mar`.

Everything we have discussed so far is not directly related to building a custom
archetype. It's all about building an Axis2 module. Now, let's see how to turn this
into an archetype by performing the following steps:

1. Go to the `com.packt.axis2.archetype.handler` directory and execute the
    following command:

    ```
    $ mvn archetype:create-from-project
    ```

2. This will generate the corresponding archetype inside `com.packt.axis2.archetype.handler/target/generated-sources/archetype` directory. Let's have a look at the `pom.xml` file created inside `com.packt.axis2.archetype.handler/target/generated-sources/archetype` directory. By default, the `artifactId` of the archetype is generated by appending `-archetype` to the original `artifactId` of the template project, which is shown as follows:

```xml
<project>
  <modelVersion>4.0.0</modelVersion>
  <groupId>com.packt.axis2</groupId>
  <artifactId>
    com.packt.axis2.archetype.handler-archetype
  </artifactId>
  <version>1.0.0</version>
  <packaging>maven-archetype</packaging>
  <name>com.packt.axis2.handler.archetype-archetype</name>

  <build>
    <extensions>
      <extension>
        <groupId>org.apache.maven.archetype</groupId>
        <artifactId>archetype-packaging</artifactId>
        <version>2.2</version>
      </extension>
    </extensions>

    <pluginManagement>
      <plugins>
        <plugin>
          <artifactId>maven-archetype-plugin</artifactId>
          <version>2.2</version>
        </plugin>
      </plugins>
    </pluginManagement>
  </build>

  <url>http://maven.apache.org</url>
</project>
```

3. To install the archetype into the `local` repository, just type `mvn install` in the command-line from `com.packt.axis2.archetype.handler/target/generated-sources/archetype`.

Now we've got our very first Maven archetype created and deployed into the `local` repository. Let's use it to generate a skeleton Axis2 module/handler project, as follows:

```
$ mvn archetype:generate -B
                -DarchetypeGroupId=com.packt.axis2
                -DarchetypeArtifactId=com.packt.axis2.archetype.
                                handler-archetype
                -DarchetypeVersion=1.0.0
                -DgroupId=com.packt.samples
                -DartifactId=my-axis2-handler
                -Dpackage=com.packt.samples.axis2
                -Dversion=1.0.0
```

 If you set `-DarchetypeVersion` to RELEASE, then the plugin will automatically pick the latest version of the archetype.

The previous command will create the following skeleton project. If you run `mvn clean install` from the `my-axis2-handler` directory, you will notice that the `my-axis2-handler-1.0.0.mar` file is created under the `my-axis2-handler/target` directory, which is shown as follows:

```
my-axis2-handler
        |-pom.xml
        |-module.xml
        |-src
            |-main/java/com/packt/samples/axis2/
            archetype/handler/SampleAxis2Handler.java
            |-main/java/com/packt/samples/axis2/
            archetype/module/SampleAxis2Module.java
            |-test/java/com/packt/samples/axis2/
            archetype/handler/SampleAxis2HandlerTest.java
```

You can find the complete Axis2 handler project at `https://svn.wso2.org/repos/wso2/people/prabath/maven/chapter07/axis2-handler`.

The archetype descriptor

The archetype descriptor is generated by the `archetype:create-from-project` goal. This is at the heart of the archetype and stores the metadata about it. The following configuration shows the `archetype-metadata.xml` file (the archetype descriptor), which was generated for our custom archetype. The file is available at `com.packt.axis2.archetype.handler/target/generated-sources/archetype/src/main/resources/META-INF/maven`:

```xml
<archetype-descriptor name="com.packt.axis2.handler.archetype " >
  <fileSets>
    <fileSet filtered="true" packaged="true" encoding="UTF-8">
      <directory>src/main/java</directory>
      <includes>
        <include>**/*.java</include>
      </includes>
    </fileSet>
    <fileSet filtered="true" encoding="UTF-8">
      <directory>src/main/java</directory>
      <includes>
        <include>**/*.xml</include>
      </includes>
    </fileSet>
    <fileSet filtered="true" packaged="true" encoding="UTF-8">
      <directory>src/test/java</directory>
      <includes>
        <include>**/*.java</include>
      </includes>
    </fileSet>
  </fileSets>
</archetype-descriptor>
```

According to the previous `archetype-metadata.xml` file, all the `*.java` files inside `src/main/java` and `src/test/java` are copied into the archetype. Also, any XML files inside `src/main/java` will be copied. During the template generation or while executing the `archetype:generate` goal, the `archetype` plugin reads `archetype-metadata.xml`.

The following lists out the complete `archetype-metadata.xml` file with all of the possible options:

```xml
<archetype-descriptor name=.. partial=.. >
```

The `name` attribute carries the name of the archetype, while the `partial` Boolean attribute indicates whether this archetype represents a complete Maven project or only a part of it.

```
<requiredProperties>
  <requiredProperty key=.. >
    <defaultValue/>
  </requiredProperty>
</requiredProperties>
```

The `requiredProperty` element carries the names of the properties required by the archetype to generate the template code. The `defaultValue` element carries the default value of the corresponding property.

```
<fileSets>
  <fileSet filtered=.. packaged=.. encoding=.. >
    <directory/>
    <includes/>
    <excludes/>
  </fileSet>
</fileSets>
```

Each `fileSet` element inside the `fileSets` parent element defines how the files located in the `jar` archetype are used to generate the template. The `filtered` Boolean attribute indicates whether the file set should be filtered or not. If set to `true`, then the selected set of files will be treated as velocity templates; if not, these will be copied as they are without any modifications. We'll be talking about velocity templates later in this chapter.

The `packaged` Boolean attribute indicates whether the file set should be packaged or not. If set to `true`, then the directory structure, which contains the file set will be prepended by the value of the `package` attribute (`-Dpackage` set along with `archetype:generate`); if not, the directory structure will be copied as it is. In our example, all XML files are copied without prepending the provided package name, as the `packaged` attribute is not set, and this means that it's set to `false`.

The `encoding` attribute indicates which encoding to be used while filtering the content.

The `directory` element indicates where the search is to be carried out and also the location to copy the files.

The `includes` element indicates the pattern used to include files while the `excludes` element indicates the pattern used to exclude files, as shown in the previous code snippet:

```
<modules>
  <module id=.. dir=.. name=.. >
```

```
    <fileSets>
      <fileSet filtered=.. packaged=.. encoding=.. >
        <directory/>
        <includes/>
        <excludes/>
      </fileSet>
    </fileSets>


  </module>
</modules>
```

The `modules` parent element is used as a container for multiple `module` child elements. This is only used in cases where we need to generate a multimodule Maven project with a single archetype. Each `module` element contains the definition of each Maven module. Next, in this chapter, we will see how to generate a multimodule Maven project from an archetype.

```
</archetype-descriptor>
```

Generating a multimodule Maven project

The process of creating an archetype that generates a multimodule Maven project is no different from what we have done previously for a single module project. You need to go inside the root of the Maven project and run the following command. We will discuss multimodule projects in *Chapter 9, Best Practices*.

```
$ mvn archetype:create-from-project
```

Let's create a multimodule project with the following steps:

1. Here, we use the `org.codehaus.mojo.archetypes:pom-root` archetype to generate the root POM file:

   ```
   $ mvn archetype:generate
        -DgroupId=com.packt.samples
        -DartifactId=com.packt.sample.multi.module.archetype
        -Dversion=1.0.0
        -Dpackage=com.packt.sample.multi.module.archetype
        -DinteractiveMode=false
        -DarchetypeGroupId=org.codehaus.mojo.archetypes
        -DarchetypeArtifactId=pom-root
   ```

2. Now, in the command-line go inside `com.packt.sample.multi.module.archetype` and then run the following command to create a child module under the parent Maven project:

```
$ mvn archetype:generate
  -DgroupId=com.packt.samples
  -DartifactId=com.packt.sample.multi.module.archetype.mod1
  -Dversion=1.0.0
  -Dpackage=com.packt.sample.multi.module.archetype.mod1
  -DinteractiveMode=false
```

This command will generate a new module with the name `com.packt.sample.multi.module.archetype.mod1` and will also update the root POM file.

3. Once again, in the command-line go inside `com.packt.sample.multi.module.archetype` and then run the following command to create another child module under the same parent Maven project:

```
$ mvn archetype:generate
      -DgroupId=com.packt.samples
      -DartifactId=com.packt.sample.multi.module.archetype.mod2
      -Dversion=1.0.0
      -Dpackage=com.packt.sample.multi.module.archetype.mod2
      -DinteractiveMode=false
```

Now we have the following project structure with a root POM file and two child modules:

```
com.packt.sample.multi.module.archetype
        |-pom.xml
        |-com.packt.sample.multi.module.archetype.mod1
                |-pom.xml
        |-com.packt.sample.multi.module.archetype.mod2
                |-pom.xml
```

The following configuration is the root POM file under `com.packt.sample.multi.module.archetype`. This has references to all of its child projects under the `modules` element:

```
<project>
  <modelVersion>4.0.0</modelVersion>
  <groupId>com.packt.samples</groupId>
  <artifactId>com.packt.sample.multi.module.archetype
  </artifactId>
  <version>1.0.0</version>
```

```
        <packaging>pom</packaging>
        <name>com.packt.sample.multi.module.archetype</name>

        <modules>
          <module>com.packt.sample.multi.module.archetype.mod1
          </module>
          <module>com.packt.sample.multi.module.archetype.mod2
          </module>
        </modules>
</project>
```

The following is the POM file under `com.packt.sample.multi.module.`
`archetype.mod1`. This has a reference to the parent POM file under the
parent element:

```
<project>
  <modelVersion>4.0.0</modelVersion>
  <parent>
    <groupId>com.packt.samples</groupId>
    <artifactId>com.packt.sample.multi.module.archetype
    </artifactId>
    <version>1.0.0</version>
  </parent>
  <groupId>com.packt.samples</groupId>
  <artifactId>com.packt.sample.multi.module.archetype.mod1
  </artifactId>
  <version>1.0.0</version>
  <name>com.packt.sample.multi.module.archetype.mod1</name>
  <url>http://maven.apache.org</url>
  <dependencies>
    <dependency>
      <groupId>junit</groupId>
      <artifactId>junit</artifactId>
      <version>3.8.1</version>
      <scope>test</scope>
    </dependency>
  </dependencies>
</project>
```

The following is the POM file under `com.packt.sample.multi.module.`
`archetype.mod2`. This also has a reference to the parent POM file under
the parent element:

```
<project>
  <modelVersion>4.0.0</modelVersion>
```

```
<parent>
  <groupId>com.packt.samples</groupId>
  <artifactId>com.packt.sample.multi.module.archetype
  </artifactId>
  <version>1.0.0</version>
</parent>
<groupId>com.packt.samples</groupId>
<artifactId>com.packt.sample.multi.module.archetype.mod2
</artifactId>
<version>1.0.0</version>
<name>com.packt.sample.multi.module.archetype.mod2</name>
<url>http://maven.apache.org</url>
<dependencies>
  <dependency>
    <groupId>junit</groupId>
    <artifactId>junit</artifactId>
    <version>3.8.1</version>
    <scope>test</scope>
  </dependency>
</dependencies>
</project>
```

4. Now we have a multimodule Maven project. Let's try to create a single archetype, which will generate the template code. In the command-line go inside `com.packt.sample.multi.module.archetype` directory, and then run the following command:

   `$ mvn archetype:create-from-project`

5. In the command-line go inside `com.packt.sample.multi.module.archetype/target/generated-sources/archetype` directory and then run the following command to install the new archetype in the `local` repository:

   `$ mvn install`

Now we've got our multimodule Maven archetype created and deployed into the `local` repository. Here, you can see the generated `archetype-metadata.xml` file, which is inside `com.packt.sample.multi.module.archetype/target/generated-sources/archetype/src/main/resources/META-INF/maven`:

```
<archetype-descriptor
  name="com.packt.sample.multi.module.archetype">
  <modules>
    <module id="${rootArtifactId}.mod2"
            dir="__rootArtifactId__.mod2"
            name="${rootArtifactId}.mod2">
      <fileSets>
```

```
        <fileSet filtered="true" packaged="true" encoding="UTF-8">
          <directory>src/main/java</directory>
          <includes>
            <include>**/*.java</include>
          </includes>
        </fileSet>
        <fileSet filtered="true" packaged="true" encoding="UTF-8">
          <directory>src/test/java</directory>
          <includes>
            <include>**/*.java</include>
          </includes>
        </fileSet>
      </fileSets>
    </module>
    <module id="${rootArtifactId}.mod1"
            dir="__rootArtifactId__.mod1"
            name="${rootArtifactId}.mod1">
      <fileSets>
        <fileSet filtered="true" packaged="true" encoding="UTF-8">
          <directory>src/main/java</directory>
          <includes>
            <include>**/*.java</include>
          </includes>
        </fileSet>
        <fileSet filtered="true" packaged="true" encoding="UTF-8">
          <directory>src/test/java</directory>
          <includes>
            <include>**/*.java</include>
          </includes>
        </fileSet>
      </fileSets>
    </module>
  </modules>
</archetype-descriptor>
```

Let's use the created multimodule archetype to generate a Maven project based on the template, as follows:

```
$ mvn archetype:generate -B
             -DarchetypeGroupId=com.packt.samples
             -DarchetypeArtifactId=com.packt.sample.
               multi.module.archetype-archetype
             -DarchetypeVersion=1.0.0
             -DgroupId=com.packt.samples
             -DartifactId=my-multi-module-project
             -Dpackage=com.packt.samples.multi.module
             -Dversion=1.0.0
```

This command will create the following skeleton project. If you run mvn clean install from my-multi-module-project directory, all the child modules will be built, which is shown as follows:

```
my-multi-module-project
        |-pom.xml
        |-my-multi-module-project.mod1
        |-my-multi-module-project.mod2
```

archetype:create-from-project with custom properties

The create-from-project goal of the archetype plugin creates an archetype project from an existing Maven project. That is exactly what we have done in the previous section. When we execute mvn archetype:create-from-project without any custom parameters, the plugin will use the default values and follow a convention.

Let's see how to create an archetype with a set of configured properties by performing the following steps:

1. In the command-line go inside com.packt.sample.multi.module. archetype, which is the archetype project we created in the previous section, and create a file called archetype.properties right under it with the following content:

    ```
    archetype.groupId=com.packt.archetypes
    archetype.artifactId=com.packt.archetypes.multi.module
    archetype.version=1.0.0
    ```

2. Run the following command from the com.packt.sample.multi.module. archetype directory:

    ```
    $ mvn archetype:create-from-project
            -Darchetype.properties=archetype.properties
    ```

3. In the command-line go inside com.packt.sample.multi.module. archetype/target/generated-sources/archetype and then run mvn install to deploy the archetype into the local Maven repository. Unlike in the previous case, the plugin won't try to generate an artifactId element for the archetype; it will simply use what is given in the archetype. properties file. In the default scenario, artifactId is com.packt.sample. multi.module.archetype-archetype; however, now it is com.packt. archetypes.multi.module.

All these properties are standard ones. You can also define custom properties as follows:

1. In the command-line go inside `com.packt.sample.multi.module.archetype` directory, which is the archetype project we created in the previous section, and create a file called `archetype.properties` right under it with the following content. Make sure that there are no periods (.) in the name of the custom property. Here, we use the `junit` version used in the project. The value of the custom property will be used as the default value:

   ```
   archetype.groupId=com.packt.archetypes
   archetype.artifactId=com.packt.archetypes.multi.module
   archetype.version=1.0.0
   junit-version=3.8.1
   ```

2. Now, we need to open up the `com.packt.sample.multi.module.archetype/com.packt.sample.multi.module.archetype.mod1/pom.xml` and `com.packt.sample.multi.module.archetype/com.packt.sample.multi.module.archetype.mod2/pom.xml` files and replace the value `3.8.1` with the `$junit-version` place holder, which is shown as follows:

   ```
   <dependency>
     <groupId>junit</groupId>
     <artifactId>junit</artifactId>
     <version>$junit-version</version>
     <scope>test</scope>
   </dependency>
   ```

3. Run the following command from `com.packt.sample.multi.module.archetypedirectory`:

   ```
   $ mvn archetype:create-from-project
               -Darchetype.properties=archetype.properties
   ```

4. Now, if you open `com.packt.sample.multi.module.archetype/target/generated-sources/archetype/src/main/resources/META-INF/maven/archetype-metadata.xml`, you will notice that the following new section is added to the `archetype-metadata.xml` file. This means that at the time you generate the template code, you have to pass a value to the custom property `junit-version`, as follows:

   ```
   <requiredProperties>
     <requiredProperty key="junit-version">
       <defaultValue>3.8.1</defaultValue>
     </requiredProperty>
   </requiredProperties>
   ```

5. In the command-line go inside `com.packt.sample.multi.module.` `archetype/target/generated-sources/archetype` directory and then type `mvn install` to deploy the archetype into the `local` Maven repository.

6. Let's use the created multimodule archetype to generate a Maven project based on the template. Note that we are passing `-Djunit-version=4.11` as an argument. If you look at the generated POM files, you will notice that the version of the `junit` dependency is set to `4.11`, shown as follows:

```
$ mvn archetype:generate -B
            -DarchetypeGroupId=com.packt.archetypes
            -DarchetypeArtifactId=com.packt.
                          archetypes.multi.module
            -DarchetypeVersion=1.0.0
            -DgroupId=com.packt.samples
            -DartifactId=my-multi-module-project
            -Dpackage=com.packt.samples.multi.module
            -Dversion=1.0.0
            -Djunit-version=4.11
```

 More details about the `create-from-project` goal is available at `http://maven.apache.org/archetype/maven-archetype-` `plugin/create-from-project-mojo.html`.

Summary

In this chapter, we focused on Maven archetypes. Maven archetypes provide a way of reducing repetitive work in building Maven projects. There are thousands of archetypes out there available publicly to assist you build different types of projects. This chapter covered a commonly used set of archetypes and later discussed how to develop your own custom archetypes.

In the next chapter, we will look into Maven repository management with the Nexus repository manager.

8
Maven Repository Management

The artifacts produced and consumed by Maven projects are stored in repositories. In this chapter, we will discuss the following topics around Maven repository management:

- Maven repositories and usage
- Repository management with Nexus
- Inclusive and exclusive routes
- Artifact indexing
- Scheduled tasks
- The repository metadata model

Maven repositories

There are two types of repositories: local and remote. The local repository is maintained in your local machine by default at `USER_HOME/.m2/repository`. Anything that you build locally with the `mvn install` will get deployed into the local repository. When you start with a fresh Maven repository, there is nothing in it. You need to download everything from the simplest `maven-compiler-plugin` to all your project dependencies. A Maven build can be an online or offline build. By default, it's online unless you add `-o` to your Maven build command. If it's an offline build, Maven assumes that all related artifacts are readily available in the local Maven repository and if not, it will complain. If it is an online build, Maven will download the artifacts from remote repositories and store them in the local repository.

The Maven local repository location can be changed to a preferred location by editing MAVEN_HOME/conf/settings. xml to update the value of the localRepository element. This is done by the code:

```
<localRepository>/path/to/local/repo</
localRepository>
```

The update policy

Does Maven always download from remote repositories even if an artifact is already available in the local repository? To answer this question correctly, we need to dig deep into how we define remote repositories in Maven.

Remote repositories can be further divided into three: release, snapshot, and plugin.

A release repository holds artifacts that have a fixed version. An artifact with the given groupId, artifactId, and version tags (GAV coordinates) is the same all the time. The following is an example of a released dependency. If you download this dependency today and then again in a month, both will be the same artifact:

```
<dependency>
   <groupId>com.googlecode.json-simple</groupId>
   <artifactId>json-simple</artifactId>
   <version>1.1</version>
</dependency>
```

A snapshot repository holds artifacts that have a special version, which ends with SNAPSHOT. Any artifact that has the SNAPSHOT version can change over time. What you download from the repository might not be the same if you download it again in a month. The following is an example of a SNAPSHOT dependency. You add a SNAPSHOT version to the project artifacts, which are still under development. As a convention, the version to be released will be postfixed by the keyword SNAPSHOT:

```
<dependency>
   <groupId>org.apache.axis2</groupId>
   <artifactId>axis2-kernel</artifactId>
   <version>1.7.0-SNAPSHOT</version>
</dependency>
```

A plugin repository is a remote repository that holds plugins. A plugin repository can be a release repository or a snapshot repository.

Maven knows about remote repository locations from the project POM file. By default, the Maven super POM file defines a set of repositories. Even if you do not define any repositories in your application POM, you will inherit what is defined in the super POM.

Repositories that are defined in the super POM file are shown in the following configuration. Here, it's the same repository that acts as the release repository as well as the plugin repository. If we set `<snapshots><enabled>true</enabled></snapshots>`, then the corresponding repository is treated as a snapshot repository; if set to `false`, then it's a release-only repository:

```
<repositories>
  <repository>
    <snapshots>
      <enabled>false</enabled>
    </snapshots>
    <id>central</id>
    <name>Central Repository</name>
    <url>http://repo.maven.apache.org/maven2</url>
  </repository>
</repositories>

<pluginRepositories>
  <pluginRepository>
    <releases>
      <updatePolicy>never</updatePolicy>
    </releases>
    <snapshots>
      <enabled>false</enabled>
    </snapshots>
    <id>central</id>
    <name>Central Repository</name>
    <url>http://repo.maven.apache.org/maven2</url>
  </pluginRepository>
</pluginRepositories>
```

Let's get back to our original question: does Maven always download artifacts from remote repositories, even if an artifact is already available in the local repository? This relies on the repository configuration. In the preceding code snippet from the super POM file, you will find the following under the `pluginRepository` section:

```
<releases>
  <updatePolicy>never</updatePolicy>
</releases>
```

The `updatePolicy` element can carry any of the values from `always`, `daily`, `interval:X`, or `never`. In this case, it is set to `never`, which means that the artifacts from this repository will be downloaded only if they are not available in the local repository. This is a perfectly valid configuration for a release repository. If this is a snapshot repository, then it won't work, and you might have to work with stale artifacts. For a snapshot repository, you have to set the value to `always`, `daily` or `interval:X`.

The `always` value means that Maven will always download the artifacts in every build. If the `updatePolicy` element says `daily`, then Maven will download the artifacts from the remote repository only once for a given day during the build. It compares the metadata associated with the local POM file with the remote one to see which has the latest timestamp. If the value is set to `interval:X` where X is an integer value in minutes, Maven will download the artifact only after this time interval.

 The default value of the `updatePolicy` configuration is `daily`.

Multiple repositories

Each Maven project has its own effective POM file. The effective POM file is the aggregated POM file from the application POM, all parent POM files, and the super POM. Finally, what matters to Maven is the effective POM, not the individual ones. Each individual POM file can have its own repositories defined under the `repositories` section, but in the effective POM file, there will be one single `repositories` section, which aggregates all the repositories defined in each POM file.

 More details about Maven POM files were discussed in *Chapter 2, Demystifying Project Object Model*.

When you have multiple repositories defined in the POM, the order in which they are defined matters. Whenever Maven detects that a required artifact is missing in the local repository, it will try to download from the very first eligible repository defined in the effective POM file. When Maven generates the effective POM, the top repositories will be taken from the application POM, then from the parent POM files and finally from the super POM. Maven will move down the repositories in the order they are defined in the effective POM if it cannot find an artifact in a given repository, as shown in the following figure:

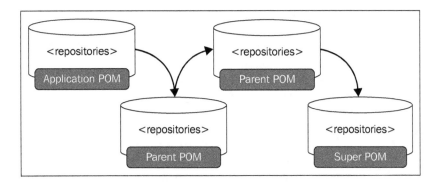

Repositories in settings.xml

You can also define repositories in settings.xml, which is available by default under the USER_HOME/.m2 directory. The repositories defined in settings.xml will get priority over all the other repositories. The following explains how to add plugin repositories to settings.xml:

1. Open USER_HOME/.m2/settings.xml and look for the <profiles> element.

2. Add the following section under the <profiles> element. When you define repositories in settings.xml, they must be within a profile element. This configuration introduces two plugin repositories and both are defined as snapshot repositories. We will talk more about Maven profiles in *Chapter 9, Best Practices*:

```xml
<profile>
  <id>apache</id>
  <pluginRepositories>
    <pluginRepository>
      <id>apache.snapshots</id>
      <name>Apache Snapshot Repository</name>
      <url>http://repository.apache.org/snapshots</url>
      <snapshots>
        <enabled>true</enabled>
        <updatePolicy>daily</updatePolicy>
      </snapshots>
      <releases>
        <enabled>false</enabled>
      </releases>
    </pluginRepository>

    <pluginRepository>
      <releases>
```

```
            <enabled>false</enabled>
         </releases>
         <snapshots>
            <enabled>true</enabled>
            <updatePolicy>daily</updatePolicy>
         </snapshots>
         <id>apache-snapshots</id>
         <name>Apache Snapshots Repository</name>
         <url>http://people.apache.org/repo/
            m2-snapshot-repository</url>
      </pluginRepository>
   </pluginRepositories>
</profile>
```

3. Go to a directory that has any `pom.xml` file and execute the following command, which will display the effective POM. Here, we are executing the `effective-pom` goal of the `help` Maven plugin with an additional argument, which starts with `-P`. The `-P` tag needs to be post fixed with the name of the profile defined in the `settings.xml`, where we have our plugin repositories. In this case, the name of the profile is `apache`(`<id>apache</id>`):

```
$ mvn help:effective-pom -Papache
```

4. Assuming that you have no repositories defined in your application POM file, the above command will display the following. This includes repositories from the `settings.xml` as well as from the super POM:

```
<repositories>
  <repository>
    <snapshots>
      <enabled>false</enabled>
    </snapshots>
      <id>central</id>
      <name>Central Repository</name>
      <url>http://repo.maven.apache.org/maven2</url>
  </repository>
</repositories>
<pluginRepositories>
  <pluginRepository>
    <releases>
      <enabled>false</enabled>
    </releases>
    <snapshots>
      <enabled>true</enabled>
```

```
          <updatePolicy>daily</updatePolicy>
        </snapshots>
        <id>apache.snapshots</id>
        <name>Apache Snapshot Repository</name>
        <url>http://repository.apache.org/snapshots</url>
    </pluginRepository>
    <pluginRepository>
      <releases>
        <enabled>false</enabled>
      </releases>
      <snapshots>
        <enabled>true</enabled>
        <updatePolicy>daily</updatePolicy>
      </snapshots>
      <id>apache-snapshots</id>
      <name>Apache Snapshots Repository</name>
      <url>http://people.apache.org/repo/m2-snapshot-
        repository</url>
    </pluginRepository>
    <pluginRepository>
      <releases>
        <updatePolicy>never</updatePolicy>
      </releases>
      <snapshots>
        <enabled>false</enabled>
      </snapshots>
      <id>central</id>
      <name>Central Repository</name>
      <url>http://repo.maven.apache.org/maven2</url>
    </pluginRepository>
  </pluginRepositories>
```

The Maven repository manager

If you are an independent developer who works according to your own schedule, you might not want to worry about a repository manager. However, if you are part of a larger team, doing day-to-day development with Maven, then you must evaluate the need for a repository manager. A Maven repository manager addresses two concerns in enterprise application development.

An organization with more than 100 developers who are continuously working on Maven based projects can easily burst out the outbound network traffic. To do an online build, it might take from 1 hour to 5 hours, based on the size of your project. This becomes much worse if you have many SNAPSHOT dependencies. The Maven repository manager, which can act as a proxy for external remote repositories, addresses this concern. With a repository manager in place, you do not need to download each and every artifact per each developer. Once a given artifact is being downloaded, it will be cached/stored at the repository manager. There is no need to go back to the remote repository and download it again and again.

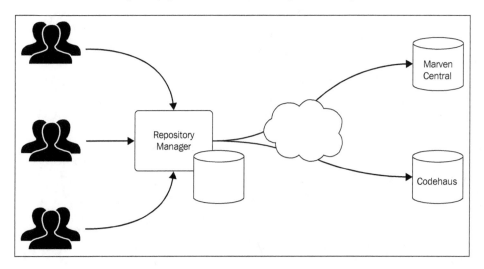

Other than just acting as a proxy, the repository manager can also act as the central point of governance. Here, you can enforce policies to specify which artifacts are allowed to use and which are not. For example, you can allow any artifact that has the Apache 2.0 open source license, but restrict anything with a GPL license. Apache 2.0 is the most business-friendly license, while GPL is a bit restrictive.

Your organization might not just be consuming Maven artifacts, but also producing some. If you produce Maven artifacts and want the public to use them, you have to make them available in a Maven repository, which is publicly accessible. This is the second concern addressed by the Maven repository manager. The Maven repository manager itself can act as a repository. This is quite useful, even for internal projects. If you have multiple internal projects where developers are simultaneously working on and sharing dependencies, you can use the repository manager to act as a snapshot repository. On a daily basis, each project can publish its artifacts to the snapshot repository, while the others that have dependencies to those can get the latest from the repository, rather than building each and every dependent project locally by each developer.

Nexus, Archiva, and Artifactory are three very popular open source repository managers. In the next section, we will have a look at the Nexus repository manager.

 A detailed feature comparison between Nexus, Archiva, and Artifactory is available at `http://docs.codehaus.org/display/MAVENUSER/Maven+Repository+Manager+Feature+Matrix`.

Repository management with Nexus

Nexus has bit of a history. The original idea was initiated by Tamas Cservenak who was working on Proximity, which was the most popular Maven proxy at that time, in December 2005. Tamas and his colleagues, who were working for a small organization, were fed up with their extremely slow ADSL connection and tried to come up with a workaround to improve the productivity. Proximity was the result. With Proximity, you do not need to always download Maven artifacts when you perform a build. These artifacts will be cached and stored locally for future use. Later in 2007, Tamas joined a company called Sonatype to build a similar product, which is the most popular Maven repository manager today, Nexus.

Nexus comes in two versions: the open source version and the Nexus professional version. In this chapter, we will only focus on the open source version.

The open source version of Nexus was released under **Eclipse Public License (EPL)** version 1.0, which is compatible with the Apache 2.0 license. The following list shows some of the key features available in the Nexus open source version. From here onwards, if we just say Nexus, it means the open source version has:

- The ability to host and maintain repositories.
- Proxying requests to remote Maven repositories.
- Grouping of repositories. With Nexus, you can group a set of repositories together and each group will have its own repository URL, which developers can use.
- The ability to host project websites.
- Fine-grained access controlling. Each action you perform on Nexus can be protected and will require a privilege check.
- The ability to search artifacts by groupId, artifactId, version, classifier, packaging, Java class names, keywords, and artifact checksums.
- Scheduled tasks for repository management.

- RESTful services to perform repository management functions.
- Extension points. The out-of-the-box functionality of Nexus can be further improved or added more by writing plugins.

Installing and running Nexus

You can download Nexus as a ZIP file distribution or as a WAR file from `http://www.sonatype.org/nexus/go`. If it's the WAR file that you download, then you have to deploy it in an application server. The zip distribution of Nexus comes with its own application server: Jetty.

 For the latest version of Nexus, you need to have Java 7.

To install from the zip distribution, you simply need to unzip it:

```
$ unzip nexus-2.9.1-02-bundle.zip
```

If it is the WAR file distribution, then you simply need to copy it to the web application deployment directory of your application server, for example, in Apache Tomcat, to TOMCAT_HOME/webapps.

You can start Nexus in two different ways. Execute the following command from the nexus-2.9.1-02 directory, which will start Nexus in the console mode. If you close the console, you kill Nexus. This is for Unix- or Linux-based systems. If you are using Microsoft Windows, you need to use the corresponding bat file.

```
$ sh bin/nexus console
```

The following command will start Nexus and will detach from the console. You close the console, but Nexus will still be running:

```
$ sh bin/nexus start
```

In the nonconsole mode, to view the startup logs, you can use the following command under a Unix- or Linux-based system:

```
$ tail -f logs/wrapper.log
```

The following command will stop the running Nexus server:

```
$ sh bin/nexus stop
```

By default, Nexus will start running on the port 8081. If you have executed the installation correctly, you should be able to access the `http://localhost:8081/nexus` URL. Now, you can log in to the system with the default username as `admin` and password as `admin123`. Once you are logged in to the system, you will see the following view. The first thing you should please delete do is to change the default password by performing the following steps:

1. Go to `http://localhost:8081/nexus/#profile;Summary`.

2. Click on **Change Password** to reset the default password:

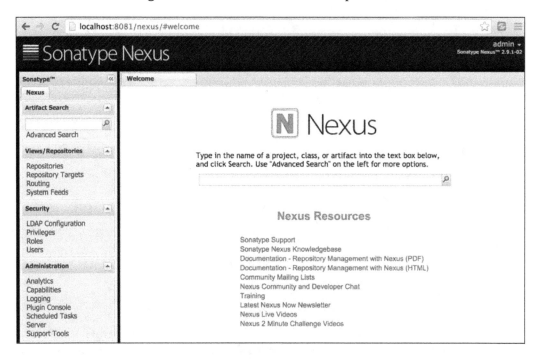

Creating a hosted repository

Let's see how to create a Maven repository with Nexus and then deploy artifacts to it:

1. Go to `http://localhost:8081/nexus` and login as `admin`.

2. Navigate to **Views/Repositories** | **Repositories** | **Add** | **Hosted Repository**.

3. Now, you will see a view as shown in the following screenshot. Fill in the required details appropriately. The default storage location is set to `file:/nexus-2.9.1-02-bundle/sonatype-work/nexus/storage/{repository-id}/`. If needed, you can override it.

4. **Repository Policy** can be either **release** or **snapshot**.

5. **Deployment Policy** can be **Allow Redeploy**, **Disable Redeploy**, or **Read Only**. If set to **Allow Redeploy**, you can deploy the same artifact again and again with the same Maven coordinates. This is needed for a snapshot repository.

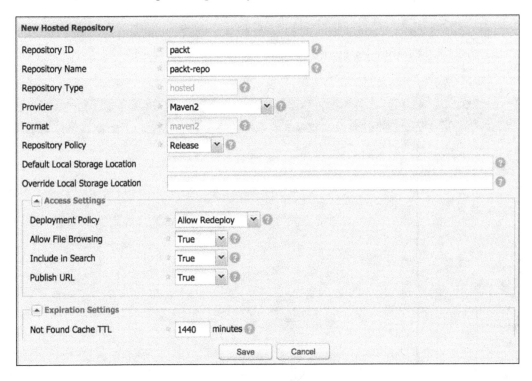

6. Now, we have configured our own Maven repository with Nexus, it is ready to use. You need to add a reference (as shown in the following code snippet) to the repository in the POM file to deploy the project artifacts:

```
<distributionManagement>
  <repository>
    <id>packt</id>
    <url>http://localhost:8081/nexus/content/
      repositories/packt</url>
  </repository>
</distributionManagement>
```

Let's create a simple Maven project and deploy the artifact it produces to the Maven repository that we just created.

The following command will create a Maven project with the `maven-archetype-quickstart` archetype. We discussed Maven archetypes in *Chapter 7, Maven Archetypes*.

```
$ mvn archetype:generate -DgroupId=com.packt.samples
  -DartifactId=com.packt.samples.archetype -Dversion=1.0.0
  -DinteractiveMode=false
```

1. You will see the following project structure that is being created with a sample POM file:

    ```
    com.packt.samples.archetype
                         |-pom.xml
                         |-src
                             |-main/java/com/packt/samples/
                             |-test/java/com/packt/samples/
    ```

2. Open the `com.packt.samples.archetype/pom.xml` file and add the following code snippet directly under the `project` root element:

    ```xml
    <distributionManagement>
      <repository>
        <id>packt</id>
        <url>http://localhost:8081/nexus/content/
          repositories/packt</url>
      </repository>
    </distributionManagement>
    ```

3. Execute the following Maven command to build the project and deploy the artifact to the Nexus Maven repository. As we discussed in *Chapter 5, Maven Plugins*, `deploy` is a phase that belongs to the Maven default lifecycle. When you execute the command, Maven will run all the plugins registered with each phase up to and including the deploy phase. The actual work is done by the `maven-deploy-plugin` registered under the `deploy` phase:

    ```
    $ mvn deploy
    ```

4. Even though you expect to see the artifact appearing in the Nexus repository, you will get the following error. The error message clearly indicates the reason for the failure. Any random person cannot deploy artifacts into the Nexus repository, only the authorized parties can do it:

```
[ERROR] Failed to execute goal org.apache.maven.plugins:maven-
deploy-plugin:2.7:deploy (default-deploy) on project com.packt.
samples.archetype: Failed to deploy artifacts: Could not transfer
artifact com.packt.samples:com.packt.samples.archetype:jar:1.0.0
from/to packt (http://localhost:8081/nexus/content/repositories/
packt): Failed to transfer file: http://localhost:8081/nexus/
content/repositories/packt/com/packt/samples/com.packt.samples.
archetype/1.0.0/com.packt.samples.archetype-1.0.0.jar. Return code
is: 401, ReasonPhrase: Unauthorized.
```

Let's see how to create a new user in Nexus and assign the user a role with the privileges to deploy Maven artifacts to the repository:

1. Go to http://localhost:8081/nexus and log in as admin.

2. Navigate to **Security Users | Add | Nexus Users**. You will see a view similar to what is shown in the following screenshot. Fill in the details appropriately.

3. Make sure the value of the **Status** field is set to **Active**.

4. Click on the **Add** button in the **Role Management** section and select **Repo: All Maven Repositories (Full Control)**, as shown in the upcoming screenshot:

5. Nexus comes with a set of roles where each role has a different set of privileges. Any user that belongs to the **Repo: All Maven Repositories (Full Control)** role has the rights to deploy artifacts into the Maven repository.

6. Once done, click on **Save** to complete the function.

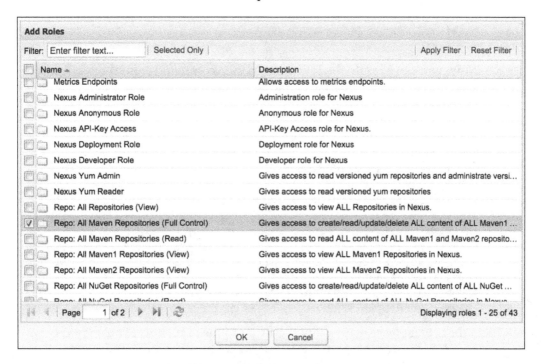

 Nexus comes with a set of built-in roles: administrator role, anonymous role, developer role, and deployment role. Based on the user's job functionality, you need to pick the appropriate role.

7. Maven repositories can be protected for legitimate access. If a given repository is protected with HTTP Basic Authentication, as in this case, the corresponding credentials should be defined under the `servers` element of `MAVEN_HOME/conf/settings.xml`, as shown in the following code snippet. The value of the `id` element must match the repository ID. How to encrypt the credentials in `settings.xml` was covered in the *Encrypting credentials in settings.xml* section of *Chapter 4, Build Lifecycles*.

```
<server>
  <id>packt</id>
  <username>username1</username>
  <password>password23</password>
</server>
```

8. Now, you can execute the following Maven command from the `com.packt.samples.archetype` directory and it should succeed this time:

```
$ mvn deploy
```

9. If you see the following error, it means that the user configured in the `MAVEN_HOME/conf/settings.xml` file might not have the required privileges to deploy artifacts:

```
[ERROR] Failed to execute goal org.apache.maven.plugins:maven-
deploy-plugin:2.7:deploy (default-deploy) on project com.packt.
samples.archetype: Failed to deploy artifacts: Could not transfer
artifact com.packt.samples:com.packt.samples.archetype:jar:1.0.0
from/to packt (http://localhost:8081/nexus/content/repositories/
packt): Access denied to: http://localhost:8081/nexus/content/
repositories/packt/com/packt/samples/com.packt.samples.
archetype/1.0.0/com.packt.samples.archetype-1.0.0.jar,
ReasonPhrase: Forbidden. -> [Help 1]
```

10. If the artifact was successfully deployed to the repository, you should be able to see it in Nexus. Navigate to **Views/Repositories | Repositories**. Click on the name of the repository that you created (**packt-repo**) and then click on **Browse Index**. You will see the artifact that we just deployed, as shown in the following screenshot:

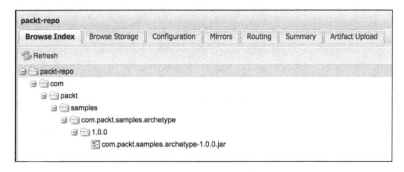

11. Let's try the command `mvn deploy` once again from the `com.packt.samples.archetype` directory. If you see the following error, when creating the hosted repository in Nexus, you have set **Disable Redeploy** as the deployment policy:

```
[ERROR] Failed to execute goal org.apache.maven.plugins:maven-
deploy-plugin:2.7:deploy (default-deploy) on project com.packt.
samples.archetype: Failed to deploy artifacts: Could not transfer
artifact com.packt.samples:com.packt.samples.archetype:jar:1.0.0
from/to packt (http://localhost:8081/nexus/content/repositories/
packt): Failed to transfer file: http://localhost:8081/nexus/
content/repositories/packt/com/packt/samples/com.packt.samples.
archetype/1.0.0/com.packt.samples.archetype-1.0.0.jar. Return code
is: 400, ReasonPhrase: Bad Request. -> [Help 1]
```

> Even though we created a hosted repository in Nexus from scratch, you do not always need to do this. Nexus comes with three hosted repositories out-of-the-box.
>
> The release repository is for the released artifacts available at `http://localhost:8081/nexus/content/repositories/releases`.
>
> The snapshots repository is available at `http://localhost:8081/nexus/content/repositories/snapshots` is for the snapshot artifacts.
>
> Nexus also comes with a hosted repository for third-party artifacts, which is available at `http://localhost:8081/nexus/content/repositories/thirdparty`.

Creating a proxy repository

By default, Nexus comes with following three proxy repositories:

- **Central**: The central proxy repository is available at `https://repo1.maven.org/maven2/`

- **Apache snapshots**: The Apache snapshots proxy repository is available at `https://repository.apache.org/snapshots/`

- **Codehaus snapshots**: The Codehaus proxy repository is available at `https://nexus.codehaus.org/snapshots/`

Let's look at how to create a set of proxy repositories in Nexus. Then we will create a group repository by combining them all. In your Maven project, you only need to add a reference to the group repository. The following steps are to be followed while creating the proxy repositories:

1. Go to `http://localhost:8081/nexus` and log in as `admin`.

2. Navigate to **Views/Repositories | Repositories | Add | Proxy Repository**. Fill in the details appropriately, as shown in the following screenshot. The remote repository URL has to be set in the **Remote Storage Location** field. Here, we are creating a proxy repository for the WSO2 nexus repository.

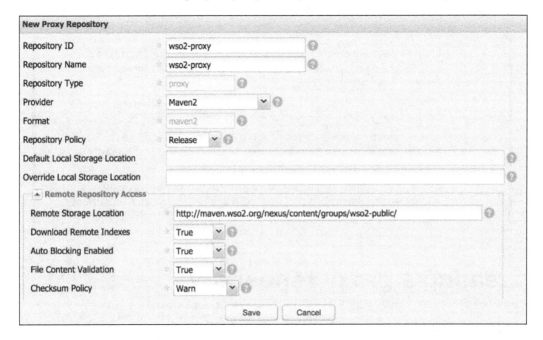

3. Click on **Save** and the proxy repository will appear under the **Repository** list. You can see that the Nexus proxy repository path is set to `http://localhost:8081/nexus/content/repositories/wso2-proxy/`.

4. Now, lets try to create a group repository by combining **wso2-proxy** repository and all the other proxy repositories that come out-of-the-box with Nexus. Navigate to **Views/Repositories | Repositories | Add | Repository Group**. Fill in the required details, as shown in the following screenshot:

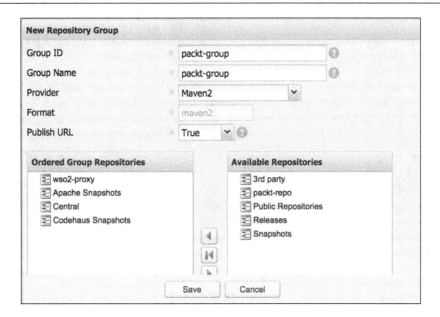

5. Make sure that you select **wso2-proxy**, **Apache Snapshots**, **Central**, and **Codehause Snapshots** proxy repositories from the **Ordered Group Repositories** panel and click on **Save**.

6. The group repository that we just created will appear under the **Repository** list, and is available at `http://localhost:8081/nexus/content/groups/packt-group/`.

7. Now, in your application POM file or in `USER_HOME/.m2/settings.xml`, you can define a single repository that points to the preceding group repository (**packt-group**):

```
<repositories>
  <repository>
    <snapshots>
      <enabled>true</enabled>
    </snapshots>
    <release>
      <enabled>true</enabled>
    </release>
    <id>packt-group</id>
    <name>PACKT Nexus Group Repository</name>
    <url>http://localhost:8081/nexus/content/groups/packt
      -group/</url>
  </repository>
</repositories>
```

8. Even though we use the same group repository for both the released and snapshot artifacts, you should avoid this. You can have one group for the released artifacts and another for the snapshot artifacts.

In the previous example, we directly changed the URL of the repository element defined in either your application POM file or the USER_HOME/.m2/settings.xml file. When you want the axis2-kernel-1.6.2.jar file, Maven will try to download it from http://localhost:8081/nexus/content/groups/packt-group/org/apache/axis2/axis2-kernel/1.6.2/axis2-kernel-1.6.2.jar. However, this is not the only way to instruct Maven to use our Nexus group repository. For example, you can define a mirror repository in the settings.xml file for a given repository in the following way, instead of directly changing its URL to Nexus. This is quite useful when you are working on a project that already defines a set of repositories. In such a case without changing any of these POM files, you can create a mirror for them, as shown in the following code snippet:

```
<mirrors>
  <mirror>
    <id>packt-group</id>
    <name>PACKT Nexus Group Repository</name>
    <url>http://localhost:8081/nexus/content/groups/packt
      -group/</url>
    <mirrorOf>central</mirrorOf>
  </mirror>
</mirrors>
```

The mirrorOf element in the preceding code snippet refers to a Maven repository that is defined under the repositories section either in a POM file or in the settings.xml file. The following code snippet shows you the definition of the Maven central repository that carries the id tag as central:

```
<repositories>
  <repository>
    <release>
      <enabled>true</enabled>
    </release>
    <id>central</id>
    <name>Maven Central</name>
    <url>https://repo1.maven.org/maven2/url>
  </repository>
</repositories>
```

This still has limitations. For each repository defined in your application POM files, you need to define a mirror repository. There are two approaches to avoid doing this. One is to use a comma separated list of the `mirrorOf` IDs, as shown in the following code snippet:

```
<mirrors>
  <mirror>
    <id>packt-group</id>
    <name>PACKT Nexus Group Repository</name>
    <url>http://localhost:8081/nexus/content/groups/packt
      -group/</url>
    <mirrorOf>central,codehause</mirrorOf>
  </mirror>
</mirrors>
```

However, when a new application POM file introduces a new repository, you need to be aware of it and then update the preceding configuration in the `settings.xml` file. You can avoid doing this by identifying all the repositories to be mirrored by `*`, as shown in the following code snippet:

```
<mirrors>
  <mirror>
    <id>packt-group</id>
    <name>PACKT Nexus Group Repository</name>
    <url>http://localhost:8081/nexus/content/groups/packt
      -group/</url>
    <mirrorOf>*</mirrorOf>
  </mirror>
</mirrors>
```

If you want to use the Nexus repository as the mirror for all the repositories, except for **codehause**, then you can use the following code snippet:

```
<mirrors>
  <mirror>
    <id>packt-group</id>
    <name>PACKT Nexus Group Repository</name>
    <url>http://localhost:8081/nexus/content/groups/packt
      -group/</url>
    <mirrorOf>*,!codehause</mirrorOf>
  </mirror>
</mirrors>
```

Creating a virtual repository

A virtual repository acts as a bridge between different types of repositories. Nexus supports bridging between Maven1 and Maven2. With a virtual directory, you can expose a Maven1 repository as a Maven2 repository. To create a virtual repository, first you need to have a hosted or proxy repository. Then you create a virtual repository on top of it:

1. Go to `http://localhost:8081/nexus` and log in as `admin`.

2. Navigate to **Views/Repositories | Repositories | Add | Virtual Repository**. To expose a Maven2 repository as a Maven1 repository, you need to select **Maven2 to Maven1** in the **Provider** field. Once you select **Maven2 to Maven1** in the **Provider** field, the value of **Format** will be automatically set to **maven1**, and all the Maven2 hosted and proxy repositories will be listed under the **Source Nexus Repository ID** field, as shown in the following screenshot:

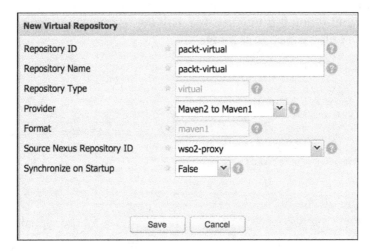

3. Once you click on the **Save** button, the virtual repository will be listed under **Repository** list and will be available at `http://localhost:8081/nexus/content/shadows/packt-virtual/`.

Blocking selected artifacts

Nexus routing rules can be used to block certain artifacts. For example, you might have a company policy to not to use any artifacts with the GPL license. In this a case, those artifacts can be blocked from the Nexus repository. The following steps show you how to block all the Apache axis2 artifacts. However, this is not a perfect example, as Apache Axis2 was released under Apache 2.0 License:

1. Go to `http://localhost:8081/nexus` and log in as `admin`.

2. Navigate to **Views/Repositories | Routing | Add**. The **URL Pattern** field carries a regular expression to the artifact path. The artifact path is everything that comes after `nexus/content`, which also includes the repository name. In this case, we use `^/org/apache/axis2/.*` as the regular expression to block any `axis2` artifact. Fill in the required details, as shown in the following screenshot:

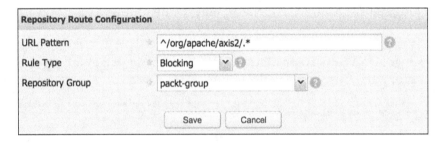

3. The value of **Rule Type** has to be set to **Blocking**. The other two options: **Inclusive** and **Exclusive**, which will be discussed later in this chapter.

4. Finally, you can select to which repository group this rule should be applied to and then click on **Save**.

5. Add the following dependency to your project and run `mvn clean install`. Maven will report an error, as it won't be able to download any axis2 related artifacts. Also, make sure that the corresponding artifact is not available in your local repository before running this command:

```
<dependency>
    <groupId>org.apache.axis2</groupId>
    <artifactId>axis2-kernel</artifactId>
    <version>1.6.2</version>
</dependency>
```

Inclusive and exclusive routing

When Maven asks for an artifact from a Nexus proxy repository, Nexus knows where to look for it. For example, we have a proxy repository that runs at `http://localhost:8081/nexus/content/repositories/central/`, which internally points to the remote repository that runs at `https://repo1.maven.org/maven2/`. Since there is one-to-one mapping between the proxy repository and the corresponding remote repository, Nexus can route the requests without much trouble. However, if Maven looks for an artifact via a Nexus group repository, then Nexus has to iterate through all the repositories in that group repository in order to find the exact artifact. There can be cases where we have more than 20 repositories in a single group repository, which can easily bring delays at the client side. To optimize artifact discovery in group repositories, we need to set the correct inclusive/exclusive routing rules.

Inclusive routing rules talk about which repositories to be included in artifact discovery, while exclusive routing rules talk about which ones to be excluded. The following steps show how to include and exclude routes:

1. Go to `http://localhost:8081/nexus` and log in as `admin`.

2. Navigate to **Views/Repositories | Routing | Add**. Fill in the required details appropriately, as shown in the following screenshot:

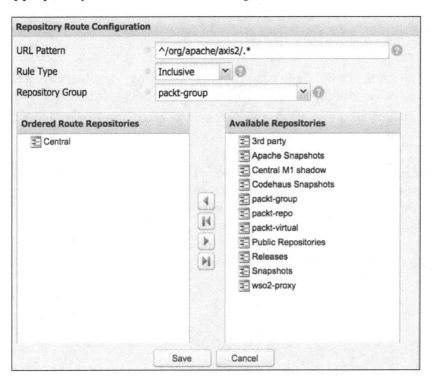

3. The **URL Pattern** field carries a regular expression to the artifact path. The artifact path is everything that comes after `nexus/content` that also includes the repository name. In this case, we use `^/org/apache/axis2/.*` as the regular expression to create an inclusive route to the `central` proxy repository.

4. Any request coming to the `packt-group` group repository, which matches the given regular expression, will now be directly routed to the central proxy repository at `http://localhost:8081/nexus/content/groups/packt-group/org/apache/axis2/axis2-kernel/1.6.2/axis2-kernel-1.6.2.jar`.

5. In the same way, we can also create an exclusive route. Here, you need to select a set of repositories from the provided list to be excluded from artifact discovery corresponding to the matching regular expression.

If you have blocked a certain artifact from a repository and you later unblock it or set a different route type for it, you might see the following exception from your Maven project, when you try to execute `mvn clean install`. As clearly indicated in the exception, the issue is related to caching. If an artifact gets blocked from a given repository, that decision will be cached until the update interval of the repository gets elapsed. In that case, you need to execute `mvn clean install -U`.

```
[ERROR] Failed to execute goal on project com.packt.samples.
archetype: Could not resolve dependencies for project com.packt.
samples:com.packt.samples.archetype:jar:1.0.0: Failure to find
org.apache.axis2:axis2-kernel:jar:1.6.2 in http://localhost:8081/
nexus/content/groups/packt-group/ was cached in the local
repository, resolution will not be reattempted until the update
interval of packt-group has elapsed or updates are forced.
```

Scheduled tasks

With scheduled tasks, Nexus gives its administrators the control to routinely perform certain tasks in an automated manner. The following steps show how to set up a scheduled task:

1. Go to `http://localhost:8081/nexus` and log in as `admin`.

2. Navigate to **Administration | Scheduled Tasks | Add**. Fill in the required details, as shown in the following screenshot:

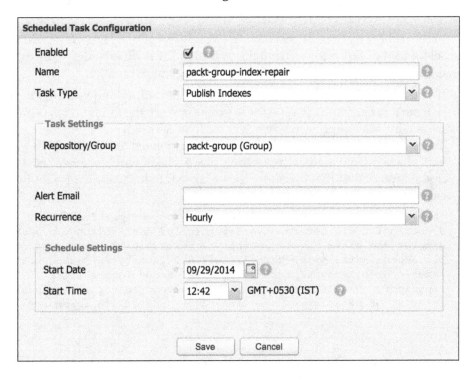

3. You can select one from the available task types from the **Task Type** field. Here, we have selected **Publish Indexes** and the task will be done in every hour starting from **09/29/ 2014, 12:42** P.M..

4. Click on the **Save** button to complete and the task will appear on the task list.

Artifact indexing

Nexus keeps an index of all the repositories managed by it. The index is maintained as a standard Lucene index. Nexus uses the created index in order to find where the requested artifacts belong, prior to talking to a remote repository.

 Apache Lucene is an open source project released under Apache 2.0 License is available at http://lucene.apache.org/.

The following list shows you how to update the index of a given repository:

1. Go to http://localhost:8081/nexus and log in as admin.

2. Navigate to **Views/Repositories | Repositories** and right-click on the repository you need. Then select **Update Index**.

3. To browse through the index of the selected repository, click on the **Browse Index** tab just below the repository list.

Nexus plugins

Similarly to Maven plugins, Nexus plugins allow you to extend the behavior of Nexus. Out-of-the-box Nexus comes with a set of plugins. To view all the plugins installed in your Nexus distribution, navigate to **Administration | Plugin Console**.

Name ▲	Version	Description	Status
Nexus Analytics Plugin	2.9.1-02	Provides support for collecting analytics data	Activated
Nexus Atlas Plugin	2.9.1-02	Provides support tools for Nexus	Activated
Nexus Capabilities Plugin	2.9.1-02	Allows Nexus to define and manage capabilities.	Activated
Nexus Content Plugin	2.9.1-02	Provides access to repository contents.	Activated
Nexus Core API (Restlet 1.x Plugin)	2.9.1-02	Provides Nexus Core REST API.	Activated
Nexus Crypto Provider Plugin	2.9.1-02	Provides support for cryptography in Nexus.	Activated
Nexus ExtJS3 UI	2.9.1-02	Provides a Nexus user interface based on ExtJS3.	Activated
Nexus Groovy Provider Plugin	2.9.1-02	Provides access to Groovy runtime.	Activated
Nexus H2 Provider Plugin	2.9.1-02	Provides access to H2 databases.	Activated
Nexus Health Check OSS Plugin	2.9.1-02	Integration with Sonatype CLM for Nexus OSS.	Activated
Nexus Indexer Lucene Plugin	2.9.1-02	Adds search capabilities for repository content.	Activated
Nexus Kazuki Plugin	2.9.1-02	Kazuki datastore provider.	Activated
Nexus LVO Plugin	2.9.1-02	Reminds about newer Nexus versions.	Activated
Nexus Logging Plugin	2.9.1-02	Allows users to control Nexus logging.	Activated
Nexus Maven Archetype Catalog Plugin	2.9.1-02	Adds a content generator for Maven archetype.xml files.	Activated
Nexus Maven Bridge Plugin	2.9.1-02	Adds an API to access maven dependency resolution for...	Activated
Nexus NuGet Plugin	2.9.1-02	Manages feeds of NuGet packages.	Activated
Nexus OSS LDAP Plugin	2.9.1-02	Adds a LDAP security realm to Nexus.	Activated
Nexus Outreach Plugin	2.9.1-02	Shows help and support content inside the Nexus UI.	Activated
Nexus Plugin Console Plugin	2.9.1-02	Adds a UI to view installed plugins.	Activated
Nexus Remote Repository Browsing Plugin	2.9.1-02	Adds support for browsing proxy repositories remote stor...	Activated
Nexus RutAuth Plugin	2.9.1-02	A HTTP header based (REMOTE_USER) realm.	Activated

A repository metadata model

If you go to `http://repo1.maven.org/maven2/org/apache/`, you will find a file called `maven-metadata.xml`. As shown in the following code snippet, the file lists out the available plugins under `http://repo1.maven.org/maven2/org/apache/`.

```
<metadata>
  <plugins>
    <plugin>
      <name>Maven XBean Plugin</name>
      <prefix>xbean</prefix>
      <artifactId>maven-xbean-plugin</artifactId>
    </plugin>
  </plugins>
</metadata>
```

If you go to `http://repo1.maven.org/maven2/org/apache/axis2`, you will again find a similar file `maven-metadata.xml` under it. This too lists out all the available plugins under `http://repo1.maven.org/maven2/org/apache/axis2`.

If you go to `http://repo1.maven.org/maven2/org/apache/axis2/axis2-kernel/`, you will see a slightly different `maven-metadata.xml`, as shown in the following code snippet. This lists out the metadata corresponding to the Maven artifact under that directory. The metadata includes the `groupId` tag, `artifactId` element and all the different versions of the artifact. In addition to these, the the value of `lastUpdated` tag indicates the time the `maven-metadata.xml` file was last updated, as shown in the following snippet:

```
<metadata>
  <groupId>org.apache.axis2</groupId>
  <artifactId>axis2-kernel</artifactId>
  <versioning>
    <latest>1.6.2</latest>
    <release>1.6.2</release>
    <versions>
      <version>1.0</version>
      <version>1.1</version>
      <version>1.2</version>
      <version>1.3</version>
      <version>1.4</version>
      <version>1.4.1</version>
      <version>1.5</version>
      <version>1.5.1</version>
      <version>1.5.2</version>
```

```
        <version>1.5.3</version>
        <version>1.5.4</version>
        <version>1.5.5</version>
        <version>1.5.6</version>
        <version>1.6.0</version>
        <version>1.6.1</version>
        <version>1.6.2</version>
      </versions>
      <lastUpdated>20120423060050</lastUpdated>
    </versioning>
  </metadata>
```

Maven allows you to store metadata at the directory level with different granularity levels. In the first example, the `maven-metadata.xml` file was available under the `org/apache groupId` path. In the second example, it was available under the `org/apache/axis2 groupId` path and in the last one, it was under the `org/apache/axis2/axis2-kernel artifactId` path. Even though the schema of the `maven-metadata.xml` file is the same for all the locations, the information kept in each file varies based on the location. If the file is under the artifact directory (`org/apache/axis2/axis2-kernel`), it will hold all the metadata related to the artifacts under it, which includes `groupId`, `artifactId`, and all the different versions of the artifact. The `maven-metadata.xml` file inside a group directory (`org/apache/axis2 or org/apache`) displays the plugin information.

In addition to the previous two examples, the `maven-matadata.xml` file can also be present in the version directory, which is available at `http://repository.apache. org/content/groups/snapshots/org/apache/axis2/axis2-kernel/1.7.0-SNAPSHOT/maven-metadata.xml`. This is mostly used for snapshot dependencies. The following code snippet shows you a sample `maven-matadata.xml` file for Apache Axis2 - 1.7.0-SNAPSHOT:

```
  <metadata modelVersion="1.1.0">
    <groupId>org.apache.axis2</groupId>
    <artifactId>axis2-kernel</artifactId>
    <version>1.7.0-SNAPSHOT</version>
    <versioning>
      <snapshot>
        <timestamp>20140921.110455</timestamp>
        <buildNumber>1943</buildNumber>
      </snapshot>
      <lastUpdated>20140921110455</lastUpdated>
      <snapshotVersions>
        <snapshotVersion>
          <extension>jar</extension>
```

```
        <value>1.7.0-20140921.110455-1943</value>
        <updated>20140921110455</updated>
      </snapshotVersion>
    </snapshotVersions>
  </versioning>
</metadata>
```

The following list shows you the complete schema of the Maven metadata model. Most of the elements here are self-explanatory and if you need any further information, you can refer to `http://maven.apache.org/ref/3.2.3/maven-repository-metadata/repository-metadata.html`.

```
<metadata  modelVersion=.. >
  <groupId/>
  <artifactId/>
  <version/>
  <versioning>
    <latest/>
    <release/>
    <snapshot>
      <timestamp/>
      <buildNumber/>
      <localCopy/>
    </snapshot>
    <versions/>
    <lastUpdated/>
    <snapshotVersions>
      <snapshotVersion>
        <classifier/>
        <extension/>
        <value/>
        <updated/>
      </snapshotVersion>
    </snapshotVersions>
  </versioning>
  <plugins>
    <plugin>
      <name/>
      <prefix/>
      <artifactId/>
    </plugin>
  </plugins>
</metadata>
```

How does Maven use `maven-metadata.xml`?

At the beginning of the chapter, we talked about two types of repositories – release and snapshot, and how to configure these repositories with an update policy. If it is an update policy for a snapshot repository, you will ideally use `always` or `daily`. This will instruct Maven to check the snapshot repositories always, or once in a given day. When Maven checks for an update, the only way it finds whether a given snapshot artifact is being updated or not is by looking at the `maven-metadata.xml` file under the version directory.

When Maven downloads a snapshot dependency, it always downloads the `maven-metadata.xml` file from the version directory, and stores it in the local Maven repository under the same directory structure by renaming the file to `maven-metadata-<repository-id>.xml`. If we use `packt-group` as the repository ID, then the filename will be `maven-metadata-packt-group.xml`. When Maven tries to update the same snapshot version once again, it will compare the timestamp of the local `maven-metadata-packt-group.xml` file to the remote `maven-metadata.xml` file.

Snapshot dependencies is not the only case where Maven downloads the `maven-metadata.xml` file from a remote repository. If you have associated a plugin with your application POM, without a version (as shown in the following code snippet), then Maven will also download the corresponding `maven-metadata.xml` file and store it locally. Only the latest released version of the plugin will be downloaded and used in the project:

```
<build>
  <plugins>
    <plugin>
      <inherited>true</inherited>
      <groupId>org.apache.maven.plugins</groupId>
      <artifactId>maven-source-plugin</artifactId>
      <executions>
        <execution>
          <id>attach-sources</id>
          <goals>
            <goal>jar</goal>
          </goals>
        </execution>
      </executions>
    </plugin>
  </plugins>
</build>
```

Maven also maintains another favor of `maven-metadata.xml` file. This is postfixed with `local`. You will find the `maven-metadata-local.xml` file in the artifact directory of your local Maven repository, when you create any local Maven artifact. This will get created when you execute `mvn clean install` against your local project, and the file will get copied to the remote repository (and might get merged too), when you deploy the artifact using `mvn deploy`.

Summary

In this chapter, we focused on the Maven repository management. We started the discussion on how Maven projects use and reference repositories within the application POM files and globally use `settings.xml`. Later, we discussed how to use Nexus as a repository manager and configure it as a hosted, proxy, and group repository. Finally, we concluded with a detailed discussion on the Maven repository metadata model. For more details about Nexus, you can check out the information at `http://www.sonatype.com/nexus/`.

In the next chapter, we will discuss the industry accepted best practices in using Maven.

9
Best Practices

In the book so far, we have discussed most of the key concepts related to Maven. Here in this chapter, we focus on best practices associated with all those core concepts. The following best practices are essential ingredients in creating a successful/productive build environment. The following criteria will help you evaluate the efficiency of your Maven project if you are mostly dealing with a large-scale, multi-module project:

- The time it takes for a developer to get started with a new project and add it to the build system
- The effort it requires to upgrade a version of a dependency across all the project modules
- The time it takes to build the complete project with a fresh local Maven repository
- The time it takes to do a complete offline build
- The time it takes to update the versions of Maven artifacts produced by the project, for example, from 1.0.0-SNAPSHOT to 1.0.0
- The effort it requires for a completely new developer to understand what your Maven build does
- The effort it requires to introduce a new Maven repository
- The time it takes to execute unit tests and integration tests

The rest of the chapter talks about 25 industry-accepted best practices that would help you to improve developer productivity and reduce any maintenance nightmares.

Dependency management

In the following example, you will notice that the dependency versions are added to each and every dependency defined in the application POM file:

```
<dependencies>
  <dependency>
    <groupId>com.nimbusds</groupId>
    <artifactId>nimbus-jose-jwt</artifactId>
    <version>2.26</version>
  </dependency>
  <dependency>
    <groupId>commons-codec</groupId>
    <artifactId>commons-codec</artifactId>
    <version>1.2</version>
  </dependency>
</dependencies>
```

Imagine that you have a set of application POM files in a multi-module Maven project that has the same set of dependencies. If you have duplicated the artifact version with each and every dependency, then to upgrade to the latest dependency, you need to update all the POM files, which could easily lead to a mess.

Not just that, if you have different versions of the same dependency used in different modules of the same project, then it's going to be a debugging nightmare in case of an issue.

With proper dependency management, we can overcome both the previous issues. If it's a multi-module Maven project, you need to introduce the dependencyManagement configuration element in the parent POM so that it will be inherited by all the other child modules:

```
<dependencyManagement>
  <dependencies>
    <dependency>
      <groupId>com.nimbusds</groupId>
      <artifactId>nimbus-jose-jwt</artifactId>
      <version>2.26</version>
    </dependency>
    <dependency>
      <groupId>commons-codec</groupId>
      <artifactId>commons-codec</artifactId>
      <version>1.2</version>
    </dependency>
  </dependencies>
</dependencyManagement>
```

Once you define `dependencies` under the `dependencyManagement` section as shown in the previous code, you only need to refer a `dependency` by its `groupId` and `artifactId` tags. The `version` tag is picked from the appropriate the `dependencyManagement` section:

```
<dependencies>
  <dependency>
    <groupId>com.nimbusds</groupId>
    <artifactId>nimbus-jose-jwt</artifactId>
  <dependency>
    <groupId>commons-codec</groupId>
    <artifactId>commons-codec</artifactId>
  </dependency>
</dependencies>
```

With the previous code snippet, if you want to upgrade or downgrade a dependency, you only need to change the `version` of the dependency under the `dependencyManagement` section.

The same principle applies to plugins as well. If you have a set of plugins, which are used across multiple modules, you should define them under the `pluginManagement` section of the parent module. In this way, you can downgrade or upgrade plugin versions seamlessly just by changing the `pluginManagement` section of the parent POM, as shown in the following code:

```
<pluginManagement>
  <plugins>
    <plugin>
      <artifactId>maven-resources-plugin</artifactId>
      <version>2.4.2</version>
    </plugin>
    <plugin>
      <artifactId>maven-site-plugin</artifactId>
      <version>2.0-beta-6</version>
    </plugin>
    <plugin>
      <artifactId>maven-source-plugin</artifactId>
      <version>2.0.4</version>
    </plugin>
    <plugin>
      <artifactId>maven-surefire-plugin</artifactId>
      <version>2.13</version
    </plugin
  </plugins>
</pluginManagement>
```

Once you define the plugins in the `pluginManagement` section, as shown in the previous code, you only need to refer a plugin from its `groupId` (optional) and the `artifactId` tags. The `version` tag is picked from the appropriate `pluginManagement` section:

```
<plugins>
  <plugin>
    <artifactId>maven-resources-plugin</artifactId>
    <executions>......</executions>
  </plugin>
  <plugin>
    <artifactId>maven-site-plugin</artifactId>
    <executions>......</executions>
  </plugin>
  <plugin>
    <artifactId>maven-source-plugin</artifactId>
    <executions>......</executions>
  </plugin>
  <plugin>
    <artifactId>maven-surefire-plugin</artifactId>
    <executions>......</executions>
  </plugin>
</plugins>
```

Maven plugins were discussed in detail in *Chapter 5*, *Maven Plugins*.

Defining a parent module

In most of the multi-module Maven projects, there are many things that are shared across multiple modules. Dependency versions, plugins versions, properties, and repositories are only some of them. It is a common as well as a best practice to create a separate module called parent, and in its POM file, define everything in common. The packaging type of this POM file is `pom`. The artifact generated by the `pom` packaging type is itself a POM file.

The following are a few examples:

- The Apache Axis2 project, available at `http://svn.apache.org/repos/asf/axis/axis2/java/core/trunk/modules/parent/`

- The WSO2 Carbon project, available at `https://svn.wso2.org/repos/wso2/carbon/platform/trunk/parent/`

Not all the projects follow this approach. Some just keep the parent POM file under the root directory (not under the `parent` module). The following are a couple of examples:

- The Apache Synapse project, available at
  `http://svn.apache.org/repos/asf/synapse/trunk/java/pom.xml`
- The Apache HBase project, available at
  `http://svn.apache.org/repos/asf/hbase/trunk/pom.xml`

Both approaches deliver the same results. However, the first one is much preferred. With the first approach, the parent POM file only defines the shared resources across different Maven modules in the project, while there is another POM file at the root of the project, which defines all the modules to be included in the project build. With the second approach, you define all the shared resources as well as all the modules to be included in the project build in the same POM file, which is under the project's root directory. The first approach is better than the second one, based on the **separation of concerns** principle.

POM properties

There are six types of properties that you can use within a Maven application POM file:

- Built-in properties
- Project properties
- Local settings
- Environment variables
- Java system properties
- Custom properties

It is always recommended that you use properties, instead of hardcoding values in application POM files. Let''s look at a few examples.

Let's take the application POM file inside the Apache Axis2 distribution module, available at `http://svn.apache.org/repos/asf/axis/axis2/java/core/trunk/modules/distribution/pom.xml`. This defines all the artifacts created in the Axis2 project that need to be included in the final distribution. All the artifacts share the same `groupId` tag as well as the `version` tag of the `distribution` module. This is a common scenario in most of the multi-module Maven projects.

Most of the modules (if not all) share the same `groupId` tag and the `version` tag:

```
<dependencies>
  <dependency>
    <groupId>org.apache.axis2</groupId>
    <artifactId>axis2-java2wsdl</artifactId>
    <version>${project.version}</version>
  </dependency>
  <dependency>
    <groupId>org.apache.axis2</groupId>
    <artifactId>axis2-kernel</artifactId>
    <version>${project.version}</version>
  </dependency>
  <dependency>
    <groupId>org.apache.axis2</groupId>
    <artifactId>axis2-adb</artifactId>
    <version>${project.version}</version>
  </dependency>
</dependencies>
```

In the previous configuration, instead of duplicating the `version` element, Axis2 uses the project property `${project.version}`. When Maven finds this project property, it reads the value from the project POM `version` element. If the project POM file does not have a `version` element, then Maven will try to read it from the immediate parent POM file. The benefit here is, when you upgrade your project `version` some day, you only need to upgrade the `version` element of the `distribution` POM file (or its parent).

The previous configuration is not perfect; it can be further improved in the following manner:

```
<dependencies>
  <dependency>
    <groupId>${project.groupId}</groupId>
    <artifactId>axis2-java2wsdl</artifactId>
    <version>${project.version}</version>
  </dependency>
  <dependency>
    <groupId>${project.groupId}</groupId>
    <artifactId>axis2-kernel</artifactId>
    <version>${project.version}</version>
  </dependency>
  <dependency>
```

```
      <groupId>${project.groupId}</groupId>
      <artifactId>axis2-adb</artifactId>
      <version>${project.version}</version>
   </dependency>
</dependencies>
```

Here, we also replace the hardcoded value of `groupId` in all the dependencies with the project property `${project.groupid}`. When Maven finds this project property, it reads the value from the project POM `groupId` element. If the project POM file does not have a `groupId` element, then Maven will try to read it from the immediate parent POM file.

The following lists out some of the Maven built-in properties and project properties:

- `project.version`: This refers to the value of the `version` element of the project POM file

- `project.groupId`: This refers to the value of the `groupId` element of the project POM file

- `project.artifactId`: This refers to the value of the `artifactId` element of the project POM file

- `project.name`: This refers to the value of the `name` element of the project POM file

- `project.description`: This refers to the value of the `description` element of the project POM file

- `project.baseUri`: This refers to the path of the project's base directory

  The following is an example that shows the usage of this project property. Here, we have a `system` dependency that needs to be referred from a filesystem path:

  ```
  <dependency>
    <groupId>org.apache.axis2.wso2</groupId>
    <artifactId>axis2</artifactId>
    <version>1.6.0.wso2v2</version>
    <scope>system</scope>
    <systemPath>${project.basedir}/lib/axis2-1.6.jar</systemPath>
  </dependency>
  ```

In addition to the project properties, you can also read properties from the `USER_HOME/.m2/settings.xml` file. For example, if you want to read the path to the local Maven repository, you can use the `${settings.localRepository}` property. In the same way, with the same pattern, you can read any of the configuration elements that are defined in the `settings.xml` file.

The environment variables defined in the system can be read using the env prefix, within an application POM file. The ${env.M2_HOME} property will return the path to the Maven home, while ${env.java_home} returns the path to the Java home directory. These properties will be quite useful within certain Maven plugins.

Maven also lets you define your own set of custom properties. Custom properties are mostly used when defining dependency versions.

You should not scatter custom properties all over the place. The ideal place to define them is the parent POM file in a multi-module Maven project, which will then be inherited by all the other child modules.

If you look at the parent POM file of the WSO2 Carbon project, you will find a large set of custom properties, which are defined in https://svn.wso2.org/repos/ wso2/carbon/platform/branches/turing/parent/pom.xml. The following lists out some of them:

```
<properties>
  <rampart.version>1.6.1-wso2v10</rampart.version>
  <rampart.mar.version>1.6.1-wso2v10</rampart.mar.version>
  <rampart.osgi.version>1.6.1.wso2v10</rampart.osgi.version>
</properties>
```

When you add a dependency to the Rampart JAR, you do not need to specify the version there. Just refer it by the ${rampart.version} property name. Also, keep in mind that all the custom defined properties are inherited and can be overridden in any child POM file:

```
<dependency>
  <groupId>org.apache.rampart.wso2</groupId>
  <artifactId>rampart-core</artifactId>
  <version>${rampart.version}</version>
</dependency>
```

Avoiding repetitive groupId and version tags and inherit from the parent POM

In a multi-module Maven project, most of the modules (if not all) share the same groupId and version elements. In this case, you can avoid adding the version and groupId elements to your application POM file. These will be automatically inherited from the corresponding parent POM.

If you look at `axis2-kernel` (which is a module of the Apache Axis2 project), you will find that no `groupId` or `version` is defined at `http://svn.apache.org/repos/asf/axis/axis2/java/core/trunk/modules/kernel/pom.xml`. Maven reads them from the parent POM file:

```
<project>
  <modelVersion>4.0.0</modelVersion>
  <parent>
    <groupId>org.apache.axis2</groupId>
    <artifactId>axis2-parent</artifactId>
    <version>1.7.0-SNAPSHOT</version>
    <relativePath>../parent/pom.xml</relativePath>
  </parent>
  <artifactId>axis2-kernel</artifactId>
  <name>Apache Axis2 - Kernel</name>
</project>
```

Following naming conventions

When defining coordinates for your Maven project, you must always follow the naming conventions.

The value of the `groupId` element should follow the same naming convention you use in Java package names. It has to be a domain name (the reverse of the domain name) that you own, or at least your project is developed under.

The following lists out some of the naming conventions related to `groupId`:

- The name of the `groupId` element has to be in lower case.
- Use the reverse of a domain name that can be used to uniquely identify your project. This will also help to avoid collisions between artifacts produced by different projects.
- Avoid using digits or special characters (that is, `org.wso2.carbon.identity-core`).
- Do not try to group two words into a single word by camel casing (that is, `org.wso2.carbon.identityCore`).
- Make sure that all the subprojects developed under different teams in the same company finally inherit from the same `groupId` element and extend the name of the parent `groupId` element rather than defining their own.

Let's go through some examples. You will notice that all the open source projects developed under **Apache Software Foundation (ASF)** use the same parent groupId (org.apache) and define their own groupId elements, which extend from the parent:

- The Apache Axis2 project uses org.apache.axis2, which inherits from the org.apache parent groupId
- The Apache Synapse project uses org.apache.synapse, which inherits from the org.apache parent groupId
- The Apache ServiceMix project uses org.apache.servicemix, which inherits from the org.apache parent groupId
- The WSO2 Carbon project uses org.wso2.carbon

Apart from the groupId element, you should also follow the naming conventions while defining artifactIds.

The following lists out some of the naming conventions related to artifactId:

- The name of the artifactId has to be in lower case.
- Avoid duplicating the value of groupId inside the artifactId element. If you find a need to start your artifactId with the value of groupId element and add something to the end, then you need to revisit the structure of your project. You might need to add more module groups.
- Avoid using special characters (that is, #, $, &, %, and so on).
- Do not try to group two words into a single word by camel casing (that is, identityCore).

Following naming conventions for version is also equally important. The version of a given Maven artifact can be divided into four categories:

```
<Major version>.<Minor version>.<Incremental version>-<Build
   number or the qualifier>
```

The major version reflects the introduction of a new major feature. A change in the major version of a given artifact can also mean that the new changes are not necessarily backward compatible with the previously released artifact. The minor version reflects an introduction of a new feature to the previously released version, in a backward compatible manner. The incremental version reflects a bug-fixed release of the artifact. The build number can be the revision number from the source code repository.

This versioning convention is not just for Maven artifacts. Apple did a major release of its iOS mobile operating system in September 2014: iOS 8.0.0. Soon after the release, they discovered a critical bug in it that had an impact on cellular network connectivity and TouchID on iPhone. Then, they released iOS 8.0.1 as a patch release to fix the issues.

Let's go through some of the examples:

- The Apache Axis2 1.6.0 release, available at `http://svn.apache.org/repos/asf/axis/axis2/java/core/tags/v1.6.0/pom.xml`.

- The Apache Axis2 1.6.2 release, available at `http://svn.apache.org/repos/asf/axis/axis2/java/core/tags/v1.6.2/pom.xml`.

- Apache Axis2 1.7.0-SNAPSHOT release, available at `http://svn.apache.org/repos/asf/axis/axis2/java/core/trunk/pom.xml`. SNAPSHOT releases are done from the trunk of the source repository with the latest available code.

- Apache Synapse 2.1.0-wso2v5 release, available at `http://svn.wso2.org/repos/wso2/tags/carbon/3.2.3/dependencies/synapse/2.1.0-wso2v5/pom.xml`. Here, the Synapse code is maintained under the WSO2 source repository and not under the Apache repository. In this case, we use the `wso2v5` classifier to make it different from the same artifact produced by Apache Synapse.

Maven profiles

We have touched the concept of Maven profiles in a couple of previous chapters, but never went into the details. When do we need Maven profiles and why is it a best practice?

Think about a large-scale multi-module Maven project. One of the best examples I am aware of is the WSO2 Carbon project. If you look at the application POM file available at `http://svn.wso2.org/repos/wso2/tags/carbon/3.2.3/components/pom.xml`, you will notice that there are more than hundred modules. Also, if you go deeper into each module, you will further notice that there are more modules within them: `http://svn.wso2.org/repos/wso2/tags/carbon/3.2.3/components/identity/pom.xml`. As a developer of the WSO2 Carbon project, you do not need to build all these modules. In this specific example, different groups of the modules are later aggregated into build multiple products. However, a given product does not need to build all the modules defined in the parent POM file. If you are a developer in a product team, you only need to worry about building the set of modules related to your product; if not, it's an utter waste of productive time. Maven profiles help you to do this.

With Maven profiles, you can activate a subset of configurations defined in your application POM file, based on some criteria.

If we take the same example we took previously, you will find that multiple profiles are defined under the `<profiles>` element: `http://svn.wso2.org/repos/wso2/tags/carbon/3.2.3/components/pom.xml`. Each `profile` element defines the set of modules that is relevant to it and identified by a unique ID. Also for each module, you need to define a criterion to activate it, under the `activation` element. By setting the value of the `activeByDefault` element to `true`, we make sure that the corresponding profile will get activated when no other profile is picked. In this particular example, if we just execute `mvn clean install`, the profile with the `default` ID will get executed. Keep in mind that the magic here does not lie on the name of the profile ID, `default`, but on the value of the `activeByDefault` element, which is set to `true` for the `default` profile. The value of the `id` element can be of any name:

```xml
<profiles>
  <profile>
    <id>product-esb</id>
    <activation>
      <property>
        <name>product</name>
        <value>esb</value>
      </property>
    </activation>
    <modules></modules>
  </profile>
  <profile>
    <id>product-greg</id>
    <activation>
      <property>
        <name>product</name>
        <value>greg</value>
      </property>
    </activation>
    <modules></modules>
  </profile>
  <profile>
    <id>product-is</id>
    <activation>
      <property>
        <name>product</name>
        <value>is</value>
      </property>
    </activation
    <modules></modules>
```

```
    </profile>
    <profile>
      <id>default</id>
      <activation>
        <activeByDefault>true</activeByDefault>
      </activation>
      <modules></modules>
    </profile>

  </profiles>
```

If I am a member of the WSO2 **Identity Server** (**IS**) team, then I will execute the build in the following manner:

$ mvn clean install -Dproduct=is

Here, we pass the system property `product` with the value `is`. If you look at the activation criteria for all the profiles, all are based on the system property: `product`. If the value of the system property is `is`, then Maven will pick the build profile corresponding to the Identity Server:

```
<activation>
  <property>
    <name>product</name>
    <value>is</value>
  </property>
</activation>
```

You also can define an activation criterion to execute a profile, in the absence of a property. For example, the following configuration shows how to activate a profile if the `product` property is missing:

```
<activation>
  <property>
    <name>!product</name>
  </property>
</activation>
```

The profile activation criteria can be based on a system property, the JDK version, or an operating system parameter where you run the build.

The following sample configuration shows how to activate a build profile for JDK 1.6:

```
<activation>
  <jdk>1.6</jdk>
</activation>
```

The following sample configuration shows how to activate a build profile based on operating system parameters:

```
<activation>
  <os>
    <name>mac os x</name>
    <family>mac</family>
    <arch>x86_64</arch>
   <version>10.8.5</version>
  </os>
</activation>
```

The following sample configuration shows how to activate a build profile based on the presence or absence of a file:

```
<activation>
  <file>
    <exists>......</exists>
    <missing>......</missing>
  </file>
</activation>
```

In addition to the activation configuration, you can also execute a Maven profile just by its ID, which is defined within the id element. In this case, you need a prefix; use the profile ID with -P, as shown in the following command:

```
$ mvn clean install -Pproduct-is
```

Think twice before you write your own plugin

Maven is all about plugins! There is a plugin out there for almost everything. If you find a need to write a plugin, spend some time researching on the Web to see whether you can find something similar — the chances are very high. You can also find a list of available Maven plugins at http://maven.apache.org/plugins.

The Maven release plugin

Releasing a project requires a lot of repetitive tasks. The objective of the Maven `release` plugin is to automate them. The `release` plugin defines the following eight goals, which are executed in two stages, preparing the release and performing the release:

- `release:clean`: This goal cleans up after a release preparation
- `release:prepare`: This goal prepares for a release in **Software Configuration Management (SCM)**
- `release:prepare-with-pom`: This goal prepares for a release in SCM and generates release POMs by fully resolving the dependencies
- `release:rollback`: This goal rolls back to a previous release
- `release:perform`: This goal performs a release from SCM
- `release:stage`: This goal performs a release from SCM into a staging folder/repository
- `release:branch`: This goal creates a branch of the current project with all versions updated
- `release:update-versions`: This goal updates versions in the POM(s)

The preparation stage will complete the following tasks with the `release:prepare` goal:

- Verify that all the changes in the source code are committed.
- Make sure that there are no SNAPSHOT dependencies. During the project development phase, we use SNAPSHOT dependencies but at the time of the release, all dependencies should be changed to a released version.
- Change the version of project POM files from SNAPSHOT to a concrete version number.
- Change the SCM information in the project POM to include the final destination of the tag.
- Execute all the tests against the modified POM files.
- Commit the modified POM files to the SCM and tag the code with the version name.
- Change the version of POM files in the trunk to a SNAPSHOT version and then commit the modified POM files to the trunk.

Finally, the release will be performed with the `release:perform` goal. This will check the code from the release tag in the SCM and run a set of predefined goals: `site, deploy-site`.

The `maven-release-plugin` is not defined in the super POM and should be explicitly defined in your project POM file. The `releaseProfiles` configuration element defines the profiles to be released and the `goals` configuration element defines the plugin goals to be executed during the `release:perform` goal. In the following configuration, the `deploy` goal of the `maven-deploy-plugin` and the `single` goal of the `maven-assembly-plugin` will get executed:

```
<plugin>
  <artifactId>maven-release-plugin</artifactId>
  <version>2.5</version>
  <configuration>
    <releaseProfiles>release</releaseProfiles>
    <goals>deploy assembly:single</goals>
  </configuration>
</plugin>
```

 More details about the Maven release plugin are available at `http://maven.apache.org/maven-release/maven-release-plugin/`.

The Maven enforcer plugin

The Maven enforcer plugin lets you control or enforce constraints in your build environment. These could be the Maven version, Java version, operating system parameters, and even user-defined rules.

The plugin defines two goals: `enforce` and `displayInfo`. The `enforcer:enforce` goal will execute all the defined rules against all the modules in a multi-module Maven project, while `enforcer:displayInfo` will display the project compliance details with respect to the standard rule set.

The `maven-enforcer-plugin` is not defined in the super POM and should be explicitly defined in your project POM file:

```
<plugins>
  <plugin>
    <groupId>org.apache.maven.plugins</groupId>
    <artifactId>maven-enforcer-plugin</artifactId>
    <version>1.3.1</version>
```

```
<executions>
  <execution>
    <id>enforce-versions</id>
    <goals>
      <goal>enforce</goal>
    </goals>
    <configuration>
      <rules>
        <requireMavenVersion>
          <version>3.2.1</version>
        </requireMavenVersion>
        <requireJavaVersion>
          <version>1.6</version>
        </requireJavaVersion>
        <requireOS>
          <family>mac</family>
        </requireOS>
      </rules>
    </configuration>
  </execution>
</executions>
    </plugin>
  </plugins>
```

The previous plugin configuration enforces the Maven version to be 3.2.1, the Java version to be 1.6, and the operating system to be in the Mac family.

The Apache Axis2 project uses the `enforcer` plugin to make sure that no application POM file defines Maven repositories. All the artifacts required by Axis2 are expected to be in the Maven central repository. The following configuration element is extracted from `http://svn.apache.org/repos/asf/axis/axis2/java/core/trunk/modules/parent/pom.xml`. Here, it bans all the repositories and plugin repositories, except snapshot repositories:

```
<plugin>
  <artifactId>maven-enforcer-plugin</artifactId>
  <version>1.1</version>
  <executions>
    <execution>
      <phase>validate</phase>
      <goals>
        <goal>enforce</goal>
      </goals>
      <configuration>
```

```
            <rules>
              <requireNoRepositories>
                <banRepositories>true</banRepositories>
                <banPluginRepositories>true</banPluginRepositories>
                <allowSnapshotRepositories>true
                  </allowSnapshotRepositories>
                <allowSnapshotPluginRepositories>true
                  </allowSnapshotPluginRepositories>
              </requireNoRepositories>
            </rules>
          </configuration>
        </execution>
      </executions>
    </plugin>
```

 In addition to the standard rule set ships with the `enforcer` plugin, you can also define your own rules. More details about how to write custom rules are available at `http://maven.apache.org/enforcer/enforcer-api/writing-a-custom-rule.html`.

Avoid using un-versioned plugins

If you have associated a plugin with your application POM, without a version, then Maven will download the corresponding `maven-metadata.xml` file and store it locally. Only the latest released version of the plugin will be downloaded and used in the project. This can easily create certain uncertainties. Your project might work fine with the current version of a plugin, but later if there is a new release of the same plugin, your Maven project will start to use the latest one automatically. This can result in unpredictable behaviors and lead to a debugging mess.

It is always recommended that you specify the plugin version along with the plugin configuration. You can enforce this as a rule, with the Maven `enforcer` plugin, as shown in the following code:

```
<plugin>
  <groupId>org.apache.maven.plugins</groupId>
  <artifactId>maven-enforcer-plugin</artifactId>
  <version>1.3.1</version>
  <executions>
    <execution>
      <id>enforce-plugin-versions</id>
      <goals>
```

```
      <goal>enforce</goal>
   </goals>
   <configuration>
     <rules>
        <requirePluginVersions>
           <message>............  <message>
           <banLatest>true</banLatest>
           <banRelease>true</banRelease>
           <banSnapshots>true</banSnapshots>
           <phases>clean,deploy,site</phases>
           <additionalPlugins>
             <additionalPlugin>
                org.apache.maven.plugins:maven-eclipse-plugin
             </additionalPlugin>
             <additionalPlugin>
                org.apache.maven.plugins:maven-reactor-plugin
             </additionalPlugin>
           </additionalPlugins>
           <unCheckedPluginList>
              org.apache.maven.plugins:maven-enforcer-plugin,org.
                 apache.maven.plugins:maven-idea-plugin
           </unCheckedPluginList>
        </requirePluginVersions>
     </rules>
   </configuration>
  </execution>
 </executions>
</plugin>
```

The following points explain each of the key configuration elements defined in the previous code:

- message: Use this to define an optional message to the user if the rule execution fails.

- banLatest: Use this to restrict the use of LATEST as the version for any plugin.

- banRelease: Use this to restrict the use of RELEASE as the version for any plugin.

- banSnapshots: Use this to restrict the use of SNAPSHOT plugins.

- banTimestamps: Use this to restrict the use of SNAPSHOT plugins with the timestamp version.

- `phases`: This is a comma-separated list of phases that should be used to find lifecycle plugin bindings. The default value is `clean`, `deploy`, `site`.

- `additionalPlugins`: This is a list of additional plugins to enforce to have versions. These plugins might not be defined in application POM files, but are used anyway, such as help and eclipse. The plugins should be specified in the `groupId:artifactId` form.

- `unCheckedPluginList`: This is a comma-separated list of plugins to skip version checking.

 You can read more details about the `requirePluginVersions` rule at `http://maven.apache.org/enforcer/enforcer-rules/requirePluginVersions.html`.

Using exclusive and inclusive routes

We discussed the Nexus repository manager in *Chapter 8, Maven Repository Management*. When Maven asks for an artifact from a Nexus proxy repository, Nexus knows where to look at exactly. For example, say we have a proxy repository that runs at `http://localhost:8081/nexus/content/repositories/central/`, which internally points to the remote repository running at `https://repo1.maven.org/maven2/`. As there is one-to-one mapping between the proxy repository and the corresponding remote repository, Nexus can route the requests without much trouble. However, if Maven looks for an artifact via a Nexus group repository, then Nexus has to iterate through all the repositories in that group repository to find the exact artifact. There can be cases where we have even more than 20 repositories in a single group repository, which can easily bring delays at the client side. To optimize artifact discovery in group repositories, we need to set correct inclusive/exclusive routing rules. This was discussed in detail in *Chapter 8, Maven Repository Management*.

Avoid having both release and snapshot repositories in the same group repository

With the Nexus repository manager, you can group both the release repositories and snapshot repositories together into a single group repository. This is treated as an extreme malpractice.

Ideally, you should be able to define distinct update policies for release repositories and snapshot repositories. This was discussed in detail in *Chapter 8, Maven Repository Management*.

Avoid having both proxy and hosted repositories in the same group repository

With the Nexus repository manager, you can group both the proxy repositories and hosted repositories together into a single group repository. It's been found that this will drastically reduce the Maven build performance, as Maven still checks in remote repositories even if the artifact is available in the hosted repository. If you still want to group all repositories, then you need to make sure you have the right setup of inclusive/exclusive rules defined. This was discussed in detail in *Chapter 8, Maven Repository Management*.

Minimizing the number of repositories

You should not let all your developers add Maven repositories as they wish. The repositories can be easily introduced by anyone via application POM files. This has to be restricted, and it's highly recommended that you define all your Maven repositories (including plugin repositories) in the parent POM file. In this way, you know where to look to make any changes.

It's even better that you completely avoid adding any repositories via application POM files, and whenever needed, introduce them via a repository manager. As in the case of the Apache Axis2 project, you can use the `enforcer` Maven plugin to ban anyone from introducing repositories. The following code shows the configuration:

```
<plugin>
  <artifactId>maven-enforcer-plugin</artifactId>
  <executions>
    <execution>
      <phase>validate</phase>
      <goals>
        <goal>enforce</goal>
      </goals>
      <configuration>
        <rules>
          <requireNoRepositories>
          </requireNoRepositories>
        </rules>
      </configuration>
    </execution>
  </executions>
</plugin>
```

Using mirrorOf instead of changing repository URLs

To point to a repository manager, you might need to change each and every repository defined in your application POM file or the `settings.xml` file. Instead of changing the repository itself, it is recommended to use a mirror.

For example, you might already have a repository under the `central` ID, as shown in the following code:

```
<repository>
  <snapshots>
    <enabled>false</enabled>
  </snapshots>
  <id>central</id>
  <name>Central Repository</name>
  <url>http://repo.maven.apache.org/maven2</url>
</repository>
```

Instead of changing the `url` tag of the preceeding configuration, you can define a mirror as shown in the following code. As the value of the `mirrorOf` element is set to `*`, any of the repositories defined in the system (or in any application POM file) will use the following mirror repository:

```
<mirrors>
  <mirror>
    <id>packt-group</id>
    <name>PACKT Nexus Group Repository</name>
    <url>http://localhost:8081/nexus/content/groups
      /packt-group/</url>
    <mirrorOf>*</mirrorOf>
  </mirror>
</mirrors>
```

Descriptive parent POM files

Make sure that your project's parent POM file is descriptive enough to list out what the project does, who the developers/contributors are, their contact details, the license under which the project artifacts are released, where to report issues, and likewise. A good example of a descriptive POM file can be found at `http://svn.apache.org/repos/asf/axis/axis2/java/core/trunk/modules/parent/pom.xml`.

```
<project>
  <name>Apache Axis2 - Parent</name>
  <inceptionYear>2004</inceptionYear>
```

```xml
<description>Axis2 is an effort to re-design and totally re-
  implement both Axis/Java......</description>
<url>http://axis.apache.org/axis2/java/core/</url>
<licenses>
  <license>http://www.apache.org/licenses/LICENSE-
    2.0.html</license>
</licenses>
<issueManagement>
  <system>jira</system>
  <url>http://issues.apache.org/jira/browse/AXIS2</url>
</issueManagement>
<mailingLists>
  <mailingList>
    <name>Axis2 Developer List</name>
    <subscribe>java-dev-subscribe@axis.apache.org</subscribe>
    <unsubscribe>java-dev-unsubscribe@
      axis.apache.org</unsubscribe>
    <post>java-dev@axis.apache.org</post>
    <archive>http://mail-archives.apache.org/mod_mbox/axis-java-
      dev/</archive>
    <otherArchives>
      <otherArchive>http://markmail.org/search/list:org.
        apache.ws.axis-dev</otherArchive>
    </otherArchives>
  </mailingList>
</mailingLists>
<developers>
  <developer>
    <name>Sanjiva Weerawarana</name>
    <id>sanjiva</id>
    <email>sanjiva AT wso2.com</email>
    <organization>WSO2</organization>
  </developer>
</developers>
<contributors>
  <contributor>
    <name>Dobri Kitipov</name>
    <email>kdobrik AT gmail.com</email>
    <organization>Software AG</organization>
  </contributor>
</contributors>
</project>
```

Documentation is your friend

If you are a good developer, you know the value of documentation. Anything you write should not be cryptic or understood only by you. Let it be a Java, .NET, C++, or a Maven project, the documentation is your friend. A code with a good documentation is extremely readable. If any configuration you add into an application POM file is not self-descriptive, make sure that you add at least a single line comment to explain what it does.

Here are some good examples from the Apache Axis2 project:

```
<profile>
  <id>java16</id>
  <activation>
    <jdk>1.6</jdk>
  </activation>
  <!-- JDK 1.6 build still use JAX-WS 2.1 because integrating
       Java endorsed mechanism with Maven is bit of complex-->
  <properties>
    <jaxb.api.version>2.1</jaxb.api.version>
    <jaxbri.version>2.1.7</jaxbri.version>
    <jaxws.tools.version>2.1.3</jaxws.tools.version>
    <jaxws.rt.version>2.1.3</jaxws.rt.version>
  </properties>
</profile>
<plugin>
  <artifactId>maven-assembly-plugin</artifactId>
  <!-- Minimum required version here is 2.2-beta-4 because
       org.apache:apache:7 uses the runOnlyAtExecutionRoot
       parameter, which is not supported in earlierversions
  <version>2.2-beta-5</version>
  <configuration>
    <!-- Workaround for MASSEMBLY-422 / MASSEMBLY-449-->
    <archiverConfig>
      <fileMode>420</fileMode>
      <!-- 420(dec)=644(oct) -->
      <directoryMode>493</directoryMode><!--493(dec)=755(oct)-->
      <defaultDirectoryMode>493</defaultDirectoryMode>
    </archiverConfig>
  </configuration>
</plugin>
<!-- No chicken and egg problem here because the plugin doesn't
expose any extension. We can always use the version from the current
build.-->
```

```
<plugin>
  <groupId>org.apache.axis2</groupId>
  <artifactId>axis2-repo-maven-plugin</artifactId>
  <version>${project.version}</version>
</plugin>
```

Avoid overriding the default directory structure

Maven follows the design philosophy **convention over configuration**. Without any configuration changes, Maven assumes that the location of the source code is `${basedir}/src/main/java`, the location of tests is `${basedir}/src/test/java`, and the resources are available at `${basedir}/src/main/resources`. Once after a successful build, Maven knows where to place the compiled classes (`${basedir}/target/classes`) and where to copy the final artifact (`${basedir}/target/`). It is possible to change this directory structure, but it's recommended not to do so. Why?

Keeping the default structure improves the readability of the project. Even a fresh developer knows where to look into if he is familiar with Maven. Also, if you have associated plugins and other Maven extensions with your project, you will be able to use them with minimal changes if you have not altered the default Maven directory structure. Most of these plugins and other extensions assume the Maven convention by default.

Using SNAPSHOT versioning during development

You should use the `SNAPSHOT` qualifier for the artifacts produced by your project if those are still under development and deployed regularly to a Maven snapshot repository. If the version to be released is `1.7.0`, then you should use the `1.7.0-SNAPSHOT` version while it's under development. Maven treats the `SNAPSHOT` version in a special manner. If you try to deploy `1.7.0-SNAPSHOT` into a repository, Maven will first expand the `SNAPSHOT` qualifier into a date and time value in **Coordinated Universal Time (UTC)**. If the date/time at the time of deployment is 10.30 A.M., November 10, 2014, then the `SNAPSHOT` qualifier will be replaced with `20141110-103005-1`, and the artifact will be deployed with the `1.7.0-20141110-103005-1` version.

Get rid of unused dependencies

Always make sure that you maintain a clean application POM file. You should not have any unused dependencies defined or used undeclared dependencies. The Maven dependency plugin helps you identify such discrepancies.

The maven-dependency-plugin is not defined in the super POM and should be explicitly defined in your project POM file:

```
<plugin>
  <artifactId>maven-dependency-plugin</artifactId>
  <version>2.0</version>
</plugin>
```

Once the previous configuration is added into your application POM file, you need to run the analyze goal of the dependency plugin, against your Maven project:

```
$ mvn dependency:analyze
```

Here, you can see a sample output, which complains about an unused declared dependency:

```
[WARNING] Unused declared dependencies found:
[WARNING] org.apache.axis2:axis2-kernel:jar:1.6.2:compile
```

 More details about the Maven dependency plugin are available at http://maven.apache.org/plugins/maven-dependency-plugin/.

Avoid keeping credentials in application POM files

During a Maven build, you need to connect to external repositories outside your firewall. In a tightened secured environment, any outbound connection has to go through an internal proxy server. The following configuration in MAVEN_HOME/conf/settings.xml shows how to connect to an external repository via a secured proxy server:

```
<proxy>
  <id>internal_proxy</id>
  <active>true</active>
  <protocol>http</protocol>
  <username>proxyuser</username>
```

```
<password>proxypass</password>
<host>proxy.host.net</host>
<port>80</port>
<nonProxyHosts>local.net|some.host.com</nonProxyHosts>
</proxy>
```

Also, the Maven repositories can be protected for legitimate access. If a given repository is protected with HTTP basic authentication, the corresponding credentials should be defined as shown in the following code, under the `servers` element of `MAVEN_HOME/conf/settings.xml`:

```
<server>
  <id>central</id>
  <username>my_username</username>
  <password>my_password</password>
</server>
```

Keeping confidential data in configuration files in **cleartext** is a security threat that must be avoided. Maven provides a way of encrypting configuration data in `settings.xml`.

First, we need to create a master encryption key:

```
$ mvn -emp mymasterpassword
{1J1MrCQRnngHIpSadxoyEKyt2zIGbm3Yl0ClKdTtRR6T1eNaEfGOEoJaxNcdMr+G}
```

With the output from the previous command, we need to create a file called `settings-security.xml` under `USER_HOME/.m2/` and add the encrypted `master` password there, as shown in the following code:

```
<settingsSecurity>
  <master>
{1J1MrCQRnngHIpSadxoyEKyt2zIGbm3Yl0ClKdTtRR6T1eNaEfGOEoJaxNcdMr+G}
  </master>
</settingsSecurity>
```

Once the `master` password is configured properly, we can start encrypting rest of the confidential data in `settings.xml`. Let's see how to encrypt the server password. First, we need to generate the encrypted password for the cleartext using the following command. Note that earlier we used `emp` (encrypt master password) and now we are using `ep` (encrypt password):

```
$ mvn -ep my_password
{PbYw8YaLb3cHA34/5EdHzoUsmmw/u/nWOwb9e+x6Hbs=}
```

Copy the value of the encrypted password and replace the corresponding value in `settings.xml`:

```
<server>
  <id>central</id>
  <username>my_username</username>
  <password>
    {PbYw8YaLb3cHA34/5EdHzoUsmmw/u/nWOwb9e+x6Hbs=}
  </password>
</server>
```

Avoid using deprecated references

Since Maven 3.0 onwards, all the properties starting with `pom.*` are deprecated. Avoid using any of the deprecated Maven properties and if you have used them already, make sure that you migrate to the equivalent ones.

Avoid repetition – use archetypes

When we create a Java project, we need to structure it in different ways based on the type of the project. If it's a Java EE web application, then we need to have a `WEB-INF` directory and a `web.xml` file. If it's a Maven plugin project, we need to have a MOJO class that extends from `org.apache.maven.plugin.AbstractMojo`. As each type of project has its own predefined structure, why would everyone have to build the same structure again and again? Why not start with a template? Each project can have its own template and developers can extend the template to suite their requirements. Maven archetypes address this concern. Each archetype is a project template.

We discussed Maven archetypes in detail in *Chapter 7, Maven Archetypes*.

Avoid using maven.test.skip

You might manage an extremely small project that does not evolve a lot without unit tests. However, any large-scale project cannot exist without unit tests. Unit tests provide the first level of guarantee that you do not break any existing functionality with a newly introduced code change. In an ideal scenario, you should not commit any code to a source repository without building the complete project with unit tests.

Maven uses the `surefire` plugin to run tests, and as a malpractice, developers skip the execution of unit tests by setting the `maven.test.skip` property to `true`:

```
$ mvn clean install –Dmaven.test.skip=true
```

This can lead to serious repercussions in the later stage of the project, and you must ensure that all your developers do not skip testing while building.

Using the `requireProperty` rule of the Maven `enforcer` plugin, you can ban developers from using the `maven.test.skip` property. The following shows the `enforcer` plugin configuration that you need to add to your application POM:

```
<plugin>
  <groupId>org.apache.maven.plugins</groupId>
  <artifactId>maven-enforcer-plugin</artifactId>
  <version>1.3.1</version>
  <executions>
    <execution>
      <id>enforce-property</id>
      <goals>
        <goal>enforce</goal>
      </goals>
      <configuration>
        <rules>
          <requireProperty>
            <property>maven.test.skip</property>
            <message>maven.test.skip must be specified</message>
            <regex>false</regex>
            <regexMessage>You cannot skip tests</regexMessage>
          </requireProperty>
        </rules>
        <fail>true</fail>
      </configuration>
    </execution>
  </executions>
</plugin>
```

Now, if you run `mvn clean install` against your project, you will see the following error message:

maven.test.skip must be specified

This means you need to specify `-Dmaven.test.skip=false` every time you run `mvn clean install`:

$ mvn clean install -Dmaven.test.skip=true

However, if you set `-Dmaven.test.skip=false`, then you will see the following error:

You cannot skip tests

You will still find it a bit annoying to type `Dmaven.test.skip=false` whenever you run a build. To avoid this, add the `maven.test.skip` property in your application POM file and set its value to `false`:

```
<project>
  <properties>
    <maven.test.skip>false</maven.test.skip>
  </properties>
</project>
```

More details about the `requireProperty` rule are available at http://maven.apache.org/enforcer/enforcer-rules/requireProperty.html.

Share resources – avoid duplicates

In many multi-module Maven projects, we have noticed that there are certain resources that need to be shared across different modules. These can be images, database scripts, JavaScript files, style sheets, or any other resources. Developers follow different approaches in sharing resources. Some of them are listed here:

- Duplicate resources in every module.
- Use constructs from the underneath source code repository to copy resources, just like `svn externals`. Here you only maintain resources in a single place, but all the modules need them, will get a copy when doing an `svn up`.
- Use the Maven remote resource plugin.

Of all the three, the use of the remote resource plugin is the best, as there is no resource duplication. With the remote resource plugin, first you need to create a Maven module, which includes all the resources that need to be shared. The following POM file defines the Maven module for all the shared resources:

```
<project>
  <groupId>com.packt</groupId>
  <artifactId>resources</artifactId>
  <build>
    <plugins>
      <plugin>
        <artifactId>maven-remote-resources-plugin</artifactId>
        <version>1.5</version>
        <executions>
```

```xml
      <execution>
        <goals>
          <goal>bundle</goal>
        </goals>
      </execution>
    </executions>
    <configuration>
      <includes>
        <include>**/*.png</include>
        <include>**/*.sql</include>
        <include>**/*.css</include>
        <include>**/*.js</include>
      </includes>
    </configuration>
  </plugin>
 </plugins>
 </build>
</project>
```

The directory structure of the shared resources project will look like following. When you build the project, Maven will bundle all the resources into a JAR file during the `generate-resources` phase of the Maven default lifecycle:

```
resources
        |-pom.xml
        |-src/main/resources/sql/*.sql
        |-src/main/resources/images/*.png
        |-src/main/resources/css/*.css
        |-src/main/resources/js/*.js
```

For any other Maven module to consume these resources, they have to take a dependency on the artifact produced by the preceding project and associate `maven-remote-resources-plugin` with the build.

The following POM file defines the Maven module to consume shared resources:

```xml
<project>
  <groupId>com.packt</groupId>
  <artifactId>consumer</artifactId>
  <dependencies>
    <dependency>
      <groupId>${project.groupId}</groupId>
      <artifactId>resources</artifactId>
      <version>${project.version}</version>
    </dependency>
```

```
      </dependencies>
      <build>
        <plugins>
          <plugin>
            <groupId>org.apache.maven.plugins</groupId>
            <artifactId>maven-remote-resources-plugin</artifactId>
            <version>1.5</version>
            <configuration>
              <resourceBundles>
                <resourceBundle>
                  com.packt:resources:${project.version}
                </resourceBundle>
              </resourceBundles>
            </configuration>
            <executions>
              <execution>
                <goals>
                  <goal>process</goal>
                </goals>
              </execution>
            </executions>
          </plugin>
          <plugin>
            <groupId>org.codehaus.mojo</groupId>
            <artifactId>sql-maven-plugin</artifactId>
            <version>1.4</version>
            <executions>
              <execution>
                <id>create-schema</id>
                <phase>process-test-resources</phase>
                <goals>
                  <goal>execute</goal>
                </goals>
                <configuration>
                  <autocommit>true</autocommit>
                  <srcFiles>
                    <srcFile>${project.build.directory}/
                      maven-shared-archive-resources/packt.sql
                    </srcFile>
                  </srcFiles>
                </configuration>
              </execution>
            </executions>
          </plugin>
        </plugins>
      </build>
    </project>
```

The `maven-remote-resources-plugin` will read the resources from the `com.packt:resources` artifact and copy them into the `${project.build.directory}/maven-shared-archive-resources` directory. As shown in the previous sample configuration, any other plugin can consume these resources, such as the `sql-maven-plugin`.

Summary

In this chapter, we looked at and highlighted some of the best practices to be followed in a large-scale development project with Maven. Most of the points highlighted here were discussed in detail in previous chapters throughout the book. It is always recommended to follow best practices, as it will drastically improve developer productivity and will reduce any maintenance nightmares.

Index

artifact indexing 229
artifact/resource filtering 152
artifacts
  blocking 225
  deploying 64
assembly descriptor 140-150
assembly help 152
assembly plugin
  about 138
  example 139
  URL 140
Axis2 distributions
  URL 148
Axis2 handler project
  URL 192
axis2-kernel module
  URL 243

B

batch mode, archetype plugin 163
best practices
  dependency management 236-238
  deprecated references, avoiding 262
  descriptive parent POM files 256
  documentation 258
  enforcer plugin, using 250, 251
  exclusive routes, using 254
  groupId element, avoiding 242
  grouping, avoiding of proxy and
      hosted repositories 255
  grouping, avoiding of release repositories
      and snapshot repositories 254
  inclusive routes, using 254
  Maven profiles 245-248
  mirrorOf, using instead of changing
      repository URLs 256
  naming conventions, following 243, 244
  number of repositories, minimizing 255
  overriding, avoiding of default directory
      structure 259
  parent module, defining 238, 239
  POM properties 239-242
  release plugin, using 249
  resources, sharing 264-267
  SNAPSHOT versioning, using during
      development 259

  unused dependencies, avoiding 260
  un-versioned plugins, avoiding 252-254
  version element, avoiding 242
build
  monitoring 11, 12
bundle plugin 114

C

Certificate Authority (CA) 52
clean lifecycle 70-73
clean plugin 96-98
cleartext 261
CN (CommonName) 52
Cocoon
  URL 167
Codehaus snapshots
  URL 219
compiler plugin 98, 99
component descriptor 79
components.xml file,
      axis2-aar-maven-plugin
  URL 83
Concurrent Versions System (CVS) 56
configuration elements, MOJO annotation
  aggregator 127
  executionStrategy 128
  inheritByDefault 128
  instantiationStrategy 128
  name 127
  requiresDirectInvocation 127
  requiresOnline 128
  requiresProject 127
  requiresReports 127
  threadSafe 128
configuration levels, Maven
  global 47
  project 47
  user 47
configuration options, assembly descriptor
  URL 148
Convention over Configuration 14, 15, 259
Coordinated Universal Time (UTC) 259
create-from-project goal
  URL 202
credentials
  exploring, in settings.xml 54-56

Thank you for buying
Mastering Apache Maven 3

About Packt Publishing

Packt, pronounced 'packed', published its first book, *Mastering phpMyAdmin for Effective MySQL Management*, in April 2004, and subsequently continued to specialize in publishing highly focused books on specific technologies and solutions.

Our books and publications share the experiences of your fellow IT professionals in adapting and customizing today's systems, applications, and frameworks. Our solution-based books give you the knowledge and power to customize the software and technologies you're using to get the job done. Packt books are more specific and less general than the IT books you have seen in the past. Our unique business model allows us to bring you more focused information, giving you more of what you need to know, and less of what you don't.

Packt is a modern yet unique publishing company that focuses on producing quality, cutting-edge books for communities of developers, administrators, and newbies alike. For more information, please visit our website at www.packtpub.com.

About Packt Open Source

In 2010, Packt launched two new brands, Packt Open Source and Packt Enterprise, in order to continue its focus on specialization. This book is part of the Packt Open Source brand, home to books published on software built around open source licenses, and offering information to anybody from advanced developers to budding web designers. The Open Source brand also runs Packt's Open Source Royalty Scheme, by which Packt gives a royalty to each open source project about whose software a book is sold.

Writing for Packt

We welcome all inquiries from people who are interested in authoring. Book proposals should be sent to author@packtpub.com. If your book idea is still at an early stage and you would like to discuss it first before writing a formal book proposal, then please contact us; one of our commissioning editors will get in touch with you.

We're not just looking for published authors; if you have strong technical skills but no writing experience, our experienced editors can help you develop a writing career, or simply get some additional reward for your expertise.

Maven Build Customization

ISBN: 978-1-78398-722-1   Paperback: 270 pages

Discover the real power of Maven 3 to manage your Java projects more effectively than ever

1. Administer complex projects customizing the Maven framework and improving the software lifecycle of your organization with "Maven-friendly technologies".

2. Automate your delivery process and make it fast and easy.

3. An easy-to-follow tutorial on Maven customization and integration with a real project and practical examples.

Apache Maven 3 Cookbook

ISBN: 978-1-84951-244-2   Paperback: 224 pages

Over 50 recipes towards optimal Java software engineering with Maven 3

1. Grasp the fundamentals and extend Apache Maven 3 to meet your needs.

2. Implement engineering practices in your application development process with Apache Maven.

3. Collaboration techniques for Agile teams with Apache Maven.

Please check **www.PacktPub.com** for information on our titles

Learning Apache
Maven 3
Kapila Bogahapitiya

[PACKT]

Learning Apache Maven 3 [Video]

ISBN: 978-1-78216-666-5   Duration: 01:59 hours

Get to grips with the basics and concepts of building a
real world Java Application with Apache Maven

1. A practical example-driven approach to
   learning Apache Maven 3.

2. Grasp the fundamentals and extend Apache
   Maven 3 to meet your needs.

3. Learn to use Apache Maven with Java
   enterprise frameworks and various
   other cutting-edge technologies.

Apache Maven Dependency
Management

Manage your Java and JEE project dependencies with ease with
this hands-on guide to Maven

Jonathan Lalou   PACKT open source

Apache Maven Dependency Management

ISBN: 978-1-78328-301-9   Paperback: 158 pages

Manage your Java and JEE project dependencies with
ease with this hands-on guide to Maven

1. Improve your productivity by efficiently
   managing dependencies.

2. Learn how to detect and fix
   dependency conflicts.

3. Learn how to share transitive relations
   and to visualize your dependencies.

Please check **www.PacktPub.com** for information on our titles